Great Holiness Classics

Volume 1

GREAT HOLINESS CLASSICS
in Six Volumes

Volume 1
Holiness Teaching—New Testament Times to Wesley

Volume 2
The Wesley Century

Volume 3
Leading Wesleyan Thinkers

Volume 4
The 19th-Century Holiness Movement

Volume 5
Holiness Preachers and Preaching

Volume 6
Holiness Teaching Today

VOLUME 1

Holiness Teaching— New Testament Times to Wesley

Edited by
Paul M. Bassett

Volume Advisors:
George Failing
William Greathouse

<!!>BEACON HILL PRESS OF KANSAS CITY
KANSAS CITY, MISSOURI

Copyright 1997
Beacon Hill Press of Kansas City

ISBN 083-411-5751
083-410-9093 (series)

Printed in the
United States of America

Library of Congress Cataloging-in-Publication Data
Holiness teaching : New Testament times to Wesley / edited by Paul M. Bassett
    p.   cm. — (Great holiness classics ; v. 1)
    Includes bibliographical references and index.
    ISBN 0-8341-1575-1
    1. Methodist Church—Doctrines.   2. Holiness churches—Doctrines.
3. Holiness—History of doctrines.   4. Church history.   5. Christian
literature.   I. Bassett, Paul M.   II. Series.
BT767.G73   1984 vol. 1
[BX8331.2]
270.6 s—dc21
[234'.8]
                                          96-44597
                                            CIP

10 9 8 7 6 5 4 3 2 1

TO
Jori
Corbin
Johnathan
Jacob
whose grandfather's fervent hope is
that they, too, will follow the Way of Holiness

Contents

Foreword

John Wesley is acknowledged and acclaimed as the chief architect of the doctrine of entire sanctification, or Christian perfection, as understood within the Holiness Movement. However, the truth this tenet expresses derives from the very heart of Scripture, and the experience and life it enshrines have been known and exemplified by the saints of every age.

Nor did Wesley give final and complete formulation of this truth. Theology is an ongoing process; it endeavors to interpret truth in language and thought forms relevant to each succeeding generation. The creativity of the Spirit is evident in the unfolding of the doctrine from Wesley to the present. The truth of Christian holiness is so grand it defies any finality of expression.

Furthermore, since saints within every Christian tradition have found this Kingdom treasure, their witness to holiness reflects the variety of these traditions. The truth of perfect love is like a sparkling diamond—to appreciate its full beauty and brilliance, we must view it from many angles.

This series of classics is designed to provide the modern reader a compact library of Holiness literature. Herein you will find, along with appropriate editorial introductions and comments, many of the significant primary documents of the Holiness Movement. I commend these volumes as a devotional treasure for those who seek spiritual enrichment as well as a resource library for teachers and preachers who would deepen and enlarge their understanding of this central truth of Scripture.

—WILLIAM M. GREATHOUSE
General Superintendent Emeritus
Church of the Nazarene

Understanding the Great Holiness Classics

Holiness

Christian holiness is a scriptural teaching to be understood and a relationship with God to be experienced. God is a holy God, and He asks His people to be like Him in this respect.

In the Old Testament we read, "Ye shall be holy: for I the LORD your God am holy" (Lev. 19:2, KJV). In teaching us about our responsibilities to God, Jesus summarized the first chapter of the Sermon on the Mount with the admonition "Be ye therefore perfect, even as your Father which is in heaven is perfect" (Matt. 5:48, KJV).

Every sincere Christian wants to know what it means to be as holy as God asks us to be. Every follower of Christ feels at times yearnings to be more Christlike, to somehow realize the Christian perfection Jesus sets before us.

It is this ideal and goal taught in the Scriptures that has, across the centuries, stirred every devout Christian who has sought and experienced God's sanctifying grace. In John Wesley's *A Plain Account of Christian Perfection* he records his own experience of discovering this truth: "I tell you, as plain as I can speak, where and when I found this. I found it in the oracles of God, in the Old and New Testament, when I read them with no other view or desire, but to save my own soul" (*Works,* 11:444).

The Holiness Classics

Following in the tradition of Wesley and other devout persons who have sought and preached Christian holiness, the publishers conceived and launched this series of six volumes of *Great Holiness Classics.* The desire and purpose was, in Wesley's words, to "spread scriptural holiness over these lands."

13

The commission given to the editors states that desire:

> To provide a representative compilation of the best Holiness literature in a format readily accessible to the average minister, thus providing: (1) the preservation of the essential elements of our Holiness heritage; (2) an overview of the broad scope of the Holiness message; (3) a norm for Holiness theology, proclamation, and practice; (4) a succinct reference work on Holiness; and (5) a revival of the best of the out-of-print Holiness classics.

What Is a Classic?

A classic work comes from the past, but simply being old does not make it classic. To be classic, a work must have enduring excellence. Its content must be so true and persuasive that succeeding generations read it and are moved to accept the truth and to shape their lives by it. Seeking after holiness as taught in a classic, one finds the truths verified both in Scripture and in his or her own experience with God. A work is classic because its truths are central to revealed and to experiential Christianity.

It is this verifying of previous experience that keeps a classic alive in the consciousness of the Christian community. There is here a principle somewhat parallel to the scientific method. In science we accept as true an experiment that can be repeated under similar conditions with the same results.

Because a Holiness classic represents such a verifiable and biblical promise of spiritual fulfillment, it becomes a typical example of true teaching and a dependable model of Christian experience. Other persons who ponder the Scripture and perform the experiment report comparable experiences of God. The accumulating testimony verifies the classic nature of the document.

A classic thus becomes an authoritative commentary on scriptural truth. It contains guidance that can be depended on to result in sound action and blessed results. The work therefore becomes a norm for future generations. It affirms to the reader, "If you approach God as I did and respond to Him, as by His Word and Spirit He led me to respond, you will discover that He works in your life as I testify He has worked in mine."

In a letter to Dr. Conyers Middleton, Wesley cites this appeal to holy living as characteristic of the Christian fathers: "What the Scripture promises, I enjoy. Come and see what Christianity has done here, and acknowledge it is of God" (*Works,* 10:79).

Selection of Materials

The editors have been guided by these concepts of classic Holiness writings. Works that have spoken to succeeding generations have endured; therefore, we have included them. Writings that present views widely held by other Holiness writers are to be considered classic. A work that stimulates the reader to try the grand experiment is classical. In Christian literature, writings that most faithfully reflect biblical teachings are classical in the best sense of being truly Christian norms.

The materials here selected as classic, then, (1) reflect accurately the teachings of the Bible, (2) have a broad and common base of Christian testimony, and (3) are in line with the best thinking of Christian leaders who have enjoyed the experience of God's sanctifying grace.

What we have chosen, we believe, gives a true account of God's plan for holy living. These writings offer a norm for Christian life that reflects God's will for His children. They lead to the greatest personal fulfillment and inspire believers to make their most effective contribution to the extension of God's kingdom.

Truth with Tolerance

Not all sincere Christians understand Bible holiness in the same way. What is here reflected is generally called the Wesleyan interpretation of entire sanctification. Even within the circle of those who follow Wesley there are some differences of interpretation. The statement of "Concepts and Identifying Terms" was drawn up as a way to reflect the widely accepted positions of the Wesleyan, Methodist tradition.

We recognize and appreciate guides to holy living from other traditions, as in the Moravian, Quaker, Mennonite, and modern Keswick movements. Much of what is here included crosses all denominational boundaries. It will therefore speak to the spirits of Evangelical Christians from most of the historic orthodox communions.

In order to avoid being too restrictive in our selections, we have sought the advice of a broad group of nearly 50 Bible scholars and churchmen whose names appear in the lists of editors and of members of the editorial and advisory boards. These persons have all been involved in a continuing consultation on the choice of materials to be included. We trust that the broad consensus further assures our choice of truly classic materials.

Editorial Policy

The editors were instructed to select writings "judged by the quality of the material and its ability to speak to this generation." Because many of the Holiness classics, especially in the first two volumes, come from an earlier period of writing, we were further given "the right to excerpt and edit the materials, updating archaic usage as needed."

Our goal has been, insofar as is possible, to let the writers speak for themselves. In excerpting we have tried to be completely faithful to the writer's views, deleting only dated, irrelevant, or duplicated materials. Our concern has always been to present as clearly as possible what the writer believed, experienced, and taught about Christian holiness.

In order to make our selections as clear as possible for today's reader, we have (1) modernized some spelling and punctuation, (2) divided some long paragraphs for greater ease in reading, (3) prepared brief introductions and analyses of the writings included, and (4) inserted center heads, side heads, and cut-in headings as brief indications of content in order to guide the reader who is looking for specific aspects of Holiness teaching.

For the historical scholar who wishes to follow in our footsteps and form his own judgment of our accuracy, we have (1) indicated our sources by title, date, edition, and page numbers from which the selection is taken (where relevant for accuracy, we have used the earliest editions of the text); (2) retained original paragraph numbers to aid the reader in locating the source of our quotations; (3) used ellipses to indicate where material has been omitted; and (4) retained italics that appear in the originals, to show what the writers sought to emphasize.

To help the reader more easily distinguish editorial comment from the classic materials quoted, we have printed the editor's additions in a slightly bolder type.

Our Prayer

The prayer of the editors and publishers is that all who read these classics of holy living may come to understand "the way of God more perfectly" (Acts 18:26, KJV).

We pray "that Christ may dwell in your hearts by faith; that ye, being rooted and grounded in love, may be able to comprehend with all saints what is the breadth, and length, and depth, and height; and to know the love of Christ, which passeth knowledge, that ye might be filled with all the fullness of God.

"Now unto him that is able to do exceeding abundantly above all that we ask or think, according to the power that worketh in us, unto him be glory in the church by Christ Jesus throughout all ages, world without end. Amen" (Eph. 3:17-21, KJV).

—A. F. HARPER
Executive Editor

Concepts and Identifying Terms

At the beginning of the project the editors were mandated to "strive for balance, reflecting the various facets of holiness—crisis and process, practice and proclamation, etc."

In order to guide us and to test the inclusiveness and balance of materials chosen, it seemed necessary to devise an instrument for reminder and measurement. We therefore developed the following list of concepts and identifying terms.

The statements are designed to indicate the teachings of the church. The identifying terms are planned as a kind of shorthand device for highlighting these truths throughout the set and in the indexes.

We believe the statements faithfully reflect what the Bible teaches and what the Church has believed and taught across the centuries. The terms are biblical and/or classical in the sense that they represent the language the Church has used to describe the various facets of the experience of God's sanctifying grace.

For convenient reference, we have used these code words as cut-in heads on pages where the related concepts are explored.

A. Doctrinal

1. The requirement of entire sanctification is rooted in God's holiness. **God's Holiness**
2. The need for entire sanctification is seen in the remaining presence of inbred sin, or carnality, in believers. The experience of entire sanctification includes cleansing from this original sin. **Carnality/ Cleansing**
3. Entire sanctification is a gift of God's grace. **Grace**
4. God provides the gift in the atonement of Christ. **Atonement**

5. To be sanctified wholly means to receive grace to love God with your whole heart and to love your neighbor as yourself. **Perfect Love**

6. At conversion, Christians receive God's Holy Spirit in regeneration, sometimes described as initial sanctification. To be sanctified wholly means to be baptized, or filled, with the Holy Spirit, as happened to the disciples in the Upper Room. **Holy Spirit**

7. To be filled with the Holy Spirit brings added power to conquer sin, to love others, and to witness for Christ. **Power**

8. God offers the ministry of the indwelling Holy Spirit to make us more Christlike. **Christlikeness**

9. We believe the doctrine of entire sanctification is taught in the Bible and is consistent with other salvation truths of Scripture. **Scriptural**

10. Entire sanctification is God's call to all Christians. **For All Christians**

11. Entire sanctification is experienced as a second blessing of grace subsequent to regeneration. **Second Blessing**

12. Because entire sanctification is God's gift in response to faith, it occurs in a moment of time, just as God's forgiveness comes in an instant. **In a Moment**

13. Entire sanctification is also known as Christian perfection, perfect love, heart purity, the baptism with the Holy Spirit, being filled with the Spirit, the fullness of the blessing, full salvation, the deeper life, Christian holiness, scriptural holiness, the rest of faith, and the promise of the Father. **Names**

B. Steps to Seeking and Finding

14. The new birth is a prerequisite to entire sanctification. **New Birth**

15. Conviction of need is a condition for the personal quest after holiness. **Hunger**

16. Full consecration is both a precondition and a gracious fruit of entire sanctification.
    Consecration

17. Faith grounded in the full-orbed purpose of Christ's death, and the fullest consecration of which we are capable, is the human condition for entire sanctification.
    Faith

18. God gives the witness of His Spirit when we are sanctified wholly.
    Assurance

C. Living the Life of Holiness

19. Christians grow in likeness to Christ, both before and after entire sanctification. Successful growth requires obedience, trust, deep devotion, and personal discipline.
    Growth

20. Being filled with the Spirit makes a difference in a Christian's attitudes.
    Attitudes

21. Holiness tends toward fulfillment of life and wholeness of human personality.
    Wholeness

22. Though sanctified wholly, men and women are still limited by their imperfections in judgment, personality, and conduct; they are still subject to all sorts of temptation.
    Humanity

23. Dangers to which the sanctified are especially vulnerable include spiritual pride and setting standards too high.
    Dangers

D. Proclamation—Witnessing

24. Testifying to God's work of entire sanctification honors God and spreads the truth.
    Witnessing

25. The truth of entire sanctification and a holy life is to be proclaimed through preaching.
    Preaching

26. Understanding of the truth of Christian holiness and hunger for the experience are communicated through teaching.
    Teaching

27. The truth of Christian holiness is spread through written testimony, exposition, and exhortation.
    Writing

28. We document and prove holiness by living holy lives and by Christian ethical behavior.
    Ethics

Acknowledgments

This is something of a hybrid work. Other people long ago wrote the basic documents, and, for the most part, they needed no introductions. Now someone has to reconstruct their historical contexts and translate them if they are to be of any use at all, and both of these tasks require interpretation. Neither the reconstructive nor the interpretive task can be carried out without expert research. So I have here stood upon the shoulders of many earlier copyists, editors, and translators, most of them anonymous. I must thank them.

And there are also some contemporaries whose names I do know whom I want to thank as well. I thank the Nazarene Theological Seminary library staff, especially Debbie Bradshaw and Dr. William Miller, for helping me acquire some needed sources. And I would like also to thank Dr. Albert Harper, the general editor of the series, for his long-suffering help. This volume is different from any other in the series both in content and in the fact that nothing here originally appeared in English. It all had to be translated somewhere, sometime, and that is painstaking work in any of its aspects. Such a process, from the selection of sources to the acquisition of critical texts to the process of translating and retranslating and checking out translations with specialists, and the submission of text, takes time that would test the patience of any editor. And from the start this work has been done in the interstices, rather than as a mainline project. That, too, tested Dr. Harper's patience. But I think we survived the ordeal as better friends than when we entered it.

Thanks are due also to the Institute for Ecumenical and Cultural Research at St. John's Abbey and University, Collegeville, Minnesota. I had the privilege of spending a semester there as a resident scholar, and while 85 percent of my very long and arduous days there were spent on another project, this one took up the other 15. And in this, the institute and the Alcuin Library of the university afforded superb resources for getting a long way on the work. Patrick Henry, director of the institute, and Dolores Schuh, his assistant, went far beyond the call of duty to see to it that I had what I needed, and more, for the main work; and it was precisely that help that unexpectedly freed me to work almost as a sort of hobby on the one that you have in your hands.

I must also thank my spouse, Pearl, but I lack the words to do it adequately. Two that do fit perfectly are *patience* and *understanding*.

Such a company of persons to thank drives one to work for perfection. But, alas, the work is not error-free. Real errors occur; and then one has made decisions that are debatable that others may rightly call errors.

But for all of that, I think the past still speaks to us substantially on its own terms here. I hope we can learn from it.

Editor's Introduction
to Volume 1

A Unique Volume

This volume of *Great Holiness Classics* marches to a beat that is a bit different from that of the others in the series. Subsequent volumes present variations on a theme well developed by John and Charles Wesley in 18th-century Britain: the doctrine of Christian perfection, with its concomitant, entire sanctification. This volume presents passages from some of the traditional sources that drew the Wesleys to their theme, aided them in understanding it, and contributed to their development of it. The volume also presents cuttings from some of the sources the Wesleys commended to others who wanted to understand Wesleyan teaching.

Both this volume and its companions relate to a distinct tradition in the history of spirituality. They are not intended to cover the broader ground represented in the splendid collection of sources currently being developed under the general title The Classics of Western Spirituality.

This volume, however, does not limit itself solely to sources with which we know the Wesleys to have been familiar. Excerpts from other sources to which they make neither reference nor allusion help us see that the Wesleys did not run on to some odd but interesting side street on the map of Christian faith. Rather, they traveled a main artery, lined, as it were, from its beginning with writings that testify confidently that the grace of God does "break the power of canceled sin" and fill His people with unconditional love for himself and for neighbor in this life. So it is that we are indebted to the Wesleys, but there are many converging paths that led to the road they traveled.[1]

---

1. Richard J. Payne, ed., The Classics of Western Spirituality: A Library of the Great Spiritual Masters (New York and Ramsey, N.J.: Paulist Press, 1980-). This collection now numbers more than 60 volumes. It is predominantly, but not exclusively, Christian. All volumes include critical introductory essays, most of which are excellent, none of which are mediocre.

Choosing the Sources

The volume editor, in consultation with the executive editor, submitted to a large ecumenical advisory committee a list of authors and works for consideration. There were 165 authors and works considered.

Three factors loomed large. First, this volume is part of a series and should conform to the page limits set for the other volumes. Second, pre-Wesleyan works do not speak Wesleyan language—at least not precisely. They speak a variety of theological and spiritual dialects. These would have to be explained if the reader who is unfamiliar with the works is to understand them. The nature of the works in this volume would require longer, more technical introductions—and more of them—than might appear in the later, post-Wesley, volumes. To a degree, the introductions in this volume must teach and prepare the reader for what is coming in language and in content. Third, since most of the readers may not have much familiarity with the language and style of pre-Wesleyan, especially pre-Reformation, writers, they would need expanded excerpts in order to understand the content.

Now came the actual reduction of the list. First, the volume editor reexamined John Wesley's works, seeking to understand his doctrine of Christian perfection/entire sanctification in the context of the rest of Wesley's thought, and then seeking to determine its major elements. Next, the editor took an incredibly enriching tour through the works of all the suggested writers and about 40 other documents (such as liturgies) from across the Christian tradition. Then, on the basis of two criteria, he cut the list of suggestions in half: (1) Works that would be difficult for the reader to obtain in their entirety and works that would require longer explanations were set aside. (2) The remaining works were then arranged chronologically—at least two from every half century up to the Reformation. These were all works the Wesleyan great tradition itself has considered to be its most influential expositions of scriptural teachings.

Sometimes the editor needed help in interpretation, so he developed and consulted a rather large secondary bibliography as well.

Then the editor undertook another round of reading. Wesley had indeed developed a distinctive understanding, but none of the distinctive elements was unique. Each had been taught throughout the history of Christianity. Wesley's genius lay in the way in which he brought the major elements together and the way in which that bringing together connects seamlessly with the great tradition. The Holiness message is clearly a development of what is already there, not a hybrid nor a novelty nor an aberration. The next step was to return to the sources to select those that best stated the distinctive elements Wesley brought together.

Quite arbitrarily, but with an eye to indicating the long continuity and mainstream character of the teachings Wesley was to synthesize, the volume editor selected at least one document or author from each century up to the Reformation. Then he selected from the 16th-century literature one Roman Catholic work, one Lutheran, one Reformed, one Anglican, and one Radical. He repeated the process for the 17th century. To round out the picture, the editor included some shorter liturgical pieces from the Early Church and three samples of spirituality from the Eastern Orthodox tradition.

This process produced a wonderfully rich collection of documents. But it was still two to three times the allowed length. So once more the collection was refined.

This is a work for pastors, students, and thoughtful laypersons, so I have omitted the scholarly apparatuses that usually accompany translations and their various introductions. I hope this neither offends nor cheapens the value of the work in their eyes.

The reader should know as well that this editor freshly translated all of the texts except Pseudo-Macarius's homilies. In each case, where scholars have published critical texts in the original or primary language, I resorted to the best available, and often to more than one. So, where possible, these translations are based upon texts in the standard critical sets such as the *Corpus Scriptorum Christianorum Orientalium, Corpus Scriptorum Ecclesiasticorum Latinorum, Sources chrétiennes,* and so on; and, of course, J. P. Migne's *Patrologia* in both the Greek and Latin series. I also consulted the best English translations of those texts for which there was one. In most cases, I had the luxury of more than one by means of which I could check my own work. I must confess that I found the line between translation and paraphrase difficult as I tried to hew to the line of readable English.

Only with Johann Arndt's *True Christianity* did I make an exception. I used the translation found in John Wesley's *Christian Library* as a way of connecting this volume to Wesley himself.

I did not use them, but a note is in order here about Wesley's translations of Macarius's homilies. Wesley seems to have edited and printed a translation done by a presbyter of the Church of England and published in London in 1721 under the title *Primitive Morality: or, the spiritual homilies of Saint Macarius . . . Done out of Greek into English with . . . emendations and enlargements.* The numbering of the homilies in that translation varies greatly from that of the critical edition used here and from all other modern editions. I retained the idea of Macarius's authorship, not because I hold it but because Wesley did, and because, even yet, the person who wishes to look more deeply into these homilies must begin with Macarius or Pseudo-Macarius to get anywhere. For a crisp readable account of the problems of authorship, and for some direction in where to find help, see Albert C. Outler, ed., *John Wesley,* A Library of Protestant Thought (New York: Oxford University Press, 1964), 9-10, n. 26.

Some readers will notice the absence of several works essential to Wesley's understanding and development of the doctrine of Christian perfection. With more than a little reluctance, I surrendered the *Imitation of Christ* and the pertinent works of Jeremy Taylor and William Law to T. C. Mitchell and his volume 2 in this series. They really belong in both volumes.

The reader really should know why, when there are English translations and paraphrases of most of these works around, I would make fresh ones. The reason is this: as with translations and paraphrases of the Bible, translations and paraphrases of the ancient sources bear the marks of the theological tradition and commitments of the translator; so it seemed appropriate that a Wesleyan/Holiness person should do the grub work that others have done—and enjoy the result!

To enable the reader to more easily distinguish the compiler's explanations from the work of the original writers, the explanations have been set in the boldface type.

About the authors' pictures. Most of them are artists' idealizations, though from about 1500 onward, we do have something of authentic physical appearances. The series editor and I debated whether to include the idealizations or not. And we decided that, in this case, something was probably better than nothing.

So you have in your hand a selection of works from the 2nd to the 18th centuries; almost all of them have come by way of centuries of copyists, editors, translators, and commentators. Still, it may be that we can hear the voices of the past giving guidance to our present and the future under the aegis of the one Holy Spirit.

—PAUL M. BASSETT

1

IDENTIFYING HOLINESS CONCEPTS FROM THE FIRST 17 CENTURIES

The Wesleys and Their Sources

Entering into John Wesley's Labor

Reading the Sources

A Theological Footnote

1

Identifying Holiness Concepts from the First 17 Centuries

The Wesleys and Their Sources

The Wesleys' genius, insofar as these volumes are concerned, lay in (1) their bonding or synthesis of earlier doctrines and experiences of Christian perfection and entire sanctification; (2) their active insistence that divine grace intended entire sanctification and Christian perfection as a gift for everyone, not simply as a reward for the heroic pieties of a few saints; and (3) their development of ways through which all could proclaim, teach, and practice holiness of heart and life. But where did they come upon this point of view? And what held them to it when some insisted that they were talking dangerous nonsense?

They certainly did not come to their conviction through the study of historical theology, systematically combing through the entire Christian tradition, gathering dispersed elements of both doctrines and their experiential expressions, then fusing them into some sort of amalgam. Nor did they come upon it in the manner of sleuths, digging through the mountains of Christian literature, seeking clues that would confirm what they suspected was true.

Rather, they came upon their "pessimism of nature and optimism of grace" (as Robert Chiles called it) as they worshiped. They came to their understandings of God, themselves, and their world, and how these related and should relate, in the context of corporate and private devotion. For them, that context had very specific dimensions. Worship of both sorts was guided by the Book of Common Prayer.

This Book of Common Prayer, first developed in the mid-16th century by Thomas Cranmer, archbishop of Canterbury, deliberately reflected the patterns and resources of monastic devotion that had developed over the previous 1,200 years. Monastic devotion aimed at a life of perfect love, of Christlikeness, even of union with God, lived in a community. The fact that monasticism often went sour or became corrupt could not hide the attractiveness of the ideal. And the ideal was that the believer would balance physical labor and prayer (corporate and private) under the governing spirit of prayer. So, the monks said, "To labor is to pray." And to study was to pray as well.

Prayer included what we would call meditation. So a regular part of prayer was the reading, or listening to the reading, of Scripture and other devotional literature. Reading was done slowly and clearly in order to allow for reflection. And it was thought best if the whole community could join in much of the reading. In fact, the readings would often be sung or chanted. In corporate worship, in which the monks engaged at least three times a day, they followed a calendar of readings that took them through the Psalms at least once a month (more usually once a week) and included passages from the Old Testament (Law and Prophets) and New Testament (Gospels and Epistles) at each gathering.

The monks did not aim at beauty in these exercises, but at encounter with the living God in company with the community. Some monastic prayer had very early taken on the narrow aim of saving one's own soul. The originators of the patterns, however, and the monastic reformers insisted that monastics were to pray primarily for the church and the world. So at their best they prayed for their own purification or sanctification in order that their prayers and labors might truly serve others.

Cranmer believed this perspective could and should be brought into the everyday life of any Christian, not just monks. Every believer should aim at a life of perfect love, of Christlikeness, lived in the everyday human community—and every believer should balance labor and worship, corporate and private, under the governing spirit of prayer. With these things in heart and mind, Cranmer created not just a book for monastics, but the Book of

Common Prayer. "Common" meant "for everyone." He intended for all, laypeople as well as clergy, to drink deeply and together from the wells of biblical and traditional piety.

This is the perspective that nourished John and Charles Wesley. Very early they disciplined themselves to engage in corporate prayer at least twice a day. Each carried forward a rigorous schedule of daily private prayer as well—all of it generally governed by the Book of Common Prayer, all of it aimed at the perfecting of the believer in unconditional love to God and neighbor. The services of morning and evening prayer and the service of Communion abounded with scripture readings, prayers and declarations promising sanctification and perfect love to believers, and exhortations to seek it in this life.

These rounds of reading, reflecting, and praying, separately and corporately, form the context for the Wesleys' spiritual development, as those disciplines had formed the context for the spiritual development of the earlier generations from whom the Wesleys would take nourishment. These rounds provided the grist for the Wesleys' understandings of who God is and who they themselves were before Him, and how they were to relate to Him and to each other. Here was the source of their understandings of Christian perfection/entire sanctification and their intense social concerns and activities. They provided the perspective on life itself for the Wesleys and their colleagues. To this they themselves testified.

Their engagement in worship had taken the Wesley brothers into their search for personal holiness and for the assurance that they had indeed attained to it. It also convinced them they were not simply chasing after some novelty or following out some personal whims; they were searching into the very heart of Christian spirituality. Their studies of the riches of the Christian tradition confirmed this for them at almost every turn. Worship, guided by the Book of Common Prayer, led them to study, guided by the consecrated intellectual wealth of the Christian past.

As is well known, John Wesley reached proficiency in the Hebrew, Greek, and Latin languages and literatures; he was, for a time, a tutor in Greek at the University of Oxford. In addition to preparing collections of notes on the Old and New Testaments, he took special interest in the Christian literature of the first five Christian centuries. He sought the ancients' help and support for his own special spiritual concerns and his work as a spiritual leader. From this literature he turned to the devotional resources of the entire Western Christian tradition.

Wesley drew upon every book in the Bible and on literature from every previous century of the Christian era to formulate his thought. He drew on writers in at least six languages and from a score of cultures to come to his understanding of the Christian faith and of the holy life.

True son of the Book of Common Prayer that he was, Wesley then sought to share with the wider community the results of those labors that had profited him. But this put him face-to-face with a difficult task. He read discriminatingly, but very broadly, and had found that some rather obscure and even unlikely sources held promise of usefulness. These works could encourage even relatively uneducated persons to genuine spirituality if someone would edit them and simplify the more difficult language. So he edited. Sometimes he used entire treatises, sometimes only short phrases. But always he edited, because his aim was not to acquaint others with the whole thought of an author, but to help the reader receive and develop the gracious gift of unconditional love to God and neighbor.

John Wesley read the entire sweep of the Christian tradition in this way. He made the gospel his authority, and this meant looking at any document from the Christian past as a mine to be explored, but not as the ore itself. He seems to have believed that almost all such resources consist of gold and dross, of food and poison (his own terms). Therefore, he edited rather freely.

And he treated his own work in the same spirit. Benevolent dictator though he was, he submitted some of it to conferences, some to empirical testing, and some to expert opinion. Most of it underwent relentless blue-penciling. As editor, he sought a language that would carry the immense variety and enormous spiritual wealth of the tradition and bring it under the control of Scripture, while at the same time allowing it to be presented as a teachable, preachable unity.

Entering into John Wesley's Labor

Like Wesley, we hope to present resources from the long and rich tradition of the Church that shed light on how God would ful-

fill our grace-given yearning to love God and neighbor uncondi-
tionally. But we will not blue-pencil the sources themselves; we
will let them say what they have to say in their own way and seek
to explain them in introductory notes.

Of course, the very process of selecting documents and portions of documents to be printed is a process of editing. Still, we
hope we have let each piece speak on its own grounds.

In every case, the editor has read all of at least the major works
of a given author to be sure the chosen selection stands in line with
the author's thought as a whole. And to avoid eccentric inclusions or
interpretations, the editor has read the principal analyzers and interpreters of each of the authors whose work appears here.

Reading the Sources

Just as special considerations governed the selection of the
excerpts presented here, so there are special considerations in
reading them.

First, take seriously the various introductions. They should
help the reader cut through the inherent foreignness of language
and thought forms of the documents in order to grasp the nub of
the matter. They do not explain everything, but they point to the
central concept.

Second, do not expect to find anything like the rounded, full,
theological expressions of the doctrines of entire sanctification and
Christian perfection to which you may have become accustomed
in reading the literature of the Holiness Movement. Of course, you
will occasionally find a rather large section that sounds very much
like something with which you are already familiar. But from this
era it is better to look for the component parts of those doctrines,
for hints and seeds. Look for intimations or even declarations of
the following:

that God has promised to, and commanded of, all believers
freedom from all sin;

that this promise and command are to be realized in this life;

that it is provided for in Christ's atoning work;

that it is essentially a cleansing from that which inclines us to
sin;

that it is a divine gifting of Christians with unconditional love
to God and neighbor;
that it is given to those already justified;
that it is given in a distinct period of time;
that it is in itself complete but always involves further growth
in grace.

Third, read the excerpts as wholes. Be careful not to get
caught up in trying to draw parallels between specific words and
phrases and the technical theological vocabulary of the Holiness
Movement. You will find hints and seeds of the concepts behind
that vocabulary in the excerpts, but usually not in word-by-word
analysis.

Here you may wish the aid afforded by the marginalia of the
other volumes in the series.

In this volume the cut-in side heads serve a different role than
in the later volumes. There the editors seek to share with the reader terms common to the American Holiness Movement. Here the
side heads are intended to identify the biblical teachings about holiness as understood in the early centuries of the Christian Church.
But those terms also reflect parallel biblical components of Wesleyan-Holiness teaching today.

The authors presented here held many different perspectives
and knew nothing of Wesleyan-Holiness dogmatics. They wrote
without Wesley or his progeny in mind. To use the same terms
here could at times be misleading. So we must be careful about
saying, "This means that," in the case of any specific word or
phrase or sentence or even paragraph—though we may well be
able to say of a larger section something like, "This excerpt does
point in the direction of the Wesleyan doctrine of instantaneous-
ness," or "This excerpt expresses an understanding of the 'secondness' of sanctification prefiguring that of Wesley."

Fourth, remember that you are sampling the main line of
Christian thought, not a bypath. The entire Christian tradition insists that God demands purity of heart of His children. It believes
that we are to be "perfect, just as [our] Father in heaven is perfect"
(Matt. 5:48, NKJV). The entire Christian tradition insists that purity
of heart is a matter of unconditional love to God and to neighbor.
It believes with all of its heart that without holiness no one will
see the Lord. The differences arise over three questions: (1) Is this
purity imputed, or is it imparted? (2) Is this purity a gift of grace or

the product of (or reward for) pious effort? (3) Is this purity to be fully realized in this life?

A Theological Footnote

Having said what we have just said, we must make two additional remarks. Both of them have to do with language.

First is an issue upon which we have already touched. Almost all of the theologizing of the Christian tradition, up until very recent times, was done in the context of ordered corporate and private worship. That context included its wealth of biblical and traditional readings and the almost indefinable but profoundly powerful influence of the presence of the entire community—including the Church Triumphant—playing upon it. Time and again the theological/spiritual writings of almost every genre produced within the tradition witness to the fact that they are in some way reflections on worship.

This means that the language of theology, in the documents presented here, is a language arising out of the encounter with the living God in community with God's people. It is essentially descriptive language. Were it not for the fact that the Bible and tradition played such important roles in worship, the language would doubtless vary even more widely than it does.

None of the authors presented here had much interest in establishing a standard vocabulary. Even Thomas Aquinas, who became a standard authority, had no interest in creating a normative theological lingo. He wanted only to be sure that we knew what he meant, and he went about it more systematically than most. But for the most part in this period we are faced with extraordinary variety—and thus some ambiguity.

However, as we noted, the roots of the theological language of our authors are one and the same for them all—the Bible and tradition understood within the context of corporate worship. So there is some continuity in the meaning of terms and ideas.

And that brings us to the second comment in this theological footnote. In almost the whole of the Christian tradition, Christian perfection and entire sanctification have been understood as two separate phenomena. And Wesleyans agree with this. But it is part of the genius of Wesley that he brought and held both together in inextricable relationship. Of course, Wesleyans believe that such is the way the Bible has it. And a great number of persons throughout the history of Christianity have seen it just as the Wesleyans later did.

But while few Christians have deliberately entirely separated the ideas of entire sanctification and Christian perfection, a large number have thought of them as only loosely connected. On the other hand, some Wesleyan Christians, and others, have sometimes talked and written as if the two terms were synonymous, as if they were but two names for the same doctrine and experience. To go either in the direction of only loose relationship or to act as if the terms were synonymous is quickly to come into confusion or to lose one or the other of the two doctrines. What we want to do is to hold them together.

Wesleyan Christians believe that one enters the "perfection" of Christian perfection through the door of entire sanctification. To speak of the experience of entire sanctification is to speak of God's ridding the believer of all that is morally unlike himself (one biblical metaphor for the experience is "cleansing"); and it is to speak of the believer's reception of the divine, gracious gift of unconditional, unqualified love of God and neighbor (a biblical metaphor for this experience is "being filled with the Holy Spirit"). The gift of cleansing and filling is received by faith, and this faith is understood to be a gracious gift—the gift of absolute assent to the will of God.

So it is that Wesleyans affirm as stoutly as do any within the Reformed and Lutheran traditions that salvation, all of it and any part of it, is by grace alone through faith. We differ with those two traditions, however, in that we believe that God gives all of us the choice either to accept or to reject the divine will at any time. When we choose to accept, the acceptance is called "faith." So faith is also a gift of grace.

In entire sanctification, the Holy Spirit, as Christ's Agent, calls us to accept the promises, gives us grace to accept them, and ushers us into the experience. Wesleyan-Holiness people believe that the Spirit does this cleansing and filling in a "moment," by which they do not mean so much a split second as they mean "at a specific time." They believe that just as there is a distinct, identifiable time at which one is born or one dies, so there is such a moment in which the cleansing, filling work is done. This moment of spiritual cleansing and filling fundamentally reconstitutes our relationships with God and others, and it opens up a moment-by-moment process of growth in grace and of demonstrations of the fruit of the Holy Spirit.

For Wesleyan Christians, then, entire sanctification is the perfecting threshold. Now the life of Christian perfection begins. One does not seek to become *more* perfect. One seeks, by grace, to express more clearly the gift of perfection that *has been given*.

Here "perfection" is understood to be a relative term. There is the perfection of the bud, and then there is the perfection of that same bud as a flower. There is the perfection of the person newly come into the experience of entire sanctification, and there is the perfection of the same person as a seasoned saint. This aligns with the typical "already but not yet" language of a number of biblical passages. In the Bible, "perfection," when used to describe our relationship to God and others, does not refer to measurement by some absolute standard nor to our mirroring some abstract ideal. It refers to the intended purpose.

Consider the most difficult biblical example: the commandment to be perfect as our Heavenly Father is perfect. Obviously this cannot mean that we are to be equal to God in perfectness—to measure up to Him. To be perfect as God is perfect would fit the definition of a God-created human as fully as He himself fits the definition of God. It would mean to serve the purposes intended for the believing human as fully as God serves His own purposes. It is only in Christ that we see into the very heart of what it is to be both a believer and to be God.

Wesleyan Christians believe God accomplishes all His purpose in us by commandeering us absolutely by divine love. As the apostle Paul puts it, "I have been crucified with Christ; and it is no longer I who live, but Christ lives in me; and the life which I now live in the flesh I live by faith in the Son of God, who loved me, and delivered Himself up for me" (Gal. 2:20, NASB). The apostle John puts it a bit differently, but the experience being described is the same work of the same Spirit: "And we have come to know and have believed the love which God has for us. God is love, and the one who abides in love abides in God, and God abides in him. By this, love is perfected with us, that we may have confidence in the day of judgment; because as He is, so also are we in this world" (1 John 4:16-17, NASB).

You and I differ in our capacity and ability to express that absolute conquest of our lives that God has made. Also the contexts in which we express it differ. Wesleyan Christians therefore do not hesitate one moment to mark the fact that Christian perfection is always perfection relative to many factors, personal and contextual. It is always unconditional love lived out in a myriad of conditions.

In the readings that follow, we will see the two doctrines, entire sanctification and Christian perfection, sometimes conjoined and sometimes separated. We will also see a number of definitions of both that are problematic. Our task will be to remain alert to the anomalies, but also to seek the main lines of any presentation. This means sometimes we will be taking an author precisely at his word; at other times, we will be able to see that the author is saying one thing and meaning another. What we will see every moment is the yearning for, and expectation of, perfection in love in this life, a perfection granted to a purified heart.

2

SIN, ENTIRE SANCTIFICATION, AND PERFECTION— THEOLOGICAL EXPRESSIONS (ca. 100—ca. 300)

Non-Christian Ideas
Gentile Beliefs
Gnosticism
Jewish Beliefs
Essential Differences

Christian Theological Expressions
THE SHEPHERD OF HERMAS
From *Shepherd of Hermas, "Mandates"* 12.2.4—6.5

IRENAEUS (ca. 180)
Against Heresies 4.20.5-6; 5.6.1-2; 5.8.1-2

CLEMENT OF ALEXANDRIA
(ca. 150—ca. 216)
Miscellanies 7.1, 3, 10

2

Sin, Entire Sanctification, and Perfection—Theological Expressions (ca. 100—ca. 300)[1]

Non-Christian Ideas

The terms "sin," "sanctification," and "perfection" had wide currency in many of the religions of the Roman Empire. So when Christians used the terms, they usually had some explaining to do, because they gave these words very different denotations and connotations from those assigned them by adherents to other faiths.

We cannot go into great detail here. But we can and should have some idea of how non-Christians used what seem to be "our" words. And we need to know that the non-Christian meanings of these terms did affect, and even to a certain degree shaped, the early Christians' use of them.

Gentile Beliefs

Almost everyone in the world into which Christianity first came, except pious Jews and Christians, believed human beings were sim-

---

1. In order to help the reader better understand how the earliest Church developed and presented its understanding of sin, entire sanctification, and perfection, this chapter is presented in a format that is not so much anthology as research essay. It is therefore rather different from those that follow.

ply expressions or aspects of nature. "So," said they, "we must live in accord with nature's design." Some preferred, when they were thinking religiously, to call nature "god," "the gods," or "the will of the gods"—or "fate," "the course of the universe," or even "reason" or "rationality"—but it was still nature of which they were speaking.

Almost everyone but pious Jews and Christians believed nature always and finally executes its design and that finally no one escapes living and dying, according to nature's design. They agreed on this much, even though they may have disagreed over the definition of nature; even though they may have disagreed over whether living according to nature was good, bad, or morally neutral; and even though they may have disagreed over whether one might adapt to nature in some really advantageous way or must simply submit and let nature do as it would.

So when the vast majority of non-Christian Gentiles heard the word "sin," they thought immediately about all attempts to avert or to avoid the course of nature. Virtue or viciousness, goodness or wickedness had to do with one's willingness and ability to adjust to nature.

Of course, as we have noted, whether one adjusted or did not adjust to nature changed nothing at all in its ultimate course. Nature had the last word. But nature, so thought our grassroots non-Christian Gentiles, is essentially orderly and rational. Refusal to adjust, therefore, is not simply refusal of nature's will or way. It bespeaks a desire to risk chaos and irrationality for the sake of one's own quirks. Such a refusal and such a desire defined sin exactly.

Of course, sin could not bring on some ultimate chaos or irrationality, but it could certainly temporarily upset things and other people. It could also put nature in a false, even a dangerous, light. And all of this would create weaknesses in what most people recognized as an already very fragile social fabric.

Holding this view of sin, the grassroots non-Christian Gentile heard the word "perfection" as a term having to do with naturality and rationality, with adjustment to nature, under whatever name. The perfect person, many thought, is one who accepts without either elation or dejection what the course of nature sends. The Stoics especially, though few in number, had influenced much of the culture to respond to the necessity for adjustment in this way. The Stoics taught that the perfect person submits—but neither sullenly nor triumphantly, neither sadly nor gladly. The perfect person submits precisely because he or she realizes that the human being is simply one expression of nature coordinating with the rest of nature. To be perfect is to be completely natural, to be completely rational.

Grassroots non-Christian Gentiles talked of sanctification, as they did of sin and perfection, but it had little or nothing to do with the Christian meaning. The term "sanctification" and its cognates almost always referred to the consecrating or hallowing of a thing, a place, or a person by means of a ritual. In this way, a person or group of persons reserved that thing, place, or person for special, and usually quite specific, religious purposes. So, for instance, a person might be set aside by special rituals as a priest, with specific rites to perform.

This "sanctifying" could be done from any number of reasons or motives: as an expression of submission to nature or to the will of the gods; as an attempt to discover the gods' intentions; as an effort to seek the gods' support; or even as an act in defiance of the gods. Sanctifying could express the deepest acceptance and adjustment, or it could express deepest rejection and maladjustment. Most viewed maladjustment with deepest fear and dread, for it threatened the peace and stability of everything.

To worship one who died as a criminal was certainly to reject all that was rational and good. It was to exhibit maladjustment.

From the pagan point of view, this was one point at which the Christian was most suspect. Christians hallowed the memory of Jesus of Nazareth. But Jesus had died as a criminal—as Christians themselves admitted. So from the pagan point of view, Christian hallowing, Christian sanctification contradicted nature or the will of the gods profoundly.

Christians were viewed as dangerously maladjusted. To the non-Christian mind, Jesus' death as a criminal had certified the folly of His life. And while non-Christians understood that some were wrongfully executed and that some types of martyrdom might be virtuous, they did not believe Jesus had been wrongfully executed nor that He was an authentic martyr. Therefore, grassroots pagans believed that Christians were engaging in the vilest and most dangerous kind of blasphemy. In the name of the highest and holiest, said the non-Christian, Christians sanctify themselves to the base and vile.

Gnosticism

The preceding was the perspective of the grass roots, the majority, however poorly many might have expressed it. And this point of view would hold its dominance for another three centuries. But at about the same time that Christianity came on the scene, some persons (they tended to be rather well educated, Jewish and Gentile) had begun to revive the ancient notion that reality does not lie ultimately in matter or nature but in the nonmaterial, in spirit or soul. And rather than advising adjustment to nature, if not identification with it, as the way to salvation, they insisted that salvation lies in escape from nature and matter to the realm of the purely and absolutely spiritual.

Since these people emphasized knowing or knowledge as the way of escape from nature or the material world or the physical, and as the way to salvation, as they understood it, they were called knowers—gnostics.

Of course, it was of the very nature of their belief that each gnostic had his or her own special knowledge. The earliest gnostics tended to avoid creeds or systematic expositions of their beliefs; and they certainly avoided creating gnostic societies. But as the second century wore on, several gnostic teachers gathered disciples, and these gnostics formed a number of schools or sects on the basis of approximate agreements. By the year 200, they seem to have grouped themselves into perhaps a half dozen such schools, and from then on the movement is sufficiently well defined to be designated with an uncial "g" (somewhat like our capital letter), as "Gnosticism."

Gnostics generally objected to attempts to catalog or to summarize their beliefs, for they believed that the work of cataloging or summarizing never really touches the essential meaning of anything. And, said they, such processes are certain to be wide of the mark in matters spiritual. But we can venture on something of a basic exposition of their thought here. And we will have to return to them from time to time.

The gnostics developed their doctrine of salvation in the light of their understanding of the structure of the universe. As they saw it, the universe consists of a number of steps or stages of reality. At one end, as it were, is God, or "the One." God, or the One, is either beyond reality (or being) or is All-Reality (or All-Being). This stage is pure spirit. At the other end, as it were, is the totally material in our world, including our physical bodies.

Salvation lies, the gnostics said, in knowing how to move from the totally material to the stage of pure spirit. Each stage except the first and the last was believed by many gnostics to be the dwelling place of a spirit, force, or god who would help the willing person understand that stage and to move on to the next. So gnostics ranked or rated themselves. Strictly speaking, a full-fledged gnostic was one who had passed into the stage of pure spirit, even if only for a moment.

Gnostic spirit-body language was not new. Most of the grass roots and their more sophisticated sources talked of spirit or soul too. They simply said that spirit or soul consists of very fine matter. But the gnostics, revivers of the ancient idea of the reality of the nonmaterial, insisted that however real matter may appear to be, it has no ultimate reality whatsoever. Ultimate reality, they said, belongs to spirit or soul, to nonmateriality. They went on to say that any material thing, including our physical bodies, has true being only insofar as it is also spirit. What is more, they said, whatever has true being is good; whatever does not have true being is evil. So spirit is good; matter is evil.

We know there are the two realms of spirit and matter, said the gnostics, because we ourselves are both spirit and matter. So the first great task of the human being is to recognize that our true reality does not lie in our physical bodies nor in the world that our senses experience, but in the realm of spirit or soul. That is difficult, they said, for we are easily beguiled into believing that the material is the ultimately real—which is to say, we are easily beguiled into believing that evil is good, the ultimate good. So off we trot into evil, which is to trot off into nothingness.

Our second great task, then, they said, is to find help for recognizing that true reality lies in the realm of the spirit. This help, said they, lies in knowing just what it is that lies between us as we now are and our being perfectly spiritual. And we must also know how to capitalize on that knowledge. Here they borrowed from the old mythological language, though they always insisted that it only pointed to reality, that it was not reality itself. They personified such things as wisdom, truth, time, mind, and peace. And they continually insisted that knowledge of the meanings behind the terms would cleanse the believer from materiality and bring him or her to the One, which is "the Truth," which is "Being Itself."

The third great task of the believer in this system was to seek to be truly real, which is to be truly good—which is to be truly spiritual. In mystical terms, this meant being at one with the One.

This way of looking at things attracted not a few first- and second- (and even third-) century Christians. After all, it was a way of salvation—salvation from the moral griminess of this world, salvation from the transitoriness of this world, salvation from the material, salvation that is truly spiritual, salvation that is eternal and good.

Several things helped the gnostic cause along among Christians, in spite of its essentially anti-Christian character. First, that which the world sees as Christian faith is but the external expression of a personal relationship with God in Christ. If there is no such relationship, there is no Christian faith, in spite of genuinely Christian external expressions. Second, the person, teachings, and work of Jesus are indeed more than meets the eye or ear. Third, the Christians' Book and their Lord are both infinitely multifaceted and multileveled. Fourth, Christianity itself believes in a Spirit who directs a continuing, creative revelation of the mind of Christ. Fifth, Christians admit that not all have the same spiritual and intellectual capacities.

We know that, even in its earliest days, some in the Christian Church were insisting that the Scriptures and the teachings of Jesus and the apostles bore under-the-surface, saving meanings that only the truly enlightened should understand. Being Christians, these persons seem seldom to have claimed that only the enlightened could be saved. They seem to have known that to be Christian (i.e., to be baptized and in good standing with the Christian community) is to be saved. Still, they made it clear that the salvation of the enlightened would be of some superior sort. It would be truly spiritual, while others would attain only to an ethical or a physical salvation, depending on their religious character.

Those who would be Christian gnostics believed that reality and true meaning lie beneath the surface of the words and deeds of this world. Often, however, they conformed only outwardly to the Church. At the most basic level, they contradicted the gospel, because the Early Church clearly declared that salvation is by divine grace through faith in Christ. Salvation does not come by knowledge. Even knowledge that is believed to be divinely revealed cannot save—except the revelation of Christ.

The gnostics who would be Christians contradicted the gospel, too, precisely at the point that is of greatest interest to this collection of documents. Perfection was a common gnostic theme. The gnostics believed that their knowledge perfected them. The way they usually said it was that their knowledge freed them from the natural or the material to be purely spiritual. And to be purely spiritual was to be perfect.

One moved toward this perfection, said the gnostics, by purifying, or sanctifying, oneself. For this, they developed special rituals, replete with special lighting effects, esoteric language, and carefully choreographed symbolic movements. Often special dieting preceded participation in these rituals. And, of course, they considered such matters sacred and therefore not to be talked about among unenlightened people.

The gnostics had a penchant for taking Christian vocabulary and filling it with their own meaning. Also, the fact that they were advocates of a way of salvation and not simply adjustment seems to have gained them great popularity among gullible Christians. By the end of the second century, thoughtful Christian leaders were recognizing that they posed a radical threat and began taking them on. We will treat the Christian response, especially at the point of conflicting views of sanctification and perfection, as we work with Irenaeus and Clement of Alexandria.

Jewish Beliefs

Far removed from the thinking of either grassroots or gnostic paganism but still opposed to Christian understandings of sin, perfection, and sanctification was Judaism. In the first century, Jewish communities existed all across the Roman Empire and beyond its boundaries. Many of these communities hummed and buzzed with fresh religious thought; the ideas of sin, sanctification, and perfection often took center stage in their discussion.

The rabbis taught that sin in essentially a disregard for the Law of Moses. On this they agreed, even where disagreement raged over the interpretation of the Law and the relationship of the tradition to it. They taught that sin is universal, but most of them did not hold a doctrine of original sin nor a doctrine of the sinfulness of our whole nature.

The rabbis ascribed the Fall to the envy of angels. These angels, having failed in their attempt to prevent the creation of the human being, upon whom they knew God intended to lavish divine love, conspired to lure Adam into sin and thus into ruin. Adam took their bait, to the great loss of the creation in general and to his own loss in particular. Creation lost the Shekinah, the full divine presence. It was taken from earth to the first heaven, from whence subsequent sin forced its moving to the seventh heaven. No longer did earth produce spontaneously and abundantly, and no longer did the heavenly bodies illumine it with anything near their full light. Adam himself lost his splendor. He lost God's presence in the whole creation, from east to west, from earth to heaven. And Adam lost endless life.

The rabbis understood that God made human beings with two inclinations, one to good and one to evil. The inclination to evil, created in us by God, is at work from the beginning of our lives. The inclination to good, also God's own creation in us, develops gradually.

The rabbis also taught that no guilt attaches to the fact that we are inclined to evil, but guilt arises when we refuse the help proffered by the Law of Moses and yield to the evil inclination. Guilt arises precisely because each of us already has the ability to study the Law and to do good works. We are born with those abilities. And God, in giving us the Law, has supplied us with that which we ought to study. In it He has shown us what good works are and how to do them. Since we are so well supplied, by our nature and by God's additional gifts to us, no blame can attach to God nor to any force either in us or outside us if we yield to our evil inclination instead of our good. Sinning is altogether a matter of refusing to heed and to use rightly that with which we have been divinely endowed for the doing of good. Sinning is essentially an act of the will.

Just as sinning is essentially an act of the will, so also is doing that which is right. The sum of doing right is loving. Loving sums up the commandments, said the rabbis. Or at least they followed Hillel, who, about 20 years before Christ's birth, had said, "Do not do to another what seems to be hurtful; that is the whole Torah. All the rest is commentary."

Perfection, said the rabbis, consists in loving the Law of the Lord without reservation and applying it faithfully. Further, they said, one cannot love the Law without faithfully applying it. But they debated whether it was possible to perfectly love it, and therefore to practice it perfectly in this life. Thus they argued the question "Is perfect love an ideal or a practical demand and possibility?"

The devout Jew sought to love the Law perfectly, whether as an ideal or a practical demand, by careful meditation and good works. One loves the Law out of one's own resources, they said. One does not ask God for love of the Law. Rather, one accepts love of the Law as one's responsibility.

The devout Jew often sensed keenly the failure to love and to practice the Law perfectly. But most did not think of this failure as rebellion against God. Rebellion would involve giving over entirely to one's evil disposition and willfully committing sin in the name of righteousness. But this, most Jewish scholars said, was further into evil than a true Jew could go. Such corruption on the part of a true Jew would be impossible, or at least implausible.

Still, they admitted they did sin, and they classified sins in terms of their presumed seriousness. Further, they believed that such sin as they committed must be atoned for. And for this, they turned to the merits of the great patriarchs, the merits one acquires through faithfulness to the commandments, and the merits accrued through "works of love" or "gifts of love." So long as merit outweighed sin, one would enter into the joys of the Lord.

So hope of reward fueled love of the Lord's Law, and this made the question of the perfect love of the Law relatively unimportant. Perfect love of the Law—such as the Scriptures declared some to have had—was to the advantage of piety but not basic to piety, a desirable characteristic of the pious but not a necessary one.

Perfection, then, bore no ultimate advantage, as the Jew saw it, for eternal blessedness could be reached without it. It was to the advantage of piety, but not of its essence.

When the Jew spoke of sanctification, the terms paralleled that of many pagans and Christians, but the meanings of the terms differed profoundly. The similarities in vocabulary led to some confusion in the early Christian communities where converted Jews and converted Gentiles worshiped together. The earliest Christian preachers often presupposed the Jewish understandings of sin and perfection and then transformed them to the Christian meaning. Gentile Christians seem sometimes to have imposed the meanings the terms held in their cultures and thus misheard the preachers.

Jews and other non-Christians would have agreed that "holy" and "sanctified" and their cognates all have roots in an idea of separation, of setting aside something or some place or someone for a special religious purpose. They would have agreed that sanctification is something human beings do. They would have agreed that sanctification demands careful, if usually simple, ritual. They would have agreed that one sanctifies another person, place, or thing in order to propitiate or otherwise satisfy whatever the sanctifier believed to be ultimate—a good, a god, or nature, or rationality, or fate.

However, quite unlike the Gentile non-Christian, the devout Jew related sanctification essentially and inextricably to morality, to ethical wrong and right. Pious Jews understood the notion of separation that is so basic to sanctification in terms of the separation between a good, holy God and evil, unholy human beings. That difference is the very definition of the separateness implied in the terms "holy" and "sanctified" and their cognates.

As the Jew saw it, the gulf between God and humanity is not altogether a result of the mere fact that God is God and humans are humans. Rather, God's separation from creation, especially from humans, arises from the free decision of humans to disobey direct commands and to attempt to establish moral autonomy. That decision put the separation on a moral basis. Humanity chose and chooses to set at naught God's absolute righteousness and to disbelieve His utter abhorrence of evil and so to separate itself from Him. God is separate from us in holiness; we are separate from Him in our unrighteousness.

But while God is absolute righteousness by very definition, said the Jew, we are not sinful by definition. The human being cannot make God to sin, cannot taint His character; but God can make the human being righteous, can change his or her very character. In fact, said the devout Jew, God commands us to be holy as He is holy. That is to say, we are to seek to end the separation insofar as it is a moral separation.

Essential Differences

So being holy or being sanctified, said the devout Jew, is a matter of our doing something. That something is living morally. Here lies an essential and fundamental contrast with the Gentile non-Christian point of view. The Gentile non-Christian saw sanctification as primarily a matter of ritual, not moral behavior.

The Jews of that early period in the Church's history understood that sanctification had to do with aligning oneself with the Law of God, which they believed to be essentially a matter of morals and ethics. Gentile non-Christians understood sanctification as having to do with aligning human desires and plans with nature, rationality, fate, or the will of the gods. The Jews understood that any relationship between themselves and their God had to do with moral character, theirs and God's. Non-Christian Gentiles understood any relationship between themselves and their god(s) to be one of an essential identity—the human being was simply one more expression of nature or rationality or fate or the will of the gods. Morality was no large issue in such a relationship. Apparently for Gentiles, moral concerns were usually little more than social conventions—instruments for self-preservation and societal preservation.

Christian Theological Expressions

Early Christians rejected absolutely the Gentile non-Christian views of sin, entire sanctification, and perfection, grassroots and gnostic, and they transformed the Jewish view radically. Most important, Christians responded to non-Christian Gentile understandings by insisting that God made human beings in the divine image. They asserted that far from being "natural," the human being has moral responsibility based upon genuine moral freedom. So sin, for the Christians, was not failure to adjust to the course of nature. Sin was the refusal to accept an appropriate relationship to God and neighbor. Sanctification, for the Christians, was not part of an attempt to placate God or the gods. Sanctification was a gift of God, cleansing and setting aside the believer for holy use. Perfection, for the Christians, was not flawless adjustment to nature. Perfection was the continuing, developing gift of unconditional love of God and neighbor.

Most important to the Christians' response to Judaism was their acceptance of the Jewish understanding that our relationship to God and to each other is essentially a matter of morality. But the early Christians transformed this understanding by making those relationships entirely dependent upon the atoning work of Jesus Christ. He makes the final and adequate propitiatory sacrifice for sin, conquers sin and death for us, and then sends the Holy Spirit to enable us to "walk not after the flesh" (Rom. 8:4, KJV).

So sin, for the early Christians, was not simply the failure to keep the moral law. Sin was a matter of living by any standard other than the "love which is in Christ Jesus" (1 Tim. 1:14, KJV).

Sanctification, for the early Christians, was not simply a matter of keeping oneself "unspotted from the world" (James 1:27, KJV). Sanctification was a divine gift of purity, given so that one may be *in* the world but not *of* the world. One would be separate from the world in moral character, but this did not presume any superiority of human capacity. Further, as the Christians understood it, sanctification intensified the social dimension of religious faith. A people bearing the holy name would bear the holy character as well. And doing this meant developing means for maintaining mutual accountability as they bore that name and character in witness to an unholy world.

Perfection, for the early Christians, was not a matter of flawless conformity to a behavioral standard. Rather, it was a matter of being graciously gifted to live a life of unconditional love. So they believed that while we do sanctify ourselves insofar as we take moral responsibility for keeping ourselves "unspotted from the world," we do not sanctify ourselves in order to be saved; God, through Christ, saves and sanctifies us, even here in this life. And while we do perfect ourselves by deliberately seeking to grow in grace, we are not perfected bit by bit until at last we are sufficiently holy to be worth saving. God graciously perfects us in love in this life by cleansing us from all sin and granting the presence of the Holy Spirit in fullness in a moment. From that moment the gift of unconditional love develops ever increasing depth and breadth.

Along with understanding that God does all this for us, the early Christians seem fully to have believed that the baptized Christian can, and should, live without sin. They also seem fully to have believed that if a person sinned after having been baptized, that person had no remaining hope of salvation.

This latter conviction would have had two sources. First, it was the common understanding that in baptism one is cleansed thoroughly from all sin. To sin after baptism would be to destroy deliberately the relationship with God and with others—a relationship that had been established in Christ. It would be a willful denial of that which one had affirmed in baptism.

The documents lead us to understand that early Christians found it inconceivable that one would accept the grace of God in Christ and then return to the enemy's service; inconceivable, and yet they recognized it as a choice that some had made—so that almost in spite of themselves, the earliest Christians found themselves asking whether there was any hope for the apostate or the backslider.

The answer that one who would make such a choice had never really been a Christian in the first place developed much later. It seems not to have occurred to anyone in that era. Rather, the early Christians deeply abhorred and lamented apostasy or backsliding, viewing them as tragedies of the most affecting sort, precisely because they believed in the power of the gospel to save and keep in all circumstances. They believed that apostasy and backsliding involved genuine Christians forsaking their name and their faith and turning back to sin.

But "Is there any hope for the apostate or backslider?" Here they faced what seemed to them ambiguity. On the one hand were two passages from what would become the New Testament that seemed to deny all hope: Eph. 5:5-6 and Heb. 6:4-6. On the other hand stood the continual word of Scripture speaking of the mercy and forgiveness of God, mercy and forgiveness extended to even the most willful, deliberate denier of grace who will repent and return to the Lord. The Church sought a better response than total rejection of those whom it had baptized who had fallen back into sin. But it sought a response that did not undercut its confidence in the power of God's grace to save once and for all or its belief in human moral responsibility.

Here was a serious pastoral problem and a very subtle one: How could they retain the deep conviction that the baptized could and should live lives of spiritual perfection, and still show the mercy and forgiveness of God to those who had failed? Perfect love was the norm, not as an ideal, but as an attainable and maintainable spiritual reality. Perfect love was the expectation, but backsliding was a reality as well.

Of special concern were those of tender conscience who could very easily believe that they had fallen back into sin when, by usually accepted Christian standards (which were quite high), they really were guilty only of bad judgment, weakness of character, or ignorance. Should the Church turn its back on them when their problem was not really sin, but overly worrisome consciences?

The Church had to raise the question of the definition of sin. Obviously, murder, fornication and adultery, lying, stealing, idolatry, blasphemy, apostasy, and some other activities and attitudes were sin. But can one always tell the difference between greed and a responsible concern for security? When does one cease being "merry of heart" and become drunk? Where is the line between rightfully leaving father and mother to serve the Lord and dishonoring parents? Is the parent with very young children who denies the faith in the face of death an apostate? On and on the questions went.

Hearing these questions, the Church struggled to maintain its norm of perfect love and its discipline while offering understanding and mercy. It directly confronted the fact that some used serious discussions of such issues as excuses for sinning or living along the edge of full consecration. And it directly confronted as well the tendency of some to nourish spiritual pride.

THE SHEPHERD OF HERMAS

Sometime in the second quarter of the second century, a certain Hermas, probably a member of the church in Rome and possibly a brother of the bishop there (Pope Pius I, as he is now known), wrote a three-part work treating these matters. Hermas was himself fully committed to the belief that Christians can and should live in perfect love, but he believed as well that the gospel has a better word than "Ichabod" for those who had backslidden or believed they had backslidden. He also believed that in any system of penance that might be established, there must not be the slightest hint that the Church endorses any level of Christian life short of perfect love.

Hermas picked up this pastoral challenge in his work titled *Shepherd of Hermas* or *The Pastor of Hermas*. This work quickly found its way across the Church, most quickly across the East, where the great majority of Christians lived. For about a century, more Christians read it and were influenced by it than by any other piece of strictly Christian literature in circulation. In fact, many Christians, including their leaders, considered it to be of equal authority with the letters of Paul, Peter, and the other works that were later to form the New Testament. But some Christians opposed it, believing it represented and encouraged a laxity in Christian morality that would destroy the faith. Even this opposition, however, recognized that the Church at large accorded it great and unique authority. Only in the sixth century did it begin consistently to lose its place among the lists of canonical New Testament books.

To meet the issue at hand, Hermas took what would have been

a novel direction by emphasizing the work of the Holy Spirit, a doctrine that was, at that time, a long way from being well developed.

Of course, Christians knew of the Spirit: from the reading and preaching of Scripture; from the creedal affirmation that Christ "was born of the Holy Spirit and the Virgin Mary"; from the creedal affirmation of belief "in the Holy Spirit"; from various liturgical acts, such as the prayer invoking the presence of the Spirit upon the waters of baptism; and from a clear sense of the Spirit's presence among them as Creator and as Lord and Giver of life. But Christians generally had as yet no fixed ideas of the role or person of the Spirit, nor of the Spirit's precise relationship to Father and Son.

Hermas himself reflects these unresolved matters in his apparent belief that the Word, before it became flesh, was the Holy Spirit and in his tendency to think of the Spirit as a composite of "holy spirits," such as faith, purity, truth, and love ("maidens," he most often calls them). But Hermas relates the work of the Spirit to the purity and perfection of believers individually and of the Church as a whole. He is clearly convinced that this work is absolutely necessary to the spiritual life of both.

"And what are these maidens?" "They are holy spirits," said the shepherd. "Except one be clothed in them, with their clothing, one
CLOTHED WITH THE SPIRIT can in no way be found in the Kingdom of God. For if you receive only the name [i.e., "Christian," at baptism] but do not receive the clothing from them [i.e., the oil poured over one who is newly baptized], you will not be benefitted at all, for these maidens are the powers of the Son of God. If you bear the name but do not bear His power, you bear His name in vain."[2]

As Hermas sees it, the Church is an organism, and a Christian is one who is uniquely alive. It is the Spirit who animates and directs both. This means that, for Hermas, authentic Christian faith springs from within the very life of the Church and the believer. We may expect that when the Spirit dwells within the Church and the believer, He will manifest His presence in good works and other pieties. These, when authentic, are manifestations of the life within.

Of course, good works and other pieties can be counterfeited

---

2. Hermas, *Similitudes* 9.8.1-2.

in attempts to gain the attention of God and others, and it is easy
for the Church and the believer to be satisfied that all is well deep
within simply because certain external standards are being met. In
fact, Hermas notes, there are even ecclesiastical officials who are
satisfied with this state of affairs. And worse, says Hermas, some
are undermining the sanctifying work that the Spirit would do by
keeping the scrupulous on the edge of doubt and despair concerning their salvation. These underminers, knowingly or not, so emphasize the external standards and impose them with such rigor
that many doubt that most believers really can fulfill the divine
mandates and live purely.

The solution to this practical spiritual problem, says the shepherd, is to remind believers of the presence of the Spirit, who will
empower them to live pure lives if they will but allow it.

From *Shepherd of Hermas, "Mandates"* 12.2.4—6.5

The Desire for Righteousness

Hermas is reporting here a conversation with the shepherd,
who is also called "the angel of repentance." The shepherd speaks
first.

"Put on, then, the desire for righteousness; arming yourself with
the fear of the Lord, resist [those evil desires, which are lethal]. Indeed, the fear of the Lord resides in good desire. If evil desire see you

HUNGER FOR RIGHTEOUSNESS armed with the fear of God and resisting, it will flee
far from you and no longer appear to you because it
fears your weapons.

"So, in triumph come to the desire for righteousness, and, hand-
ing over your conquest, serve the desire for righteousness as it pleases.
If you serve the desire for good and submit to it, you will overcome
the desire for evil and subdue it as you please."

I [Hermas] said, "Sir, I would like to know how I should serve
the desire for good." He said, "Listen! Practice righteousness and
virtue, truth and fear of the Lord, faith and meekness, and whatever
other good things there be that are like them. By practicing these
things, you will be a well-pleasing servant of God, and you will live to
Him. In fact, whoever serves the desire for good shall live to God."

So it was that he [the shepherd, the "angel of repentance"] finished his 12 commandments. Then he said to me, "You have these
commandments; walk in them and exhort those who hear so that

their repentance may be guilt-free for the remainder of their lives. Take care to fulfill this ministry which I give you, and give your labors to it, for you will find favor with those about to repent, and they will do what you say, for I will be with you and will compel them to be persuaded by you."

I said to him, "Sir, these commandments are great and beautiful and glorious, and 'they are able to make glad the human heart' if one might keep them. But I do not know whether these commandments can be kept by human beings—they are so very difficult."

IF YOU BELIEVE He said in response, "If you determine that they can be kept, you will easily keep them. They will not be difficult. But if your heart is already receptive to the idea that human beings cannot keep them, you will not keep them.

"I tell you right now, if you do not keep them, but, rather, neglect them, you will not be saved, nor will your children, nor your household, because you have already decided on your own authority that these commandments cannot be kept by human beings."

Now, he [the shepherd] said these things to me with great anger. His appearance changed so that a human being could not bear his ire. That confounded me, and I feared him very much.

But when he saw that I was quite disturbed and confused, he began to speak to me more gently and cheerfully. He said, "Fool, without understanding and double-minded, don't you understand the glory of God—how great and mighty and wonderful it is? After all,

GOD GIVES THE POWER 'God created the world' for the sake of humanity, and God placed all of the creation in subjection to humanity and gave the human being all power to master all that is under heaven.

"If then," he [the shepherd] said, "the human being is lord of all of God's creatures, and masters them, should it not be possible to master these commandments as well? One who has the Lord in his heart is able to master all things—including all of these commandments.

"But for those who have the Lord on their lips yet have hardened hearts, those who are far from the Lord, these commandments are difficult and impossible.

"So, you, one empty in mind and a lightweight in the faith, put the Lord in your heart. Then you shall know that nothing is easier or sweeter or more gentle than these commandments.

"You who walk in the devil's commandments, commandments

which are difficult and bitter and cruel and foul, be converted, and do not fear the devil. He has no inherent power against you.

"That is because I, the angel of repentance, who masters him, will be with you. The devil can only cause fear, but the fear which he causes has no binding power. Therefore, do not fear him and he will fly from you."

I [Hermas] said to him, "Sir, listen to my short speech." "Feel free," he [the shepherd] said. I said, "Sir, the human being is willing to keep God's commandments, and there is no one who does not pray to the Lord in order to be made strong in His commandments and to submit to them. But the devil is unyielding and oppresses them."

He said, "He is not able to oppress those servants of the Lord who hope in the Lord with all of their heart. The devil can wrestle with them, but he cannot throw them down. So, if you 'resist him' he will be conquered and 'flee from you' in shame. But to **WITH ALL THE HEART** those who are hollow, I say fear the devil as if he had power.

"When a person fills with good wine a large number of vessels, among which are a few already half empty, he turns his attention to those half-empty vessels and worries lest they have gone sour, for empty vessels quickly go sour, and the flavor of the wine is spoiled.

"So also the devil. He comes to all servants of God, tempting them, and as many as are full of faith withstand him powerfully. He leaves them, having no room for entry. Then he comes to those who are half empty, and, finding room, he enters into them and does what he wishes in them. And they become his menial slaves.

"But I, the angel of repentance, say to you, do not fear the devil, for I was sent to be with those of you who repent with all of your heart. I was sent to strengthen you in the faith.

"So, believe in God. Though you have renounced your true life by way of your sins, and though you have even added to your sins and have made your life onerous, believe that if you 'turn to the Lord with all of your heart and do that which is right' for the remaining days of your life, and if you serve Him in uprightness, according to His will, He will heal your past sins, and you shall have power to overcome the works of the devil. And do not fear the devil's threat at all, for he is as powerless as the sinews of a dead man.

"So listen to me and fear Him who has all power 'to save and to destroy,' and keep these commandments, and you shall live unto God."

And I said to him, "Sir, I have now attired myself in the Lord's full righteousness. And because you are with me, I know that you will break down all of the devil's power, and we shall master him and have

FULL RIGHTEOUSNESS, PURE HEARTS

power against all of his deeds. And I hope, sir, that I shall now be able to keep these commandments of yours, the Lord granting me strength."

He said, "You shall keep them if your heart be pure toward the Lord. And all who ever purify their hearts from the vain desires of this world shall preserve them and shall live unto God."

IRENAEUS (CA. 180)

Irenaeus, bishop of Lyons

Irenaeus, probably bishop of the Christian community around Lyons in Gaul (now France), is one of the most attractive figures in the second-century Church. He was born far to the east of Lyons, in Smyrna, on the Aegean coast of the Roman province of Asia Minor, sometime around 115, probably to Christian parents. His bishop in his youth seems to have been Polycarp, who was himself quite possibly a disciple of the apostle John.

Irenaeus began his ministry in Asia Minor at about the time that a Christian named Montanus, from Phrygia, the next provincial subdivision to the east, gained a significant number of disciples and began to disturb church meetings and congregations.

We know of Montanus and his work only from his enemies, so we must be careful not to write as if our conclusions were incontrovertible. But what we are sure of is that he was an enthusiast, a fanatic, if you will, for the gospel. Especially important to him was what he perceived to be the loss of spiritual fervor and freedom in the churches. He seems to have believed that the Church had gotten so preoccupied with explaining its beliefs and in developing more or less standardized liturgies and forms of church government that it had ignored the Holy Spirit. The Church was no longer the free fellowship of the free Spirit, he said. He and his followers seem to have claimed a number of new advices and messages from the Holy Spirit aimed at reviving the Church, especially in preparation for the end of the age—the Second Coming.

The Montanists did pose a threat to order, they sometimes claimed new revelations that seemed outlandish, and they sometimes expressed themselves in extreme ways. But as Irenaeus and some others saw it, they were not heretical. The Christians of Asia Minor seem to have sent Irenaeus to Rome, urging the Church there to take the Montanists' point seriously—to discipline them, but not harshly. He was only partially successful.

After a period of study and teaching in Rome, Irenaeus went to Lyons. And in Lyons he remained for the rest of his life.

In Lyons, Irenaeus may have put his concern with Montanism aside. At least he now turned most of his attention to a full-scale attack on gnosticism, a movement he seems to have taken to be far more inimical to the Christian faith. He had probably had some brushes with the gnostics as a young pastor in Smyrna, but it is as a mature, very knowledgeable leader that he wrote his great work opposing them, *Against Heresies.*

In this book, Irenaeus attacked gnosticism on several fronts at once and in the process touched on many matters in such a way that he affected almost every basic aspect of doctrine, church life, and structure for a long time to come. Of course, our concern here is his contribution to the doctrines of Christian perfection and entire sanctification.

Critical to that contribution was Irenaeus's notion of "recapitulation." The gnostics believed matter to be ontologically nothing and therefore evil. So, they said, it is impossible that the God of the Old and New Testaments created "the heavens and the earth" (Gen. 1:1, NIV), it is impossible for the true God ever to stoop to being incarnated, and it is impossible to believe in any physical resurrection of Jesus or of us.

Over against these views, Irenaeus confessed one God who is the Creator of the world. He also affirmed that the visible world was created good, not evil. The evil that is now in the world is not a consequence or a reflection of something originally and essentially evil in the creation. The evil now at work in the world is the consequence of both angelic and human misuse of reason and moral freedom (free will). Both the devil and Adam willfully disobeyed God, and through Adam's disobedience in giving heed to the devil, the entire created world fell. The one and only God created the universe, including the human being, intentionally. He made the human in "the image and likeness of God" (Gen. 1:26). And Irenaeus believed in the solidarity of the human race—all subsequent human beings "participate" in Adam, that first human being. So when Adam sinned, all subsequent human beings sinned. To cite but one of many places in which Irenaeus made this point, we note *Against Heresies* 5.16.3: "In the first Adam, we offended God, not fulfilling His command."

However, God has acted to undo the consequences of Adam's sin. God the Father sends Christ, who is also truly God, as the Second Adam: "Because of His measureless love, He became what we are in order to enable us to become what He is" (*Against Heresies* 5.preface). Just as Adam held in himself all of his progeny, so (according to the genealogy recorded in Luke) Jesus Christ "recapitulated in himself all the dispersed peoples dating back to Adam, all languages and the whole human race, even Adam himself."

Just as Adam originated a disobedient race, one doomed to death, Christ has redeemed that race and transformed it into a new humanity. The great instrument of that transformation is His passion, death, and resurrection. "In wiping out the disobedience of Man, originally enacted on the tree [in Eden], He [Christ] became obedient unto death, even the death on the cross, healing the disobedience enacted on the tree by obedience on a tree" (*Against Heresies* 5.16.3). Adam introduced sin and death into the race; Christ reintroduces life and immortality.

At the heart of this recapitulation is restoration of full fellowship with God and restoration of the "image and likeness of God" in us. It is here that Irenaeus most severely criticized the gnostics. They typically talked of flesh, soul, and spirit as something that human beings possess, like mouth, ears, and neck; many of them even went on to talk of three types of human beings—fleshly, soul-type, and spiritual persons. Irenaeus very firmly insisted that while we may for practical purposes talk of our flesh, our soul, or our spirit, these are not finally parts in any significant sense, and they certainly do not designate types of persons. A human being is flesh and soul and spirit—all of them together. We do not have such parts, we *are* all of them together. That is how God made us. And this flesh-soul-spirit human being is made in His image and likeness.

Irenaeus usually distinguished between "likeness" of God and "image" of God. The "likeness" in which we are made is the supreme gift of the Spirit; it is perfection, which, since it refers to God, who *is* perfection, is perfection in love—or moral perfection. Irenaeus sometimes connected the term "image" of God with the body—it is the body that He fashioned in the beginning, and it is the body into which He breathed the breath of life. This breath gave the human being life, and it revealed the human to be a rational being. But usually Irenaeus used "image" to denote the whole person. And when he did this, "image" included "likeness," for while "likeness," being a divine gift to us, is not an aspect of our nature, it is integral to being truly human.

The possibilities of grace are great indeed precisely because the complete human being, made in the image of God and having been gifted with His likeness, is a truly spiritual being capable of perfection. Irenaeus put it in terms of a parallelism between the breath of life and the Holy Spirit.

[The Ebionites, whom Irenaeus accounts as gnostics] fail to understand that as at the beginning of our creation, in Adam, the breath of life from God joined with the created substance, animated man, and made him a rational animal, so at the End [i.e., in the incarnation of the Word] the Word of the Father and the Spirit of God united **MAN IS CAPABLE OF** ed with the ancient substance of that which pro- **PERFECTION** ceeded from Adam and made a living and perfect man, one receiving the perfect Father. So, as in the animal we were all dead, in the spiritual we are all made alive. For Adam never escaped those hands of God to whom the Father had said, "Let us make man after our own image and likeness." Therefore, in the end, it was not by the will of the flesh, nor by the will of a man, but by the decree of the Father that His hands perfected a living man, so that Adam should be in "the image and likeness of God" (*Against Heresies* 5.1.3).

The point of Irenaeus's doctrine of recapitulation is that the incarnation of the Word in Christ Jesus institutes a new creation. And as it was Adam's sin that ruined the first creation, so now Christ's victory has to do precisely with sin and sin's sting, death. As it was precisely our "likeness" to God (i.e., the divine gift of spiritual perfection) that Adam's sin corrupted, it is precisely that gift that may now be restored, thanks to Christ's coming as the Second Adam and His identification with us.

As Irenaeus saw it, then, the Father sent the Son, the Word, to become a man, to suffer and die, and to be resurrected, for the sole purpose of re-creation. Irenaeus saw the Incarnation as a remedy that made the patient better than he or she had been prior to the onset of the disease. He recognized the importance of Christ's second coming as the consummation of recapitulation; but he insisted that the First Coming had brought and wrought all that was essential or fundamental to that consummation.

It is probably quite clear by now just how important the doctrines of sanctification and perfection were to Irenaeus. They stand at the center of the divine purpose for the human being. The work of Christ makes little sense apart from them. Irenaeus would wonder at the understanding and faith of those who insist that sinfulness for the Christian believer is inevitable. To insist thus would be to give away too much to the gnostics with their absolutely impassible, uncreating God and their necessarily evil creation.

But did Irenaeus speak of or imply a "second definite work of grace, subsequent to regeneration"? Did he talk of entire sanctification?

The answer to both questions is yes and no. And it is a bit complex.

The basic data to keep in mind are these:

1. All believers in Christ are being "deified." "Christ was made human that we might be made divine."
2. This deification refers to our essential moral character, not to our physical, intellectual, or emotional capacities.
3. The agent of this work is the Holy Spirit, who simply culminates in the believer the plan and work of the creating Father and the redeeming Son.
4. While the deifying work is in one sense completed only when we "see him [Christ] as he is" (1 John 3:2, RSV), it is also perfect and perfected from the very start. It is perfect in that it is God's work, through Christ, by the Spirit. The Spirit prepares us "for God." That is, we are made one in Christ so that as He is one with the Father, so may we be. To accomplish this, the Father gives the Spirit to the Son so that the Son may give the Spirit to believers.
5. This sanctifying work is perfected from the start in that it is

essentially the fullness of the Holy Spirit filling all of the believer's life.

As did most of the Early Church, Irenaeus saw this sanctifying, perfecting work in the context of baptism. So he says, "Through Baptism, our bodies are united with God and receive life that is incorruptible. Our souls receive it by the Spirit. Both [baptism and the gifting by the Spirit] are necessary. And through them we obtain the life of God" (*Against Heresies* 3.17.2). Irenaeus seems to be referring to the "secondness" of sanctification in the context of baptism in the following passage as well.

Through the effusion of the Spirit, the human being becomes spiritual and perfect. This is what brings the believer to the image and likeness of God. But if the Spirit is not united to a person's soul,

BY THE EFFUSION OF THE SPIRIT that person is imperfect. That person goes on in sensuality and carnality. Of course, such a person carries about the image of God in his or her flesh, but has not received the likeness of the Spirit (*Against Heresies* 5.6.1).

These passages seem to refer rather clearly to the two "acts" of baptism, which topic we dealt with a bit earlier. It implies, at least, that the fullness of the Spirit comes as a "second work of grace," as a divine gift to those already redeemed through Christ.

One seeks in vain for particular passages of any great length in which Irenaeus expounds his understandings of sanctification and perfection. Either that, or one may look at much of what Irenaeus wrote as considerations of these topics. An analogy would be reading through all of Shakespeare's writings for specific passages of some length expounding his love of the English language.

Nonetheless, in addition to the passages already cited in our exposition of Irenaeus, we offer the following cuttings, which show the richness of his thought with respect to our being made godly through the work of Christ by the work of the Spirit.

Against Heresies 4.20.5-6

God Gives Himself to Those Who Love Him

"No man can see God and live," as He is in His marvelous greatness and glory, because the Father is incomprehensible. But in His love and in His humanity, and because He can do all things, He has granted precisely this to those who love Him. They can see God, just as the prophets foretold. "What is impossible to men is possible to God."

Of course, of himself man cannot see God. But when God wills it, He is seen by men. He is seen by those whom He wills, when He wills it, and in the manner in which He wills it, for God has power to do anything.

He is seen in a prophetic way through the Spirit. He is seen through the Son in an adoptive way. And in the kingdom of heaven, he will be seen in a paternal way. It works this way: the Spirit prepares persons for the Son of God; the Son leads a person to the Father; and the Father grants that person incorruptibility for eternal life. And this incorruptibility comes to the person because that person sees God.

Just as those who see the light are in the light, participating in its splendor, so those who see God are in God—participating in His splendor. Now this splendor gives them life. That is how those who see God participate in life. This is why He who is incomprehensible and intangible and invisible gives himself to be seen, to be understood, to be comprehended. He would give life to those who comprehend and see Him by faith. For, just as His greatness is unfathomable, so His goodness is ineffable—that goodness by which, being seen, He gives life to those who see Him. Now, it is impossible to live without life, so the very possibility of life comes from participation in God. And to participate in God is to know Him and to enjoy His goodness.

Thus those who truly live see God in such a way as to live; made immortal by the sight of God and by truly attaining to Him.

Against Heresies 5.6.1-2

A Full Salvation

God shall be glorified in that which He has wrought, for it is modeled after the likeness of His own Son. It is conformable to Him. For man—not merely a part of man, but man—was made in the likeness of God by the hands of the Father. (That is, by the Son and by the Holy Spirit.) Now the soul and the spirit are surely a part of man, but they are certainly not the man as such. For the perfect man is made up of the intermixture and of the union of the soul's receiving the Spirit of the Father along with the blending of the fleshly nature, which has been formed according to the image of God.

This is why the apostle declares: "We speak wisdom among

those who are perfect." He calls "perfect" those who have received the Spirit of God, those who speak so that everyone knows what they are

PERFECTED BY THE SPIRIT OF GOD

saying, as Christ himself also used to speak. Likewise, we have also heard many in the church who have prophetic gifts, who, through the Spirit, speak all sorts of languages and reveal the secrets of some for the benefit of all.

The apostle calls these persons "spiritual" because they partake of the Spirit, but not because they have been divested of their flesh and thus become purely spiritual. In fact, if anyone takes away the substance of the flesh—which is to take away some of the handiwork of God—and thinks that then he has reached the purely spiritual, maybe even the Spirit of God, he must know that he has reached only the human spirit. But when this spirit, blended with the soul, is united to [the divine] handiwork, one is made spiritual and perfect, thanks to the outpouring of the Spirit. And such a person is one who has been made in the image and likeness of God. But if the soul lacks the Spirit, one is truly animal, and being left fleshly, this person shall be an imperfect being. This person really does have the image [of God] in form, but the similitude has not come through the presence of the Spirit. So, such a being is imperfect.

Furthermore, if anyone should take away the image and set aside the handiwork, that person cannot then say that this is a human being. It is, then, either some part of a human being, or, as I have said, it is something other than a human being. Flesh which has been molded is not a perfect human being as such, but a human body, part of a human being. Neither is a human soul in itself a human being; it is a human soul and part of a human being. Nor is a spirit a human being; it is even called a spirit and not a human being. Rather, it is the intermixture and union of all of these that constitutes the perfect human being.

This is why the apostle, explaining himself, makes it clear that the saved human being is a complete human being as well as a spiritual human being. So he says in 1 Thessalonians: "Now the God of peace sanctify you wholly; and may your spirit, and soul, and body, be preserved in integrity to the coming of the Lord Jesus Christ."

Now, to what end did he pray that these three—soul, body, and spirit—might be preserved to the coming of the Lord unless he knew about the reintegration and uniting of the three in one and the same salvation? This is why he also declares that those who are "the perfect" are those who present the three to the Lord without reservation. "The perfect," then, are those in whom the Spirit of God remains, preserving their bodies and souls blameless; they hold fast the faith of God—i.e., faith directed Godward—and are upright in their dealings with their neighbors.

It is on this basis that he also says that this handiwork is the "temple of God." So: "Do you not know that you are the temple of God and that the Spirit of God dwells in you? Therefore, God will destroy any person who would defile the temple of God; for the temple of God is holy. And you are that temple."

Here, he clearly declares that the body is the temple in which the Spirit abides. And the Lord says the same thing concerning himself: "Destroy this temple, and in three days I will raise it up." And he says this of the temple of His body. Still, not only does [the apostle] acknowledge our bodies to be a temple; but he even recognizes that they are the temple of Christ. So he says to the Corinthians: "Do you not know that your bodies are members of Christ? Should I then take the members of Christ and make them the members of a whore?"

[The apostle] does not say these things in reference to some sort of spiritual man, for such a being could have nothing to do with a prostitute. Rather, he says, "our body": that is, the flesh. It continues to be "the members of Christ" in holiness **WE DEMONSTRATE HOLINESS BY LIVING HOLY LIVES** and purity. When it joins itself to a harlot, it becomes members of the harlot.

This is precisely why he said: "If anyone defile the temple of God, him will God destroy."

So, would it not be the height of blasphemy to allege that the temple of God—in which the Spirit of the Father dwells—and the members of Christ do not partake of salvation but are derogated to perdition? Further, our bodies are not raised of themselves but by the very power of God. As [the apostle] says to the Corinthians: "Now the body is not for fornication, but for the Lord, and the Lord for the body. For God has both raised up the Lord and shall raise us up by His own power."

Against Heresies 5.8.1-2

Made Holy in This Life

Even now we receive a certain portion of His Spirit, inclining us toward perfection and preparing us for incorruption [i.e., the incorruption of our resurrection bodies]. Little by little, we are being conditioned to receive and hear God. What we so far have, the apostle calls "an earnest," a part, of the honor that God has promised us. So, in his Epistle to the Ephesians, he says: "[In this hope also] you, having heard the word of truth, the good news of your salvation, believed, and have been sealed with the Holy Spirit of promise, which is the earnest of our inheritance." Thus, this earnest abiding in us renders us spiritual even now. That which is mortal is swallowed up in immortality. So he declares: "For you are not in the flesh, but in the Spirit, if it be true that the Spirit of God dwells within you."

Now, this cannot happen by a discarding of the flesh. It happens by the impartation of the Spirit. For, those to whom [the apostle] was writing were not without flesh. Rather, they were those who had received the Spirit of God, "by which we cry Abba, Father."

Now if at the present, having the earnest, we do cry "Abba, Father," what shall it be like when, rising again, we behold Him face-to-face? When all of the members shall burst forth in a continuous hymn of triumph, glorifying Him who raised them from the dead and gave them the gift of eternal life? For if the earnest, pulling one into itself, even now makes one cry out, "Abba, Father," what shall the perfect grace of the Spirit, given by God to human beings, bring about? It will render us in His likeness and accomplish the will of the Father. For it will make man after the image and likeness of God.

So, because the Spirit abides in them, the apostle properly terms "spiritual" those persons who have the earnest of the Spirit and are not enslaved by the lusts of the flesh, those who are subject to the Spirit and who walk in all things according to the light of reason. Now, spiritual persons will not be incorporeal spirits. Rather, our substance—the union of flesh and spirit—taking in the Spirit of God constitutes the spiritual person. But those who indeed turn away the counsel of the Spirit and are the slaves of fleshly lusts, and lead lives contrary to reason, who dive pell-mell into their own yens and have **CARNAL PERSONS** no yearning for the divine Spirit, live like pigs and dogs. These, the apostle very properly calls "carnal," because they think of nothing but carnal things.

CLEMENT OF ALEXANDRIA (CA. 150—CA. 216)

No one knows just how far back we must go to find the roots of the belief that salvation comes as a result of knowledge. We know that even in the earliest days of the Christian Church some were insisting that the Scriptures and the teachings of Jesus and the

apostles bore under-the-surface, saving meanings that the truly enlightened would understand. However, since they knew all persons
were called to be Christians, they seldom claimed that only the enlightened would be saved. Still, they made it clear that the salvation
of the enlightened would be of some superior sort. It would be truly
spiritual, while others would attain only to an ethical salvation or a
physical one, depending on their religious character.

Since these elitists believed that true salvation, or at least their
supposedly superior form of it, comes by way of a superior knowledge, they bore the name "gnostic." This placed them in the broad
and diverse movement of which we have already spoken, though
most of that movement made no Christian claims whatever.

They were often highly influential within the Church and quite
difficult to counteract where that was necessary. This was so because those gnostics who would be Christians often conformed
outwardly to the Church. After all, they said, the Church does give
opportunity, in its worship and in its teaching, to get to the reality
and true meaning that lie beneath the surface of the words, deeds,
and institutions of this world. But at the most basic level, these
would-be Christian gnostics contradicted the gospel. The Church
declared clearly that salvation comes by divine grace through faith
in Christ. It flatly declared that salvation does not come by knowledge, not even divinely revealed knowledge. Still, gnosticism
flourished here and there within the Church—and was a danger almost everywhere.

Clement's Alexandria, Egypt, was a hotbed of gnosticism of
various sorts, including would-be Christian forms of it. And it was
proliferating rapidly in the latter half of the second century.
Clement, a Christian lay teacher of whom we know tantalizingly little, saw both the danger and the implicit anti-Christianity in its
teachings and in its perspective. In responding to it, he became
Christianity's first systematic theologian.

A common Christian strategy for combating the gnostics in the
years around 200 was to stifle speculative thought and to advocate
simplistic faith. Clement thought this strategy quite inadequate and
proposed instead the argument that the Christian is the true gnostic. The Christian, said he, is the true knower of the knowledge that
saves. That knowledge is the knowledge of faith, the knowledge of
Jesus Christ, who is the great true Gnostic and Master of gnostics.
Christ knew the very mind of God and revealed it, he said. In fact,

Christ *is* the very Mind of God—so Christ is both the Instructor in true knowledge and the Content of that knowledge. To know Him is to know the one thing necessary to salvation. And it is to know as well the true value of all else and how all fits together. Even more profound, to know Christ is to be a dwelling place of the Holy Spirit, whose presence puri-

TO KNOW CHRIST IS TO BE A DWELLING PLACE OF THE HOLY SPIRIT

fies the one in whom He dwells.

The gnostics commonly con- sidered the theme of purification, because purification was neces- sary, they said, for the reception of saving knowledge. Clement saw true purification as a divine gift to all Christians by means of which they may here and now love God and neighbor perfectly. This gift is given in baptism, he said; and this makes it a gift given to all Christians, since all Christians become Christians by bap- tism.

The gnostics also commonly considered the theme of perfec- tion. They believed their knowledge perfected them. Most of them would say that their knowledge or insight freed them from the nat- ural or the material so that they could be purely spiritual and therefore perfect.

Clement agrees that knowledge perfects us, but by way of the biblical text, he transforms the terms. It is God's knowledge of us and our knowledge of God that perfects us, he says. And this knowledge is given only in Jesus Christ, who, as God and as hu- man, reveals that knowledge to us by revealing himself. Truly knowing Christ, we truly know both ourselves and God, and this sets us free. It perfects us. But our freedom is not freedom from the natural or the physical. It is freedom from sin. And this perfects us. Truly knowing God and ourselves, through Christ, does not destroy our connection with the material world. Rather,

FREEDOM FROM SIN PERFECTS US

it makes our bodies and our world means of grace, just as Jesus Christ, the enfleshed Cre- ator/Word, transformed the whole creation.

From the Enlightenment to the First World War, scholars al- most universally looked upon Clement as a Platonist operating, however sincerely, under a thin veneer of Christianity. So they tended to look upon his works as attempts to make Christianity in- tellectually respectable to the Greeks and spiritually respectable to the gnostics. However, since about 1940, scholars have developed more and more convincingly the thesis that Clement was profoundly Christian. Further, they have argued that his works are thoroughly Christian pieces intended to show the intellectual weaknesses of the Greeks and the spiritual fatuities of the gnostics. Clement's writings do this, it is argued, by way of a thorough transformation of classical language to Christian uses.

Miscellanies 7.1

Scripture Guides Our Teaching

It is now time to say to the Greeks (the false gnostics) that the [true] gnostic (the Christian, the true "knower") is the one who is truly spiritual and religious. We do this so they may learn what a true Christian is. The philosophers may then condemn their own stupidity for recklessly and thoughtlessly persecuting the Name (i.e., Christians). They will then know that they have irrationally called impious those who know the true God. And I suppose that I must use more lucid arguments in dealing with the philosophers . . .

So, in order not to interrupt the continuity of discussion, we shall summarize the philosophers' position as we describe Christianity. And, rather than continually referring to prophetic sayings, we shall refer to the Scriptures at appropriate points. Then we shall consider biblical evidences altogether, since the philosophers do not understand what the Scriptures are saying. And we will still present proofs to those who believe, after we have done as we have said.

Now, if what we say appears to anyone to be different from what the Lord's writings say, we want you to know that our words depend upon the Lord's writings for their breath and life. Yet, while they take their rise in the Lord's writings, they attempt to interpret the sense, not merely to analyze the words, of that writing. But one must not go much beyond the immediate sense. . . . That would not be reasonable, and you are right to believe that doing so is superfluous. However, not to take a look at those issues that would press us is indolence; and it is a defect. Further, "truly blessed are those who, observing His testimonies, seek Him with all of their heart." The Law and the prophets are those testimonies to the Lord.

What we propose to do then is to prove that the [true] gnostic alone is holy and pious and worships the true God as befits Him.

CHRISTIANS ARE THE TRUE GNOSTICS And we propose to prove as well that loving and being loved by God follow that worship that befits Him. So it is that He accounts all excellence as honorable, but

He accounts it as varying in worth. So, according to His judgment, among the things that we perceive by our senses, we are to more highly esteem rulers, parents, and the aged. Among those things in which we are instructed are the most ancient wisdom and primeval prophecy [the Bible]. Among [basic] ideas, we accept the Son as the First Principle, the Beginning of all Existence.

And from the Son, we are to learn the more distant Cause, the Father of the universe, the Most Ancient and Most Beneficent, whom we cannot describe in words. He is to be venerated above all and reverenced in awe and silence and holy wonder. He [the Father] it is who is declared by the Lord. And He is comprehended up to the level of their capabilities by those who learned to comprehend Him (i.e., those whom Jesus taught during His earthly ministry); and He it is who is understood by those to whom the Lord chooses to grant knowledge—"whose senses have been trained to discern," as the apostle puts it.

FROM JESUS WE LEARN ABOUT GOD

For the [Christian] gnostic, then, the service of God is a continual occupying of the soul in study of the Deity, in ceaseless love. And on the basis of this it can be said that there are two kinds of service bestowed upon humans, one whose aim is improvement [growth through learning], the other whose aim is ministerial [serving]. The first is illustrated by the medical art and by philosophy: the medical art has as its object the improvement of the body; philosophy, the betterment of the soul. Ministerial service is illustrated by the service rendered by children to parents and by subjects to rulers.

So it is also in the church. The elders take care of matters which aim at [moral and spiritual] betterment, the deacons to those that are ministerial. The angels serve God in the management of affairs on earth in both of these forms of service. And the [Christian] gnostic himself ministers to God and shows people the strategy for betterment according to the terms of his appointment as one who disciplines others in amending their lives. For the only [truly] pious person is one who serves God rightly and without blame in human affairs. As that husbandry is best that uses its knowledge and skill to produce and gather in fruits so as to benefit human beings, so that piety is best that skillfully attains the best harvest, accruing the fruits of the saving knowledge attained by those (more than a few) for whom the gnostic has been a means of belief.

GODLINESS IS LOVING GOD

And since godliness is the disposition that preserves that which befits God, it must be said that the godly person is the only [true] lover of God. That is what one will be who knows what is befitting both as to knowledge and as to the kind of life that is to be lived— one who is destined to become like God and is already being taken into God. That is to say, such a person is first of all a lover of God. As one who honors his father is a lover of his father, so one who honors God is a lover of God.

Miscellanies 7.3

Perfected and Made like the Lord

For now, I pass by some things without comment (though I praise the Lord for them) in order to affirm the fact that [Christian] gnostic souls continue to be honored by their identity with all excellence. The grandeur of their contemplation surpasses even the lifestyle of the (so-called) holy ranks among whom the blessed dwellings of the gods are distributed according to status; they are accounted holy among the holy; and, being transferred whole (i.e., not simply in soul or spirit or intellect) from among the "whole," they reach places better than the "better places" (as defined by the so-called gnostics); they embrace the divine vision, not in mirrors or by means of mirrors, but in the surpassingly clear and absolutely pure, insatiable vision that is the privilege of ardently loving souls; and they celebrate forever. For they are all accounted worthy to dwell in identity [with the One] and in transcendence.

Such is the vision that the "pure in heart" may come to—directly.

It is the role of the [true] gnostic, who has been perfected and made like the Lord to the measure possible to him, to converse with God in thoroughgoing service to Him, through the Great High Priest. [This is] a service that sees to the salvation of others through teaching and through a certain benevolence in what he does. The [true] gnostic

WE GROW IN GRACE THROUGH PRAYER AND SERVICE TO GOD

even shapes and creates himself, and, moreover engraces those who hear him, as God would do. There are two reasons for this: first, to the degree that it be possible, he takes to himself, through practice, the kind of moderation that tends to bring one to impassibility [peace of mind]—that is, to the impassibility that belongs to God by nature; and second, he has uninterrupted converse and fellowship with the Lord.

In my opinion, mildness, philanthropy, and notable piety govern this [true] gnostic assimilation. I would affirm that these virtues are a "sacrifice acceptable in God's sight." Each one who is given entrance to holiness is enlightened in order that the union (with God) may be indissoluble—as the Scripture says, "God's sacrifice is the humble heart, which understands aright." For both the gospel and the apostle command us "to bring [our]selves into captivity" and to put ourselves

BECOMING FREE FROM SIN

to death, slaying "the old man, who is corrupt through lusts" and raising the new man from death ("from the old way of life") by abandoning the passions and becoming free from sin. . . .

For reasons now obvious we quite appropriately do not offer sacrifice to God (who, needing nothing, supplies everyone with everything). Rather, we glorify Him who gave himself in sacrifice for us, and we sacrifice ourselves. So the process moves toward ever higher levels of freedom from want and from passion, because that in which God delights is our salvation. . . .

GOD DESIRES RIGHTEOUSNESS

Neither sacrifices nor offerings on the one hand nor glory and honor on the other can win the Deity over. He is not influenced by such things. Rather, He appears only to the excellent and good. . . .

But, there are those who do not think there is a God. . . . On the same level as these are the opinions of those who say that either there is no God, or that any God who might exist simply does not keep an eye on everything. They say this, having fallen into licentiousness in their pleasures or into serious accidents or pains in the course of daily living. . . . This sort of person is even unwilling to believe that one who is changeless in justly granting goodness is the one true God.

So, we are vindicated in saying that the [Christian] gnostic who cares first for himself and then for his neighbor, with an eye toward our reaching the highest standard of excellence, is truly pious. It is as a son who tries to please a worthy father by demonstrating that he is

YOU SHALL BE HOLY, FOR I AM HOLY

himself virtuous and like his father; or it is as a subject who tries to please a good ruler. After all, belief and obedience are our own to command.

But what of the one who believes that the cause of evils lies in the weakness of matter? Or in the willy-nilly impulses of ignorance? Or in the irrational forces that victimize us where our intellectual incapacities lay us open? We answer: the true gnostic (the Christian) gets the better of these uncontrollable factors by his learning and helps all who are willing to be helped, as best he can. He imitates the divine purpose for human beings. Put him in a position of authority, and he will rule as Moses ruled: with an eye to the salvation of his subjects. And he will quash whatever is brutal and perfidious by honoring the best and by punishing the evil with the kind of punishment that truly educates.

After all, the soul of a righteous person is an image of the divine; it is made like God himself. For it is placed in its sanctuary and is consecrated by means of obedience to the commands of the Ruler of all, mortal and immortal; the Ruler and Sire of all that is noble, who is True Law and Ordinance and Eternal Word; the One Savior of each individually and of all altogether. Truly, He is the Only-begotten, the express Image of the glory of the universal King and Almighty Father.

He stamps on the mind of the [Christian] the perfect vision, which is according to His own image, so that we now see the divine image in a third embodiment [i.e., in the character of the true gnostic]. Because of Him we [true gnostics] live true **I WILL PUT MY LAW IN THEIR MINDS** life, imitating the example of the One who is made to us knowledge, having converse with that which is unchanging and unchangeable.

So, being in control of himself and of all that belongs to him, and having a firm grasp of divine science, the true gnostic sincerely moves toward truth. Now the term "science" applies to the empirical knowledge and systematic understanding of intellectual objects. With respect of divine things, its role is to investigate several **KNOWLEDGE OF GOD** matters: what is the First Cause, that through which all things were made and that without which nothing has been made; what are the things that hold the universe together, partly by penetration, partly by closing, some in combination, some apart; and what is the location and capacity of each, and the service contributed by each.

With regard to the human being: what is he in himself, and what is in accord with his nature or, conversely, opposed to it; how he comes to act or be acted upon—his virtues and vices, **KNOWLEDGE OF PERSONS** the roles of good, evil, and ambivalence; and what of those things having to do with being human, with prudence and temperance, and with the supreme absolutely perfect virtue, justice.

The true gnostic uses prudence and justice to acquire wisdom and true humanity. This he does not only in enduring misfortunes, but also in governing pleasure, desire, pain, and anger; and generally in withstanding all that rocks the soul, whether by force or by guile. For we must not simply endure vices and evil; we must cast them off.

ADD TO YOUR FAITH ... PERSEVERANCE We reserve endurance for things that cause fear. And even suffering is found to be useful—in medicine, in education, in punishment. For through suffering, our characters are made better for the sake of mankind.

[The true gnostic, the Christian] is a world citizen, but not of this world only; rather of a higher order, in which he does all things in the appropriate order and with that degree of interest that each merits, never acting amiss in any way. Because of his knowledge of the absolute God, he covets nothing, he has few wants, and he enjoys more than enough of every good. He is rich in the highest sense. And the first consequence of his righteousness is that he loves to be with

RICH TOWARD GOD those that are like himself. He loves to converse with them, both on earth and in heaven.

This is why he also stands ready to share with others all that he has. And, being one who loves others, he profoundly abhors evildoing of any sort. This comes of his having learned that one should be faithful to oneself and to one's neighbors, as well as being obedient to the commandments, for one who is willingly directed by the commandments may be called a servant of God. But one

PURE IN HEART, FRIENDS OF GOD who is already pure in heart—for the sake of knowledge [of God] by itself, not because of the commandments—is a friend of God.

For we are not born good; nor is goodness a product of natural growth, as if it were like a body part (which would mean that virtue is neither voluntary nor praiseworthy); nor is it acquired and perfected by social contact, as if it were like speech (in fact, vice, not virtue, originates in this way).

And, along the same line, true knowledge is not derived from skills that are related to our aptitudes or to physical abilities that we have developed. Were it derived in this way, we might be satisfied simply to shape and hone the soul. In fact, the laws of the country might perhaps restrain wicked practices. But arguments that are compelling only from the standpoint of logic are too superficial to establish the truth scientifically. Still, Greek philosophy does, as it were, provide for the soul the preliminary cleansing and training necessary to receiving the faith; and on this foundation, truth constructs the edifice of knowledge.

Here we find the true wrestler, the one who is crowned in the amphitheater of this wondrous universe for genuine victory over all his passions. The president is Almighty God; the umpire is the only-begotten Son of God; and the spectators are angels and gods. Our great contest—one utilizing all weapons—is not carried on against flesh and blood, but against the spiritual power of inflamed affections that are at work in the flesh. And this is God's unerring decision concerning our reward: it will be His most righteous prize. The Christian soldier will win immortality when he comes away safely from these

FIGHT THE GOOD FIGHT OF FAITH mighty battles having vanquished the tempter, who has challenged us to them.

God has laid down the same conditions for all participants, so He cannot be accused of injustice. The person who is able will make his choices, and the person who truly wills to prevail will prevail. It is in order that we may know what we are doing that we have received the gift of reason. And just here the maxim "Know thyself" means that we should know why we are made—which is to obey the commandments. And if we choose to will salva-

COME NOW, AND LET US REASON TOGETHER tion, we will obey them. This, I think, is the genuine inescapable necessity (to borrow and transform a Stoic term); we cannot escape from God.

So the spectators have been called to watch the contest. The wrestlers in the arena contend. And now the prize is won by the one who has obeyed the trainer's orders. So our work as humans is to submit to God, who has revealed a many-dimensioned salvation by way of commandments. And our recognition of this is God's good pleasure. Now the Benefactor begins the kindness; a faithful person is one who ardently accepts that kindness and keeps careful account of it by observing the commandments; but that person rises to the dignity of being a friend who returns the kindness to the best of his ability, with love.

The single most appropriate human return of the divine kindness is to do those things that are pleasing to God. Accordingly, the Master and Savior accepts all that is done to help and to improve humanity as a favor and an honor to himself. He accepts it as if it were His own doing and in certain respects as an effect related to its Cause, just as He accepts the wrongs done to those who believe in Him as instances of thanklessness and insult to himself. . . .

LOVE OF GOD AND OF OTHERS It is, after all, impossible to make a full return, one corresponding to the benefit received from God, for so great a gift. . . . As the sun lights up both the heaven and the entire world, shining on both land and sea . . . so the Word, being shed abroad in every direction, illuminates even the tiniest details of our actions.

Miscellanies 7.10

Faith Made Perfect

Gnosis is a kind of perfection of the human as human. It is in tune with itself and, with respect to the bent and manner of life and of speech, consistent with the Holy Word. Thanks to the knowledge of divine things. For it is by insight that faith is made perfect. In fact, this is the only way that a person of faith becomes perfect.

Now faith is an inward good. Without undertaking a search for God, it both confesses His existence and glorifies Him as existent. So, one must begin with his faith and, having grown strong, by the grace of God, must come to insight concerning God insofar as that be possible.

However, we understand that there is a difference between insight and the kind of wisdom attained by education. Insofar as anything merits the name "insight," it is certainly wisdom as well. But it is not necessarily true that all wisdom is insight. Wisdom depends upon language to explicate its meaning; the basis of insight is having no doubt about God and trusting Him implicitly. Of insight, Christ is both Foundation and Superstructure—Christ, by **HAVE NO DOUBT ABOUT GOD** whom are both Alpha and Omega. Now the limits, the alpha and omega, faith and love, are not matters for instruction but are *gnosis*. They are handed down as tradition by the grace of God and entrusted as a *depositum* to those who prove themselves worthy of the instruction. And from this teaching the value of love shines ever more brilliantly. So it is said, "To him who has shall be added." Knowledge is added to faith and love to knowledge; and to love, the heavenly inheritance.

This occurs whenever anyone clings to the Lord by faith and knowledge and love and ascends with Him to the very presence of God, the Keeper of our faith and love. He is the ultimate Source of the knowledge imparted to those who are **CLING TO THE LORD BY FAITH AND KNOWLEDGE** equipped and approved to receive it. And they need further preparation and training for both the hearing of the spoken word and the sobriety of life necessary to cautious advance beyond the point of the righteousness of the law.

This *gnosis* leads us on to that perfect end that knows no end. It teaches us here the nature of the life that we shall hereafter live with gods [i.e., persons who have become like God] according to the will of God. This we will come to when we have been delivered from all of the salutary chastening and punishment brought on us by our sins. Following this rescue, rank and honors are assigned to those who are perfect, those who are finished with purification and all other ritual—even that which is holy among the holy. At last, when they have been made pure in heart by their nearness to the Lord, their final restoration attends on their unending contemplation of God.

MADE PURE IN HEART

The name "gods" is given to those who shall hereafter be enthroned with the other gods, who first had their stations assigned to them beneath the Savior. So *gnosis* is swift to purify, and it is fitting for the welcome change to the higher state.

So, too, it easily transplants one to that divine and holy state that is related to the soul. By its own illumination, it carries one through the mystic stages till it restores one to the crowning dwelling place of rest, having instructed the pure in heart to look upon God face-to-face with understanding and absolute certainty. For herein lies the perfection of the [true] gnostic soul: having transcended all purifications and rites, it should be where the Lord is, in unmediated subordination to Him.

THE PURE IN HEART SHALL SEE GOD

In the next chapter we will hear how Clement related sanctification and baptism.

3

SIN, ENTIRE SANCTIFICATION, AND PERFECTION IN EARLY CHRISTIAN WORSHIP
(ca. 100—ca. 300)

An Early Baptismal Liturgy
HIPPOLYTUS OF ROME
The Apostolic Tradition 15-21
Freedom from Sinful Attitudes

Baptism, Sanctification, and Perfection
JUSTIN MARTYR (ca. 100-165)
Biographical Note
Apology 1.61
How We Dedicate Ourselves to God
CLEMENT OF ALEXANDRIA (ca. 150—ca. 216)
Biographical Note
Paedagogos 1.6.25.1—32.1
To Be Perfect Is to Be What God Wants Us to Be
TERTULLIAN (ca. 160—ca. 225)
Biographical Note
On Baptism 4-8
The Spirit Sanctifies

A Developed Baptismal Liturgy
The Apostolic Constitutions 3.16.3-4; 17.1-4
There Is a Baptism of the Spirit
The Apostolic Constitutions 7.41.1—45.3
Grant Me a Pure Heart

3

Sin, Entire Sanctification, and Perfection in Early Christian Worship (ca. 100—ca. 300)

Early Christian writers seldom took occasion to present full-blown theological or philosophical treatises. They usually wrote in response to specific issues, and in doing so, they assumed their Christian readers understood the basic lines of the gospel.

So the writings of early Christians do not fully explain what they believed about sin, entire sanctification, or Christian perfection. Rather, we find the most complete expressions of these beliefs in liturgical fragments, in descriptions of corporate worship, and finally in the full liturgies we have from the very end of the second century.

This should not surprise us, for the gospel of Jesus Christ came not as a single, authoritative systematic theology, but as a saving revelation. Thus it came to "Parthians and Medes and Elamites, and residents of Mesopotamia, Judea and Cappadocia, Pontus and Asia, Phrygia and Pamphylia, Egypt and the districts of Libya around Cyrene, and visitors from Rome, both Jews and proselytes, Cretans and Arabs" (Acts 2:9-11, NASB). And believers responded first of all by worshiping. The second- and third-century writers were worshipers before they became writers. And when they wrote to Christians, they were writing to persons whose faith rooted itself in worship.

The Church of the second and third centuries intentionally expressed its faith primarily in its corporate worship and in its ethic, which it understood to be the practical extension of its worship. So it proclaimed the gospel to the world. And those early Christians understood their daily lives to be extensions of this intentional proclamation and ethic.

The theologians themselves understood that corporate worship lay at the heart of their work—that all else radiated from corporate worship and built upon it. They understood, then, that corporate worship transcended—and fed—intellectual reflection and emotional experience as the great expression of the Christian revelation and Christian faith. And they understood that the moral aim of corporate worship was our freedom from sin and our perfection in love.

It would have been impossible for believers in that era to speak of personal religious experience apart from reference to corporate worship. For while it was certainly true that the individual confessed the faith as a personal act, it was equally true that confession of the faith was made to the church in the context of corporate worship and as an act of corporate worship. From the moment that one expressed positive interest in the faith until he or she died in the faith, the internal life of the church bore on the believer as a life of mutual accountability.

What we know of second- and third-century Christian worship tells us that Christians worshiped as joyful penitents, forgiven and "filled with the Holy Spirit" (Acts 2:4; 4:31, NASB). They made it clear that God in Christ, quite contrary to what they deserved, had taken the initiative and done the salvation work for, in, and through them. They worshiped as an act of praise and thanksgiving and as an act of confession. They understood, too, that in worship God would continue to reveal himself.

At worship with others, the Christian discovered what it meant to be one of the holy people encountered by the living, holy God. The early Christian believed that in corporate worship one experienced that unique relationship and received those absolutely necessary gifts that one needed truly to live a daily life as it was meant to be lived. In this way corporate worship was to govern every dimension of daily life, including its encounter with a God who calls us to be holy and offers His own presence that we might be holy.

Within the practice of corporate worship, no activities were more important than those that symbolized entry into the Christian community. These were the great divine acts of redemption and reconciliation that had given believers true life and now sustained them. It was simply unthinkable that one could become a Christian and therefore a member of the Christian community apart from baptism. And it was unthinkable that one could remain Christian apart from participation in the Lord's Supper, which they were inclined to call Eucharist (meaning "Thanksgiving").

Christians called these rites of entrance and continuing grace "mysteries" and "symbols," but not because they were private or abstract. Rather, they called them "mysteries" because they believed the Holy Spirit took ordinary matter, in the form of water and bread and wine, and made it reveal the very heart of God and carry forward the divine purpose. By an act of divine grace, these common elements carried profoundly uncommon and transforming meaning and divine action—and so the participating (communing) Church, as body and as individuals, found that same Spirit to have taken the initiative again. They found themselves transformed and made profoundly uncommon, made bearers of the divine action of forgiving, and made a vehicle for the sanctifying presence of the Holy Spirit in the world.

The Church called the rites "symbols," because by making use of them we are taken to the very center of the meaning of God's redeeming character and deeds. This is to say that the term "symbol" held for them almost the exact opposite of the meaning it holds today. For us it means an abstraction, a certain extraction of the essence of something. For them, a "symbol" partook of the very nature and meaning of that which it symbolized. So since Jesus had commanded water baptism as the symbol of entry into the kingdom of God, one could not enter the kingdom of God apart from water baptism. Since Jesus had said of the bread and the wine, "This is my body; this is my blood," and had also said that He was our Life and the Bread of Life, it was impossible for one to think of calling himself or herself a Christian apart from participating in the meal that Christ had provided for us. God had taken the initiative graciously to transform the water and the bread and the wine into vehicles of grace.

Therefore, as the earliest Christians saw it, the symbol actually participated in the very character of the thing or idea symbolized. They believed that the plain water used in baptism really did participate in the very real washing away of original sin. The ordinary bread and wine used in the Eucharist really did somehow participate in the body and blood of Christ. Whatever the philosophical or "scientific" issues such a belief entailed, the believer began with confidence in the gracious initiative of God.

At the heart of it all was the Incarnation, in which "the Word was made flesh, and dwelt among us" (John 1:14, KJV). And then by

His death and resurrection, the Word who became flesh reversed the whole procedure. Irenaeus, the second-century Christian writer and bishop we met in chapter 2, put it in terms of basic principle and expressed the understanding of the entire tradition to his time when he said, "God became man that we might become God." (See chap 2, pp. 62-67.) The coming of Christ as the God-man had completely overthrown all the old notions of the impossibility of any direct relationship between God and the human being, between God and creation, between spirit and body, between heaven and earth.

So it was that early Christianity challenged the conventional wisdom. Such conventional wisdom carefully guarded the idea of the absolute distinction and therefore of the impossibility of relationship between a true God and creation, between spirit and body, between heaven and earth. In contrast, Christianity continually spoke of God's loving desire to establish a direct relationship with human beings precisely to bring about transformation, change, renewal, rebirth, and regeneration. Everywhere in its early worship and its literature, Christianity's language is that of complete victory over sin in this life, of radical transformation of the human moral character in this life, of the fullness of the presence of the Holy Spirit within and among believers in this life. Of course, that language does recognize that temptation is subtle and strong, and it recognizes that some believers will struggle with sin in their lives. But never once is it even hinted that the believer's normal or necessary condition in this life is suppression of personal sinfulness. The language is that of new birth and victory over sin here and now.

Early Christians, then, understood liturgical acts to speak that language, to be its very dictionary, as it were. Those acts took the believer right on into the life of new birth and victory over sin and sustained the believer there.

In an anthology of Holiness works, this perspective leaves us with a dilemma. To present evidence concerning ideas of entire sanctification in the second and third centuries, we will have to print liturgies and explain them. But this involves a certain betrayal of meaning, for the earliest Christians developed the liturgies, especially the sacramental forms, because they understood rational, verbal explications of the faith to be severely limited. They used symbols precisely because the character of God and the nature of our redemption by God's grace are ineffable. Symbols finally defy merely rational explanation or description.

The tendency of the second- and third-century writers was to take the theology of entire sanctification/Christian perfection for granted in their writings. If the liturgies deliberately transcend and defy the merely rational, that means that the ideas of entire sanctification and Christian perfection appear everywhere and nowhere in the literature. They appear nowhere insofar as no known treatises, no known sermons, and no known letters explicitly discuss them. They are everywhere insofar as they are necessary presuppositions to almost all the ethical teaching of the Church. And they are everywhere implied as the norm for Christian living in those portions of the second-century liturgies that remain to us.

The place in which they appear most clearly is the liturgies for baptism. Here rebirth-transformation-victory language appears in very vigorous and uncompromising form, and even more powerful symbolic acts accompany it. It is in this union of word and symbol that we find the clearest, most persuasive source of the Early Church's understandings of sanctification and Christian perfection outside of the writings that would later come to form the New Testament.

Not that baptismal liturgies were everywhere the same. Until around the middle of the second century, except for the universal use of water and (from probably the 80s onward) the universal invocation of the Trinity, baptismal liturgies were not at all uniform. Practices varied from congregation to congregation and within congregations from time to time.

Still, the Christian emphasis on unity often translated itself into a concern for uniformity, especially in those rites that everyone understood to be so basic to the faith. So, from the mid-second century onward, for the next two centuries or more, congregational differences more and more gave way to regional preferences. Thus one could find relative uniformity within a geographical area—and the geographical areas in which one could find uniformity grew and became larger and fewer as well.

Yet even in the period of greatest variety, Christians everywhere understood baptism to be the saving moment, the moment in which one is born again. And it was the act of salvation. It was a human act, but essentially it was the presence of the Holy Spirit on the baptismal water itself, making it effective in cleansing the baptizand. So it was also a divine act. Christians called it an illumination of the mind, the new creation, the new birth, the sealing of the soul to eternal life, the restoration of the divine image, sanc-

tification and deification. It was the process in which believers
were made "Christ."

When the Christian congregation gathered for a baptism, they
understood that the person being baptized would now enter into the
kingdom of God. In the case of a baptizand old enough to make his
or her own confession of sin and then of faith in God's gracious forgiveness, baptism symbolized repentance and the washing away of
sin. From the standpoint of the Church's proclamation of the gospel
of Jesus Christ, baptism symbolized Christ's burial and resurrection—
the baptizand would die with Christ to sin and would be raised with
Christ to new life. No one understood baptism to be an abstraction or
simply a testimony—it was a way into spiritual reality itself; the early
Christians understood baptism to be a saving moment.

And they understood baptism, taken in its entirety, to be a
sanctifying moment as well. It symbolized the death and resurrection of Christ, and it symbolized the coming of the Holy Spirit upon the believers at Pentecost.

Apparently by about the middle of the second century, Christians almost everywhere, whatever the variety in ritual, had come
to understand baptism to be a sort of drama in two acts, each act
having two scenes, as it were. You will see this rather clearly in the
two baptismal liturgies we present here.

Act 1, Scene 1: the prebaptismal liturgy. Here the bishop or
priest blessed the water and prayed for the Holy Spirit to descend
upon it to sanctify it, so that the rite really would confer spiritual
blessing. Then the candidate disrobed as a symbol of having come
into life with nothing and of leaving life in that way. The disrobing
also symbolized two other related ideas: the disclaiming of material goods and having "put off the old man" (Col. 3:9, KJV; cf. Eph.
4:22). Then followed a renunciation of Satan. And finally, the bishop or priest anointed the baptizand with oil to symbolize the exorcism of all of Satan's hosts, and delivery from their power. Now
the baptizand was properly ready to be presented to Christ.[1]

Act 1, Scene 2: baptism itself. First the baptizand confessed the
faith, either in a series of questions and answers or by a brief recita-

1. The language is ambiguous with respect to the baptism of infants. The evidence tells
us that while the early Christians apparently did think about baptism primarily in terms of
conversion, they also apparently practiced infant baptism quite early (how early, we do not
know for sure), and this they did apparently without the slightest ripple of objection to it.

tion of a formal statement. (One of the oldest of these statements was apparently first developed in Rome and came to be very similar to what we now call the Apostles' Creed.) Then came a triple immersion (or, in some places a pouring or sprinkling) in the name of each of the Persons of the Trinity, successively.[2] The baptism itself was followed by an anointing with the oil of thanksgiving, with prayers, and with scriptures. Then the baptizand dried himself or herself and was clothed in a white robe, symbolizing having "put on the new man" (Eph. 4:24; Col. 3:10, KJV) and being clothed with righteousness or with the wedding garment or the Spirit (the biblical passages for each of these were probably read). Then the newly baptized one was led into the congregation, symbolizing his or her membership among them.

Act 2, Scene 1: the postbaptismal liturgy. Surrounded by the congregation, the bishop or priest laid his hand on the head of the baptized one, prayed for the infilling of the Holy Spirit, poured a generous amount of oil over the baptizand's head, symbolizing the entrance of the Spirit in fullness into the baptizand, and made on his or her forehead the sign of the cross. This was followed by the kiss of peace.

Act 2, Scene 2: Eucharist. The newly baptized one then took Communion for the first time, with the congregation.

No one said that the use of water and certain words themselves regenerate the baptizand, but early Christians everywhere believed that regeneration took place in baptism—that baptism was the means by which, and the moment in which, regeneration and cleansing were effected. Reflecting on such passages as John 3:5, Eph. 5:25-27, and Heb. 10:22, and recalling the Lord's command that His disciples baptize, early Christians felt baptism was a part of the very act of salvation: no baptism—no salvation; no symbol—no reality.

---

2. We know from the sources that two things very early became essential to baptism. First, it was to be done in or with water, but there is no clear evidence supporting any particular mode of baptism. Some of the language leads us to think of immersion; some, of pouring; and some, of sprinkling. Each one symbolized a different aspect of what baptism meant.

Second, the name of each Member of the Trinity was to be invoked. There is evidence that some very early baptisms were done in the name of Jesus only. This, however, seems to have been limited to believing Jews. The evidence seems to be overwhelming on the side of the Trinitarian formula as the usual form. But while the Trinitarian formula seems to be usual, we cannot be sure just how many times the water was administered to the baptizand. Again, the language is ambiguous. Some apparently applied the water once, some thrice. It is clear that Christians had come to believe that Jesus himself had commanded them to baptize "in the name of the Father, and of the Son, and of the Holy Spirit."

Likewise, no one said that the anointing with oil and the laying on of hands themselves sanctified the newly baptized believer. But early Christians everywhere believed that sanctification took place in the baptismal ritual, following the baptism itself. They believed that the anointing and the laying on of hands were the means by which, and the moment in which, sanctification was effected. So they said—reflecting such passages as Acts 8:14-17—that anointing with oil and the laying on of hands is the point at which the Spirit comes in fullness in the very process of one's receiving salvation: no anointing and laying on of hands—no sanctification; no symbol—no reality.[3]

Very early then, Christians expressed a conviction that God's grace in Christ is twofold: it brings justification and regeneration, and it brings as well the presence of the Holy Spirit in fullness to empower and direct the believer in a holy walk. The early liturgies thus show both the distinction between the two blessings of redemption and also their intimate connection.

An Early Baptismal Liturgy

Our description of the preceding early Western or Roman baptismal liturgy comes from Hippolytus, a Greek-speaking elder in the church of Rome about A.D. 200. But we must not think that it was used only in Rome. The church of Rome, being the church in the imperial capital, kept contact with the Church in many other places. And being a rather conservative church, it invented very little in those days with respect to either liturgy or doctrine. Rome tended to reflect what was going on in the rest of Christendom, and its baptismal liturgy would be no exception to this point. In fact, Hippolytus, a true son of the Roman church, had no interest in novelty or in being unique. He was sure the liturgy he presented was very ancient and commonly used in other parts of the world. And it is likely he was correct.

---

3. As more and more adult Christians saw to the baptism of their children, it became increasingly common for the church to celebrate the entire baptismal liturgy only for those making their confessions of faith for themselves. When it celebrated the baptism of an infant, it increasingly postponed Act 2 (both scenes) until such time as the child could make his or her own profession. And it became increasingly customary for the bishop to preside only over the celebration of Act 2. In time, Act 2 came to be called Confirmation, but the Early Church never called it that.

The two aspects of this liturgy most significant to our present study are the emphasis on exorcism[4] and the fact that the ritual had the two distinct parts or "acts" of which we have already spoken. Both of these bear clear, if undeveloped, signals regarding the earliest Christians' understanding of entire sanctification and Christian perfection. It is also important to recognize that, in large part, the Early Church finally developed its understanding of the person and work of the Holy Spirit, including the relationship of the Spirit to the Father and the Son, from its study of Scripture and its reflection upon the celebration of baptism.

You will also want to notice the union of instantaneous and progressive elements. While in one sense baptism is a momentary act, it also stretches out over a period of days, and its effects are to deepen through a lifetime.

Further, you will note that while the application of water in the name of the Trinity was at the center of the rite, other acts, especially the anointings, were considered equally necessary to it.

HIPPOLYTUS OF ROME

The Apostolic Tradition 15-21

Freedom from Sinful Attitudes

Now, when those who are to receive baptism are selected, [you are to] examine their lives: Have they lived morally good lives as catechumens? Have they honored widows? Have they visited the ill? Have they done all kinds of good works?

When their sponsors respond by saying, "He has," let them hear the gospel.[5]

From the time that they are set apart [for baptism], let hands be laid upon them daily as they are exor-

Statue of Hippolytus at the entrance to the Apostolic Library, Vatican City, Italy.

---

4. Exorcism meant the expulsion of evil. The Church believed that without the destruction of evil and the indwelling of the Spirit, Christian life and growth were impossible.

5. "The gospel" probably refers to a reading of the account of Jesus' baptism by John.

cised. And as the day of their baptism nears, the bishop shall exorcise each of them, so that he may know that each is pure. And if anyone is not good or not pure, let that one be set aside, for that one has not heard the Word with faith. It is, after all, impossible that the alien (Satan and his influence) conceal himself forever.

Those who are to be baptized should be instructed to bathe and wash themselves on the Thursday preceding their baptism. And if a woman is in her menstrual period, let her be set aside to receive baptism another day. On the preceding Friday, those who are to receive baptism shall fast. That Saturday, those who are to receive baptism shall gather at a place decided upon by the bishop. They shall all be told to pray and to kneel, and the bishop shall lay his hand upon them and exorcise all alien spirits[6]—that those spirits

FREEDOM FROM ALL SINFUL ATTITUDES may flee from them and never return. And when he is done exorcising them, the bishop shall breathe on their faces; and when he has signed [with the sign of the cross] their foreheads, ears, and noses, he shall raise them to their feet.

They shall then spend the entire night in vigil; they shall be read to and taught. Those who are to be baptized shall bring with them nothing other than that which each brings for the Eucharist, because it is appropriate that one who has been made worthy should then offer an offering.[7]

At cockcrow, let prayer first be made over the water. Let the water be flowing in the font or poured into it. Let it be done this way unless there is some need to do otherwise; if there is permanent or urgent need to do otherwise [e.g., if there is no font or tank], use whatever water you can find. Those receiving baptism shall disrobe. Baptize the little ones first. All who can speak for themselves shall do so. Parents or someone from their family shall speak for those who cannot speak for themselves. Then baptize the men and lastly the women, who shall have loosened all of their hair and taken off any gold or silver ornaments. Let no one take any alien material object down into the water.[8]

At the time set for baptizing, the bishop shall give thanks over the oil, which he puts in a cruse (one calls this the "oil of thanksgiving"). Then he shall take some more oil and exorcise it (one calls this the "oil

---

6. An alien spirit was a sinful spirit, an attitude contrary to the Spirit of God. Thus, the bishop as God's representative invoked His power to free the new Christian from all sin.

7. Customarily, the baptizand partook of his or her first Communion immediately following his or her baptism, and the newly baptized usually supplied the bread and the wine for it.

8. Apparently some wanted to carry certain objects into the water, believing it would give the objects magical powers.

of exorcism"). Now a deacon takes the oil of exorcism and stands on the priest's left; and another deacon takes the oil of thanksgiving and stands on the priest's right. As the priest takes [the hand of] each one of those who is to receive baptism, he shall bid each one to renounce, saying:

"I renounce you, Satan, and all your service and all your works."

And when each one has renounced all of this, the priest shall anoint each one with the oil of exorcism, saying:

"Let every spirit [of evil] depart from you."

In this way, the priest shall hand the baptizand, naked, over to the bishop or to the priest who stands by the water to baptize. In the same way, a deacon shall descend with the baptizand into the water and say, helping the baptizand to say:

"I believe in one God, the Father Almighty . . ."

And the one receiving baptism shall say, affirming all of this:

"I believe in this way."

"I BELIEVE" IS COMMITMENT TO THE CHRISTIAN FAITH And the giver [of baptism], having placed his hand on the baptizand's head, shall baptize the baptizand once.

And then he shall say:

"Do you believe in Christ Jesus, the Son of God, who was born from the Holy Spirit of the Virgin Mary, and was crucified under Pontius Pilate, and died, and rose again on the third day alive from the dead, and ascended into heaven, and sits at the right hand of the Father, and will come to judge the living and the dead?"

When the baptizand has said, "I believe," he shall be baptized again. And [the giver of baptism] shall say:

"Do you believe in the Holy Spirit and the holy Church and the resurrection of the flesh?"

Then the baptizand shall say, "I believe," and shall be baptized a third time. And then, when the baptizand has emerged, he shall be anointed with the oil of thanksgiving by the priest, who says:

"I anoint you with holy oil in the name of Jesus Christ."

Then each of the baptizands shall dry himself and put on his clothes and enter into the church.

Then the bishop shall lay his hands on them and invoke, saying:

"Lord God, You have made these worthy to receive remission of sins through the washing of the regeneration of the Holy Spirit; send upon them Your grace, that they may serve You according to Your will; for to You is glory, to Father and Son with the Holy Spirit in the holy Church, now and to the ages of ages. Amen."

Then, pouring the oil of thanksgiving into his hand and placing his hand upon the head of the baptizand, the bishop shall say:

"I anoint you with holy oil in the name of God the Father Almighty and Christ Jesus and the Holy Spirit."

And, having signed the baptizand on the forehead, the bishop shall give him a kiss and say:

"The Lord be with you."

And the one who has been signed shall say:

"And with your spirit."

So let the bishop do with each one. And then they shall pray with all the people. They do not pray with the faithful until they have carried out all these things. And when they have prayed, they shall give the kiss of peace.

[Then follows the eucharistic service, with the newly baptized as full participants for the first time.]

As we noted earlier, the liturgy that Hippolytus describes was not new in his day; nor, in spite of regional differences, would it have been notably unique. A Christian visiting Rome from some far corner of the empire would have felt at home with it, because most of the regional differences lay in the order in which certain things were said and done. Only a few differences lay in the words and acts themselves.

Baptism, Sanctification, and Perfection

JUSTIN MARTYR (CA. 100-CA. 165)

Biographical Note

The Church's theologians, seeking to articulate the faith ever more clearly and to help others do so, could not help but reflect on such an important moment as a baptism and then to express its implications in words. In time, the theologians' reflections came to enrich the liturgies as well.

Justin,
apologist and martyr.

In this section we shall present passages from three theologians as they do some of that reflecting. You will see the growing understanding of baptism as a work of the Holy Spirit. You will also see the increasing clarity with which they understood the act of anointing to symbolize the coming of the Spirit in fullness, entirely sanctifying the believer and empowering that believer to live a life of unconditional love to God and neighbor.

After we have presented these pieces from the theologians, we shall present a liturgy from about A.D. 380 that shows the influence of such theological reflection. You will see in it the clear commitment of early Christianity to the doctrine and experience of entire sanctification/Christian perfection.

Justin Martyr taught in both Palestine and Rome. He was an exceptionally well educated person who may have been teaching philosophy even before his conversion to Christianity. As a Christian, he wrote treatises that attempted to present his faith to both Jews and to Gentiles, especially to the well educated.

The work that is usually called the *First Apology* is addressed to Roman Emperor Antoninus Pius and his son Marcus Aurelius. Justin probably wrote it while he was in Rome in A.D. 152.

Both Antoninus Pius and especially Marcus Aurelius had deep religious and philosophical interests and were well educated. With great sophistication they would argue that human beings are simply "natural" beings, that true morality is a matter of adjusting to whatever nature or the will of the gods has in store. Justin agreed with them that we have little to do with our own coming into the world. And he understood how helpless we can feel to change the course of nature or the unfolding of history. But he very stoutly insisted that we are not mere products of nature. We are special creations of God, deliberate creations, children of God. So we bear moral responsibility for the way in which we live. We were born in sin, and we may continue to be mired in it and dominated by it. But, he says, that is not our necessary destiny. God in Christ has offered us new birth. We were born ignorant of all that could rescue us from sinfulness, but God has sent us light and true wisdom.

When Justin turned to tell his readers just how it is that one receives the new birth and its enlightenment, he described Christian baptism. The rite itself is not central, but its meaning is. Baptism is washing and illumination, says Justin. The believer is free from sin and able now, by the indwelling Spirit, to walk as one thus freed.

Justin could be reflecting a stage in the development of baptismal liturgies just a bit earlier than that described by Hippolytus, and he could be describing the situation in Palestine instead of Rome—but probably not. The outline of the liturgy seen here, and the understanding of the meaning of the rite, differ very little from Hippolytus.

You will want to note especially Justin's emphasis on baptism as "illumination" and the relationship of that emphasis to exorcism. The act of exorcism marked a very dangerous moment in the baptismal process, for it dealt directly with Satan, the enemy, who is bent on the destruction of Christian faith. Positively, exorcism included anointing with oil, a symbol of the coming of the Spirit into the life of the believer. Christianity offered both a vacating and a filling.

Several of the religions of Justin's time used the term "illumination." For most, it denoted the moment in the ceremony of initiation in which the one being initiated came to understand the basic truth or key concept of that religion. That person would then seek to live all of life in the light of that illumination. Justin, and Christians generally, used the term to denote the moment in which one truly understood who Jesus Christ is and what He has done, and received Him fully into his or her life. The Christian point was that illumination was not knowledge or understanding of a truth or a concept; it was a life-changing encounter with a Person. The encounter then entailed a holy life, sustained by the Eucharist, by "feeding on Christ."

By Hippolytus's time, if not already by Justin's, Christians believed that one could not enter the faith without exorcisms. For without the expulsion of evil and the indwelling of the Spirit, illumination was impossible.

Apology 1.61

How We Dedicate Ourselves to God

I shall explain how we dedicated ourselves to God and how we were made new through Christ, for should I omit this, I might seem to be insincere in this explication of the faith.

Those who are persuaded and believe to be true the things that we teach, and who promise to live according to them, are enabled and taught to pray and, with fasting, to ask God for forgiveness of their past sins. We pray and fast with them.

This done, they are led by us to a place where there is water, and in the manner in which we were regenerated they are regenerated, for at that time they are washed in the water in the name of God the Master and Father of all, and of our Savior Jesus Christ, and of the Holy Spirit. This is in keeping with what Christ said: "Unless you are born again, you shall not enter into the kingdom of heaven."

SALVATION THROUGH JESUS CHRIST AND THE HOLY SPIRIT

Now it is quite clear that those who have already been born cannot reenter the wombs of those who bore them. Yet, my previous citation from Isaiah the prophet did indicate how those who have sinned and repent shall be freed from their sins: "Wash yourselves, be clean, take away evildoing from your souls. Learn to do good. Be an advocate for the orphan. Defend the widow's cause. Come and let us reason together, says the Lord. For though your sins be as scarlet, I shall make them as white as snow. If you will not listen to me, the sword will eat you up, for the mouth of the Lord has spoken these things."

We learned this reason for baptism from the apostles: at our first birth, we came forth of necessity, apart from our knowledge, from the moist seed of the intercourse of our parents with each other. We grew up in bad habits and in evildoing; yet, we were not to remain children of such mere necessity and ignorance. Instead we were to become children of our free choice and knowledge, so that we might obtain remission of the sins that we had already committed. The name of God, the Father and Master of all, is named over him who has chosen to be newborn and has repented of his sinful deeds. . . . This washing is called illumination, since they who learn these things are inwardly illumined. The illumined one is also washed in the name of Jesus Christ, who was crucified under Pontius Pilate, and in the name of the Holy Spirit, who foretold all about Jesus through the prophets.

Here Justin plunges into several chapters on counterfeits of Christian baptism developed under demonic influence. One of the principal points he makes is that Christian baptism is of such importance and power in the ongoing life of the believer that the

demons do their worst to confuse matters. In chapter 65, he returns to his main theme, baptism itself.

After baptizing in this way the one who has believed and affirmed the faith, we escort him to the place where those whom we call brethren have come together. There we offer up sincere corporate prayers for ourselves, for the newly baptized, and for all others in every place, so that having found the truth, we may be considered good citizens and keepers of the law. This is how we attain salvation. Prayers concluded, we kiss one another in greeting.

Then the president is presented bread and a chalice containing wine, mixed with water. He takes these and offers up praise and glory to the Father of all, through the name of the Son and the Holy Spirit; then he recites long prayers of thanksgiving to God in the name of those to whom such favors have been granted [i.e., the baptizands]. At the close of these prayers and thanksgivings, everyone there expresses approval by saying "Amen." This Hebrew word, "Amen," means "so be it." Then, when the president has celebrated Eucharist, they whom we call deacons permit each one present to partake of the bread and wine.

And they carry it to the absentees as well. . . .

We call this food "Eucharist." And only one who has confessed the truth of our teachings, who has been cleansed by baptism for the remission of sins and for regeneration, and who disciplines his life by the principles that Christ set forward can partake. We do not partake of them as if they were ordinary bread and ordinary drink. Rather, just as our Savior Jesus Christ became incarnate through the Word of God and took flesh and blood upon himself for our salvation, so (we have been taught) the food that has been made the Eucharist by the prayer of His Word [i.e., by Jesus' words of institution] and nourishes our flesh and blood by being assimilated is the flesh and blood of that very Jesus who was made flesh.

CLEMENT OF ALEXANDRIA (CA. 150—CA. 216)

Biographical Note

Our next theological reflection on baptism is short, but it is important. Clement shows a deepening of Justin's understanding of baptism as illumination, and he expresses—more clearly than the Roman liturgy reported to us by Hippolytus—the meaning of the Spirit's work in baptism. We also read here one of the earliest reflections on the relationship between Jesus' baptism by John and our own baptism.

Clement of Alexandria of whom we wrote earlier, lived at about the same time as Hippolytus, but at the eastern end of the Mediterranean. Alexandria took more interest in intellectual matters than any other city in the Roman Empire, except perhaps for Athens. And in fact, Clement may originally have come from Athens. Apparently, like Justin, he was exceptionally well educated and was thoroughly acquainted with the great philosophical tradition of Greece and its Roman adaptations. As in the case of Justin, it is probable that Clement taught philosophy before his conversion to Christianity.

As we have already noted, Clement concerned himself most with the rapidly rising new school that called itself Knowledge or Wisdom, the perspective we now call gnosticism. And while Justin had known gnosticism in a rather early form, Clement confronted it as a fully developed worldview.

We have already noted some of the characteristics of gnosticism. Now we look even more deeply into the gnosticism that Clement knew.

Most gnostics believed that the world we experience with our senses misleads us, because it is a world of partial realities and shadows, not the world of ultimate reality. It is a world of many things, when we really want or need unity. The common run of persons, they said, take the world for ultimate reality and are satisfied in their ignorance. But there are some who sense the world's illusoriness and yearn for the "Ultimate," for the "One."

There is hope for these who have such sensitivity, because that sensitivity comes from our spirit, and that spirit is our connection with ultimate reality, with God. If one properly develops the spirit, one may be saved. To be saved, this sensitive (or spiritual) person must (and here the gnostics loved to quote the Bible) "walk not after the flesh, but after the Spirit" (Rom. 8:1, 4, KJV).

For the gnostic, salvation meant learning all about the long chain of "energies" or "powers" that emanate from the "Ultimate" or the "One," as we have indicated. Salvation meant learning to exploit these energies so that we might learn ever more, until at last we come to know Reality, God, without any intermediary. Salvation is unmediated knowledge of the One.

For the gnostic, sin was any attachment to the material world, especially any attachment to the body when there was a subsequent refusal to cultivate our spirits and to develop a spiritual reading of all things. At its more subtle levels, sin was willful satisfaction with anything less than unmediated knowledge of the One. Entire sanctification would be a complete freeing (probably coming in a moment of profound mystical insight) from this material world and absolute knowing of the Ultimate. Perfection would be living out the implications of that moment of freeing and knowledge.

We have already hinted at the reason that impelled Clement to fight gnosticism so ferociously. Gnostics could, and did, use all of the Christian vocabulary. But they denied that the true God would create anything material, and they denied that He would ever call matter "good" or have the slightest concern for it. They thought the first two chapters of Genesis to be blasphemous and the Christian doctrine of the Incarnation to be unthinkable. Gnosticism rejected much of the creed that baptizands recited: "I believe in God the Father Almighty, Maker of heaven and earth; and in Jesus Christ, His only Son, our Lord: who was conceived by the Holy Ghost, born of the Virgin Mary, suffered under Pontius Pilate, was crucified, dead, and buried; . . . the third day He rose again from the dead; . . . and I believe in . . . the resurrection of the body."

Clement sought to refute the gnostics with their own ideas. He told these persons who pretended deep and mysterious insight that they simply had not thought deeply enough. God had taken the initiative and revealed himself—the Ultimate Reality—in Christ. And through Christ, God had made saving illumination possible, which is not only knowledge, but righteousness. The believer does not simply know God, nor is the believer absorbed into Him; the believer is being remade in God's very likeness. For all of this, Christ is the Teacher—by His person and His work, including His teachings.

Further, while Clement clearly recognized varying levels of understanding of the faith among believers, he insisted that in Christ the grace of God has been extended to all. He assumed that there probably is an intellectual elite even in the Church—but that no believer is any less saved than the elite and that all bear a moral responsibility to grow in grace and in the knowledge of Christ.

Clement wrote his *Paedagogos* (The Teacher) sometime after A.D. 180. Book 1 of this work, from which we quote, bears the title "Christ the Educator." In chapters 2—4, Clement moves into his theme: Christ is the true Tutor, the very Word made flesh is our Teacher, and He has come from the Father, who is not some impassible, too-sublime-to-care Being, but a good and tender Father, whose children we all are. In chapters 5 and 6, including the passage presented here, Clement refutes the gnostics who say that the Christian use of the term *nēpioi* (little children) in baptism proves that there are two sorts of believers—the perfect and the imperfect. Clement insists that in a very real sense all believers are perfected in their baptism and that they are required to continue that perfecting throughout their lives. He speaks of the "seeds of perfecting" being planted in baptism. So perfection is not by knowledge—it is by grace. It is not for the elite only—it is for all. It is not absolute—it is relative. And it is intimately associated with baptism and the giving of the Spirit there.

Paedagogos 1.6.25.1—32.1

To Be Perfect Is to Be What God Wants Us to Be

We have abundant ways of countering those given to quibbling. We are not called children and infants (in the baptismal ritual) because of the elementary or meager nature of our education, as those who are puffed up by their knowledge allege. Immediately upon our being newborn [i.e., immediately upon baptism], we attained the perfection for which we had hoped, for we were illuminated, which is to know God. One who knows what is perfect is not imperfect.

Now do not scold me when I profess to know God, for the Word [Christ] is unrestricted and already reckoned it appropriate that we might speak to Him. This is so because, at the moment of the Lord's baptism, there sounded a voice from heaven as a witness to the Beloved, saying, "Thou art my beloved Son, today have I begotten thee."

So, let us pose this question to the "wise," "Is Christ, begotten today, already perfect or (monstrous thought) imperfect?" If the answer is "Imperfect," there is something that He has yet to do. But to say that He must add to His knowledge is absurd, for He is God.

Now, no one can be superior to the Word—the Teacher [Christ], the only True Teacher. So, won't the "wise" at least admit, however re-

luctantly, that the perfect Word, born of the perfect Father, was begotten in perfection, according to the predetermined strategy? And if
He was perfect, why was He baptized? "Ah," say the "wise," "it was
necessary, to show that He was indeed fully human." Very well! So
then I say, "Does Christ become perfect simultaneously with His baptism by John?" And the answer is, "Manifestly." "He could not then
learn anything more from John?" And the answer is, "Certainly not."

SANCTIFIED BY THE SPIRIT But now comes this question: "Is Christ perfected
by the washing (of John's baptism) alone, and is He sanc-
tified by the descent of the Spirit?" The answer is, "Yes!"

The same things also take place in our case, for whom the Lord
has become the Pattern. Being baptized, we are illumined; being illumined, we are made children; being made children, we are perfected;
being perfected, we are made immortal. As he says, "I have said that
you are gods, and all sons of the highest" (Ps. 82:6).

This work [i.e., baptism, considered in its ritual entirety] is vari-
ously called a "gift of grace," "illumination," "perfection," and "washing." It is the washing through which we are cleansed of our sins; the
grace gift by which the penalties for our sins are remitted; the illumination through which we see the holy light of salvation, that is, the illumination by which we see God clearly.

Now we call "perfect" that which lacks nothing. So what is lacking to one who knows God? It would be truly monstrous to call that
which is not complete a gift, or act, of God's grace. He, being perfect,
bestows perfect gifts. Just as all things were made at His command, so
the perfecting of His grace follows on His merest desire to bestow
grace. The power of His will brings the essence of the future into the
present.

Even further, release from evils is the beginning of salvation. So,
only those of us who have first touched the very limits of life [i.e.,
have passed from the old life into the new] are already perfect. Those
of us who are separated from death already live. After all, salvation is
SALVATION IS IN FOLLOWING CHRIST a matter of following Christ, "for that which is in
him is life." "Truly, truly I say to you, the one who
hears my words and believes on him who sent me
has eternal life. He does not come into condemnation but has passed
from death to life." So, simply to believe and to be reborn is perfection in this life.

God never changed in this matter, for as the creation of the
world expresses the working of His will, so His salvation, which is

called "the Church," expresses the working of His counsel. He knows whom He has called and whom He has saved, for at one and the same time, He called and saved them.

"You are," says the apostle, "taught by God." It is not permissible to think that what He teaches is imperfect. What is learned from Him is the eternal salvation of the eternal Savior, to whom be thanks for ever and ever. Amen. And only he is [has real life] who is regenerated and enlightened [i.e., baptized]. He is delivered on the spot from darkness and in that instant [of baptism] receives the light.

So then, those who have shaken off sleep become entirely alert— or, rather, those who try to remove a film from the eyes do not turn up the light, but they seek to remove the film so that the pupil may be free. Thus we who are baptized, having wiped away the sins which have obscured the light of the divine Spirit, have the eye of our spirit freed. We are unhampered, and full of light, by which alone we contemplate the Divine, the Holy Spirit, who flows down on us from above.

This is the eternal modification of our sight, which enables us to see the eternal light. That which is holy loves that from which holiness proceeds, which has appropriately

HOLINESS IS LOVE FOR GOD AND COMES FROM GOD

been called light: "Once you were darkness; now are you light in the Lord." I believe that it was because of this that the ancients called the human being phos [phōs = light; phós = a man].

"But," say the "wise," "this person still has not received the perfect gift." And with this I agree. But that person is in the light, and the darkness does not overcome him.

There is nothing intermediate between light and darkness. So while it is true that ultimate completion[8] is reserved until the resurrection of believers, reception of the perfect gift[9] is nothing other than the obtaining of that which was previously promised. Now, this is not to say that both the arrival at the end and the earnest of that arrival are the same, for eternity and time are not the same. And neither are the undertaking and the final result the same. But both refer to the same thing, and it is one and the same person who is involved in

---

8. "Ultimate completion" seems to mean what theology today calls final salvation in heaven.

9. The "perfect gift" surely refers to salvation through Christ, perhaps intended to include "the gift of the Father" (see Acts 2:4) that Jesus had previously promised to His followers (Luke 24:49, NEB).

both. Faith, so to speak, is the undertaking generated in time; the final result is the attainment of the promise, which is forever secured.

Now the Lord himself very clearly revealed that salvation is equal for all when He said, "This is the will of my Father: that everyone who sees the Son and believes on him should have everlasting life. And I will raise him up in the last day." We believe that insofar as it is

MADE PERFECT IN THIS WORLD possible in this world (which is what He means by "the last day"), to the time that the world, preserved by Him, shall end, we are made perfect. For that reason, He says, "He that believeth on the Son has eternal life."

If, then, those who have believed have life, what remains beyond the possession of eternal life? Nothing. Nothing is lacking to faith, for faith is perfect and complete in itself. If it lacks anything, it is not wholly perfect. Nor is it truly faith if it be in any way defective. There is not a different sort of thing awaiting those of us who have believed in this life after we have departed from it. Faith here, among us who have believed, is a pledge and foretaste of the same nature as its fulfillment. So,

GRASPED BY FAITH without distinctions among us, having in anticipation grasped by faith that which is yet to come, we receive it, after the resurrection, as present, so that the word that was spoken may be fulfilled: "Be it according to your faith." Where faith is, there is the promise; and the consummation of the promise is rest.

So then, in illumination [i.e., baptism] we receive knowledge, and the purpose of knowledge is rest—rest being conceived as the final object of hope. As experience brings an end to inexperience and a solution brings an end to perplexity, so darkness disappears because of illumination. Darkness is ignorance, by which we stumble into sins, absolutely blind as to the truth. Knowledge is the illumination that we receive. It makes ignorance disappear, and it endows us with clear vision. Moreover, to desert the bad is to adopt the better, for what ignorance has ill tied, knowledge well releases. Human faith and

HUMAN FAITH AND DIVINE GRACE divine grace swiftly loosen our shackles, our transgressions having been removed by a single medicine, the baptism of the Word.

We are washed from all our sins. We are no longer enmeshed in evil. This [i.e., baptism] is the one grace of illumination; our characters are not the same as before washing. And since knowledge springs up with illumination, shining its beams about the mind, we, who were untaught, become disciples in the moment we hear.

Now, I ask, does this occur at the moment of this instruction? It is impossible to say just when it happens because instruction leads to faith, and faith, together with baptism, is tutored by **TUTORED BY THE HOLY SPIRIT** the Holy Spirit. And that faith is the single universal salvation of the human race. As the apostle most clearly demonstrated, speaking to this very point, there is equality before the righteous and loving God, and He retains the same kind of fellowship with all persons. First the apostle said: "Before faith came, we were kept under the law, shut out of the faith which would later be revealed, so that the law became our schoolmaster to bring us to Christ, so that we might be justified by faith. But after that faith [i.e., that faith "which would later be revealed"] is come, we are no longer subject to a schoolmaster." Do you hear? We are no longer under that law, which was accompanied with fear, but we are subject to the Word, the master of free choice.

Then, second, the apostle said this, which is free of all partiality: "For you are all the children of God through faith in Jesus Christ. For **ALL OF GOD'S GRACE FOR ALL OF GOD'S PEOPLE** as many as were baptized into Christ have put on Christ. There is neither Jew nor Greek, neither bond nor free, neither male nor female, for all of you are one in Christ Jesus." There are not, then, in the same Word [in Christ], "some illuminated, and some animal-level people." Rather, all who have abandoned the desires of the flesh are equal and "spiritual" before the Lord. Again, elsewhere, the apostle writes: "For by one spirit we are all baptized into one body, whether Jews or Greeks, whether bond or free; and we have all drunk of one cup."

TERTULLIAN
(CA. 160—CA. 225)

Biographical Note

Tertullian, from the North African city of Carthage, was another of earliest Christianity's exceptionally well educated adherents. Like Justin and Clement, he converted to Christianity as an adult—like them, at about age 30. It appears that he practiced law before taking Christian ordination, and he could never seem to satisfy

Tertullian of Carthage

his need for careful definitions of terms nor his conviction that Christianity's "rules," both doctrinal and behavioral, must be maintained to the letter. Yet no one who has left us any writings argued more vigorously or effectively than he that the Church, with its penchant for structure in all things, must not quench the Spirit.

Over the issue of obeying the Spirit, Tertullian left the church in Carthage to become a Montanist, and he apparently eventually left Montanism to join an even stricter group. The Montanists in some places and at some times developed outlandish notions, or at least they used outlandish language. But their primary concern found great sympathy in the Church: they wanted a Church obedient to the Holy Spirit. But they believed that the Spirit's principal characteristic is freedom and that His principal gift to believers is freedom. By freedom they seem to have meant openness to new revelations and ecstasies—the more unusual the better. Here, of course, is where they got into trouble, for these revelations and ecstasies often interrupted the usual course of corporate worship, and they allowed all too little room for examination (or, as the Early Church called it, "discernment of spirits").

At least at first, the Montanists drew their understanding of the Holy Spirit from Christian corporate worship, especially the Bible readings and the sacramental celebrations. Later they looked to their own ecstasies.

Tertullian's tract on baptism appears at first reading to have nothing whatsoever to do with Montanism. And, in fact, he may have written it even before he had heard much about that sect. But the concerns he expresses relate quite directly to issues raised later by the Montanists and by the mainline Church's response to them.

Heretics, perhaps gnostics, had questioned the usefulness of Christian baptism. They made sport of the Christian claims concerning the effects of baptism, especially since the ceremony had no drama in it and involved nothing more than common water and very plain words.

Tertullian writes to help resolve the doubts of those who are about to receive baptism and of those already baptized whose faith the critics have threatened. His basic response is very simple: God always does His earthly work through simple earthly means, using seeming foolishness to perplex the worldly-wise. In the divine strategy, supernatural effects do not depend upon supernatural materials. What we really must reckon with in baptism is the person and work of the Holy Spirit.

Here Tertullian begins to reflect upon the baptismal ritual. The Holy Spirit is invited to come down and sanctify that common water, so that the water may itself sanctify the one baptized in it. As common water washes away external physical dirt, so sanctified water washes away the sin that is within us. But that is only the beginning, says Tertullian. Baptism in sanctified water prepares us then to receive the Holy Spirit in fullness. But, writes Tertullian, we do not actually receive the Spirit then. We actually receive the Spirit in fullness in the second part of the ritual. First, as we emerge from the water of baptism, we are anointed with oil in the name of the Trinity. This makes us receptive to the coming of the Spirit. So now the bishop lays hands on us, blesses us, and calls the Spirit down upon us. This thoroughly sanctifies us.

On Baptism 4-8

The Spirit Sanctifies

Sufficient proof of our argument may be seen in a selection of prefigurations in which the rationale of baptism is recalled. The first of them is that the Spirit of God, who from the beginning rode upon the waters, would as Baptizer abide upon waters. Long ago, its place in Scripture made this a prophetic indication and type of baptism. A holy thing, in fact, was borne upon a holy thing. That is to say, because lower matter simply must take to itself the quality of that which is above it, the water acquired holiness from that which it bore [i.e., the Spirit of God]. It is especially true that corporeality must take on spirituality. And because of its subtlety, spirituality easily penetrates and inheres. So it is that the nature of the waters, having received holiness from the Holy, absorbs power to make holy.

Now, let's not have anyone saying, "Does this not logically mean that we must be baptized in the very waters that were there in the beginning?" Not the very same and yet still the same, the very same to the extent that the species is one, though there are many individual instances, and whatever becomes an attribute of the species abounds in the individuals. Therefore, it makes no difference whether one is washed in sea or pond, river or spring, cistern or tub. And there is no difference between those whom John baptized in the Jordan and those whom Peter baptized in the Tiber unless you want to argue that the eunuch whom Philip baptized in water, come upon accidentally, obtained a higher or lower degree of salvation on that account.

When God is invoked, all waters . . . acquire the privileged sacred significance, [because] the Spirit descends from heaven and rests upon the waters, sanctifying them His very own self. And when they are sanctified in this way, they absorb sanctifying power. Moreover, the simile would apply as well to the simple act; that as we are defiled by sins as though with filth, we are washed clean with water. But just as sins in the flesh are not visible—for instance, one does not find the stains of idolatry, adultery, or embezzlement on one's skin—persons who sin in these ways are filthy in spirit, which is where sin originates. The spirit is the master, the body the servant. And yet, each of these imparts its guilt to the other, the spirit by its exercise of authority, the flesh by its responsive service. So it is that when the waters have in some way acquired healing power by the intervention of an angel, the spirit is corporally washed and the flesh spiritually cleansed in them. . . .

Why have we referred to such matters? So that no one will believe it difficult for the holy angel of God to be there to put the waters in motion for man's salvation even when an evil angel of the profane one often does business with that same element to the ruin of man. If it be considered unusual that an angel invade the waters, we would declare that a foreshadowing of the future has already occurred. An angel, invading, used to move the pool of Bethsaida. Those complaining of ill health watched for it. For if one preceded the others down there, he gave up his complaints after washing. This example of physical healing foretold spiritual healing according to the pattern that physical things, as figures, precede spiritual.

Therefore, the grace of God, moving all things forward, has approached more nearly the significance of the waters and the angel. They were formerly used to remedy the defects of the body, now the spirit is healed; they used to be busied with temporal health, now they transform the eternal; they used to free one person once a year, now they save many people, extinguishing death by the washing away of sins. Evidently, as the guilt is taken away, the penalty is taken away as well. Thus man is restored to God, to the likeness of him who earlier had been in the image of God. The image in semblance is esteemed as the eternal likeness, for he regains that very Spirit of God that he had at that long-ago time received by God's breathing, but had later lost through sin.

Not that we acquire the Holy Spirit as a result of [baptism in] water, but that in the water, being made clean by the angel, we are **MADE READY FOR** made ready for the Holy Spirit. Here, too, a type **THE HOLY SPIRIT** has come first. As John was the forerunner of the Lord, preparing His ways, so also the angel, the mediator of baptism, coming suddenly, makes straight the ways for the Holy Spirit. This is accomplished by the abolition of sins, which faith obtains, signed and sealed in the Father, Son, and Holy Spirit. For if every word be established by three witnesses, how much more the gift of God? By way of the blessing, we have as Mediators of the faith the same Persons that we have as Guarantors of salvation. The number of divine names also gives hope to confidence. Moreover, because the calling down of faith and the pledging of the solemn promise of salvation are done in the name of the three, one must add mention of the Church, for where the three are—that is, Father, Son, and Holy Spirit—there is the Church.

So it is that when we come up from the washing, we are thoroughly anointed with a blessed anointing like that given by earlier custom, following Moses' anointing of Aaron, in which one is anointed by the priest with oil out of an animal horn. This is the origin of the name "Christ"; it is from "chrism," the Greek word for "anointing." That is, of course, the name we apply to our Lord. Anointing is a spiritual act, for our Lord was anointed with the Spirit by God the Father. As it says in the Acts: "Thy holy servant Jesus, whom you anointed." So it is in our case as well; the unction flows over flesh, **SET FREE** but it profits spiritually. We are immersed in water in bap-**FROM SIN** tism itself as a fleshly act; but the spiritual effect is that we are set free from sins.

Then a hand is laid upon us by way of blessing, summoning, and inviting the Holy Spirit. There is good reason for this. Human character is allowed to call the Spirit down into the water; and the laying on of hands, the conjoining of water and Spirit and our meager spirit, brings life. Surely one would allow God to bring about something spiritually sublime with His own chosen instrument, through holy hands. The origins of this act are found in the ancient sacred rite in which Jacob blessed his grandsons, Ephraim and Manasseh. He crossed his hands in that act, reversing the natural order. Thus he prefigured Christ and portended the future blessing in Christ.

Then the most Holy Spirit descends freely from the Father upon

CLEANSED AND BLESSED bodies cleansed and blessed. And as He abides there, it calls to mind again His unsullied throne. He came down upon our Lord in the form of a dove, clearly declaring in this way His nature through a simple, innocent creature. . . . So he says, "Be simple, like doves."

This, too, has its earlier type. After the waters of the Flood had washed away ancient iniquity—or, so to say, after the baptism of the world—a dove, having been sent forth from the ark and having returned with an olive leaf, announced to the earth, as a herald, the pacification of the heavenly wrath. This sign of peace was held out to the heathen too.

Continuing the same theme, the dove, the Holy Spirit, is sent forth from heaven, where the Church is prefigured by the ark; it flies to earth, that is, to our flesh, as that flesh is emerging from the washing away of our ancient sins, and it brings the peace of God.

Someone says, "But the world is sinning again, which makes the comparison between baptism and the Flood a bad one." In fact, this world is destined for the fire. And so is the one who resorts to his transgressions after baptism. So we must take baptism as an admonitory sign.

A Developed Baptismal Liturgy

By the end of the 300s the interaction between the reflections of the theologians and the various developing baptismal rituals reached a kind of maturity. Neither theological reflection nor liturgical development stopped, but the sense of a need for uniformity had led to considerable standardization—especially in the case of baptism and the Lord's Supper. On the eastern end of the Mediterranean, where at that time the great majority of Christians lived, it would seem that three liturgies, each with only slight variation from the other two, were in the process of being fused into one.

No one knows who shaped these liturgies, but we know that one of them is probably based upon the one described by Hippolytus and that another comes from Syria—probably from the Greek-speaking city of Antioch. The third leaves us only guessing.

All three of these liturgies, in the process of being fused, appear in a work called the Apostolic Constitutions (AC), a work written in the East, probably in Syria or Palestine, in the 380s. This was a period of both political and theological unrest. The AC meant to impose liturgical order in a confused situation, and it meant to do so by enhancing the role of the bishop and by claiming to be a document issuing from a meeting of the original apostles in Jerusalem. The AC reflects older practice. How much older we do not know, though some of what it reports seems to be taken from documents reaching back into the first century. Its novelty lies in its attempt to meld various earlier strands.

The AC gives special attention to the doctrine of the Holy Spirit. In the case of baptism, that concern spells itself out precisely in the book's description of what we have earlier called the "second act" in the rite of baptism—the anointing with oil and the laying on of hands by the bishop. In book 3, chapter 16, paragraph 4, that anointing is called "a type of the baptism of the Spirit." In 3.17.1, it is said to be given "in place of the Spirit," seeming to mean "as a symbol of the Spirit's coming." But at that point a problem arises, for it would appear that the anointing comes before the actual baptism.

This apparently odd sequence has not gone unnoticed. Across 1,600 years most interpreters have said that the passage itself confuses the initial anointing(s), which have to do with exorcism of malign spirits, and the later one, following baptism, which has to do with the reception of the Holy Spirit in fullness and therefore makes much of the laying on of hands by the bishop. Most of these interpreters suggest that the reason for the confusion lies in the AC's near preoccupation with strengthening the place of the bishop. This seems reasonable, especially since this account is clearly related to that of Hippolytus.

Hippolytus seems clearly to distinguish between the meanings of the two types of anointing, but in either case the ritual actions themselves are similar—anointing with the laying on of hands. By the time of the writing of the AC, Christians (at least in the East) associated laying on of hands with the giving of the gift of the Spirit in fullness, an association that Hippolytus granted only to the postbaptismal anointing. They missed the difference that Hippolytus described.

So we have here a puzzle regarding the texts. Historically the church has not worried about it. It has simply accepted some of the theological reflection presented in the AC, and even some of the AC's purposes, but it has followed Hippolytus's description of the order of things as normative: earlier anointings are for exorcism. And the laying on of hands has to do with the work of the Holy Spirit in cleansing the believer of evil. The anointing with the laying on of hands, signifying the coming of the Holy Spirit to dwell in the believer in fullness, follows baptism; spiritually, it cannot precede it.

Sanctification can occur only after one has been "buried with him [Christ]" in baptism and raised to new life in Him (Rom. 6:4, KJV). The old "life" cannot be sanctified. In 7.22.2, then, in spite of the apparent confusion in the order of events, the anointing with the laying on of hands is called "the seal of the covenants." This is another way of saying that it is the fulfillment, and promise of further fulfillment, of the divine promises concerning our redemption—the Spirit has come and will abide as "Creator Spirit."

The Apostolic Constitutions 3.16.3-4; 17.1-4

There Is a Baptism of the Spirit

Now, the bishop shall anoint [the baptizand's] head during the laying on of hands, as it used to be done for kings and priests. Not that those now baptized are ordained priests. Rather, because as anointed persons in the train of the Anointed One, they are a royal priesthood, a holy nation, the Church of God, the pillar and ground of truth. Those who once were not a people are now beloved and chosen. So, Bishop, according to that typology you shall anoint with holy oil the heads of those baptized, men or women, as a type of the baptism of the Spirit. Then, either you, Bishop, or the presbyter acting for you, saying and pronouncing over them the holy invocation of the Father and of the Son and of the Holy Spirit, shall baptize them in the water. Then let a deacon receive the men, a deaconess the women, so that the conferring of this inviolable seal may occur with due dignity. And after all of this, the bishop shall anoint the newly baptized with the holy oil.

. . . Baptism, then, is given in symbol of the death of the Son, the water symbolizes entombment, the oil symbolizes the Holy Spirit, the seal symbolizes the Cross, and the holy oil represents chrism, the confession [of faith]. We remember the Father as Author and Sender, and, together with Him, the Holy Spirit as Witness. The descent [into the water] symbolizes our dying together [with Christ]; the ascent [from the water], our rising together with Him. The Father is God over all; Christ is the only begotten God, the beloved Son, the Lord of glory; and the Holy Spirit is the Paraclete, sent and revealed by Christ, and is Christ's Messenger.

The Apostolic Constitutions 7.41.1—45.3

Grant Me a Pure Heart

So let the candidate for baptism declare this in a renunciation: "I renounce Satan and his works and his pomps and his angels and his wiles and all things that are subject to him." And after the renunciation, let the baptizand declare his adherence, saying: "And I attach myself to Christ; and I believe and am baptized into one unbegotten One, the only true God, the Almighty, the Father of Christ, the Creator and Maker of all, from whom are all things.

"And [I am baptized] into the Lord Jesus Christ, His only begotten Son, the Firstborn of the whole creation, who before all ages was begotten, not created, by the good pleasure of the Father, through whom all things were made, those in heaven and those on earth, visible and invisible; who in the last days descended from heaven and took flesh, and was begotten of the holy virgin Mary, and lived a holy life according to the laws of His God and Father; and was crucified under Pontius Pilate and died for us, and rose again from the dead the third day after His passion, and ascended into the heavens, and is seated at the right hand of the Father, and is to come again with glory at the end of the world to judge the living and the dead; of whose kingdom there shall be no end.

"And I am baptized into the Holy Spirit, the Paraclete, who worked in all of the saints from the beginning of the **BAPTIZED INTO** world but was later sent also to the apostles by the Fa-**THE HOLY SPIRIT** ther, according to the promise of our Savior and Lord, Jesus Christ; and after the apostles to all those that believe in the holy, catholic, and apostolic Church. And I am baptized into the resurrection of the flesh, and into the remission of sins, and into the kingdom of the heavens, and into the life of the world to come."

After this confession, as the order would have it, the baptizand comes to the anointing of oil. This oil is blessed by the priest for the remission of sins and as a preparatory step to baptism. For the priest calls upon the unbegotten God, the Father of Christ, the King of all beings that have been granted perception and intelligence, in the name of the Lord Jesus, to sanctify the oil and to impart to it the grace of the Spirit, efficacious strength, the remission of sins, and a predisposition for the baptismal confession, so that the one who is

FREED FROM ALL UNRIGHTEOUSNESS anointed, being freed from all unrighteousness, may become worthy of initiation according to the command of the Only Begotten.

After this, the baptizand comes to the water. The priest blesses and glorifies the Lord God, the Almighty, the Father of the only begotten God. He gives thanks that God has sent His Son to become human for us in order that He might save us, and that He has authorized Christ to become obedient to the laws of the Incarnation in all things, to proclaim the kingdom of heaven, the remission of sins, and the resurrection of the dead.

For all of these things, the Father adores the only begotten of God himself, who is after the Father's likeness, and because of the Father, did what He did, and for His sake, giving the Father thanks that He endured the death of the Cross for all, and has appointed baptism to be a type of the new birth.

And He glorifies as well because God the Lord of all, in the name of Christ and of the Holy Spirit, has not cast mankind away. He has varied His providence, at first giving paradise to Adam for his dwelling and well-being, and then chasing him out, justly, after his offense. Yet, in goodness not absolutely tossing [man] away, but teaching his descendants in various ways. On [their] account, as the world was coming to its end, He sent His Son to become human for humans' sake, sent Him to take upon himself all human passions—without sin.

So, let the priest now call upon Him, with the baptism in mind, saying: "Look down from heaven and sanctify this water. Give it grace and power, so that the one who is to be baptized according to the commandment of Your Christ may be crucified with Him and

TO DIE TO SIN die with Him, and be buried with Him, and rise with Him, to be adopted in Him, to die to sin and to live to righteousness."

And after this, when he has baptized that person in the name of the Father, and of the Son, and of the Holy Spirit, he shall anoint the baptizand with chrism, saying: "O Lord God, without generation, without superior, Lord of all, Wafter of the aroma of the knowledge of the gospel in all nations, grant now that this chrism may be efficacious on this one being baptized. In the way in which the scent of the oil permeates, so may the sweet aroma of Your Christ continue upon this one, firm and fixed. And grant that having died with Him, this one may rise with Him and live with Him."

Let the priest say these things and things like them, for such is the power of the imposition of hands on each. Unless a prayer of this sort is said by a pious priest over each of these, the candidate for baptism descends into the water only as the Jews do and only puts off the filth of the body, not that of the soul.

After this, let the baptizand stand up and pray the prayer that the Lord taught us. One who is risen again must stand up and pray, because one who is raised stands upright. Now, let the baptizand pray facing the east, for it is written in the Second Book of the Chronicles that after King Solomon finished building the Temple of the Lord, at the very Feast of Dedication, the priests and the Levites and the singers stood up with cymbals and psaltries, faced east, and praised and confessed, saying: "Praise the Lord, for he is good, for his mercy endures forever."

And let him pray thus after this preceding prayer: "O God Almighty, Father of Your Anointed One, Your only begotten Son,

GRANT ME A PURE HEART AND YOUR HOLY SPIRIT grant me an undefiled body, a pure heart, a watchful mind, knowledge without error, and the presence of Your Holy Spirit. These things [I pray] in order that I may be established in the truth and may have full assurance of it, through Christ, through whom be glory to You, in the Holy Spirit, for ever. Amen."

4

GREGORY OF NYSSA
(ca. 331/40—ca. 395)

Biographical Note and Introduction

On Perfection

4

Gregory of Nyssa
(ca. 331/40—ca. 395)

Biographical Note and
Introduction

Among the many saints and heroes in the history of Christianity, Gregory of Nyssa stands as one of the most attractive. And since the end of World War II, research has shown him to be of far more importance in both his own time and the subsequent history of Christian thought than had previously been supposed. He has been discovered to be one of the most creative and profound thinkers in the history of Christianity, a true teacher and father of the Church.

The depth of his influence is most clearly seen in studies of the relationship between philosophi-

St. Gregory of Nyssa, detail of a miniature in the 11th-century Menologion of Basil II (Vat. Gr. 1613).

cal currents and Christian theology and spirituality from the late 4th century to the early 10th century. However, his direct impact on Western European Christianity began to fade after the 10th century. In fact, until recently Gregory's influence had all but disappeared except in medieval mysticism, some of the technical debates of the 11th and 12th centuries, and in a continuing shadow in Anglicanism.

In Eastern Christianity Gregory's direct influence has ebbed and flowed but has never come even near to disappearing. His work is especially significant in the areas of Christology, the discussion concerning the relationship of divine providence to human freedom, and considerations of the nature of the Christian life.

Abridged though they must be, the excerpts from his reflections on Christian perfection and entire sanctification presented here will clearly demonstrate his significance as a source of the Wesleyan perspective.

Gregory was the youngest of a trio of superlative churchmen who served in fourth-century Cappadocia (now east-central Turkey). All three took serious part in the theological wrangles of the day. And in their part of the world, theological wrangles were also political wrangles involving the highest levels of church and government bureaucracy.

History knows these three as the Cappadocian Fathers: Gregory, his brother Basil (330-79), and their mutual friend Gregory (ca. 329-90). Basil became bishop of the important see (a bishop's area of responsibility) of Caesarea, Cappadocia, in 370 and is usually known as Basil of Caesarea or Basil the Great. Their mutual friend Gregory served as bishop of Constantinople from 379 to 381. He is known, however, as Gregory Nazianzus (or Nazianzan), because he was earlier an auxiliary bishop in the Cappadocian town of Nazianzus. After serving in Constantinople, he returned to Nazianzus and was elected bishop there.

Basil and Gregory of Nazianzus struck up a deep and lifelong friendship when both were students of rhetoric in Athens. As an expression of that friendship, they spent several years together in monastic retreat, studying Scripture and the tradition, and praying.

Gregory of Nyssa, unlike his brother and their friend, did not gain his education at one of the great centers of higher learning. Nor did he take the monastic path. For a time, he stepped away from ecclesiastical vocation and taught rhetoric. This is to say that he taught young men to understand and speak to public issues. Thus they shaped public opinion, especially in public institutions such as the courts, and on public occasions such as funerals of prominent persons and installations into various offices. To do this, one had to steep himself in the full range of classical literature and to demonstrate exceptional social skills as well. Thus, Gregory of Nyssa became a man of affairs, and so he remained for the rest of his life, even after he returned to ecclesiastical office and became bishop of Nyssa in 372.

He was an ecclesiastical man of affairs. But at least initially Gregory was no mere administrator. His strength lay in his preaching skills, diplomacy, theology, and the promotion of spirituality. In each of these he demonstrated an exceptional ability to address all classes of people. We would say that he was charismatic and carried high credibility.

Before we look more closely at Gregory's work, we need to consider the context in which he carried it forward.

Constantine I was named coemperor on the death of his father, Constantius I Chlorus, in 306. It seems quite clear from this distance that radical reform of the Roman Empire was the principal item on Constantine's agenda. From the first he bent his efforts toward the reestablishment of a unified Roman Empire with a well-organized administrative structure that would operate by the book. He legitimized the Christian Church in A.D. 311 or 312 and called for Christians to resolve their theological differences through a council of bishops coming from all over the Roman Empire and just beyond its borders. He also removed the capital of the Roman Empire from Rome to Byzantium (soon to be named Constantinople). Here, radical reform of the empire was carried out in a period of less than 25 years.

Thus, Gregory and his closest colleagues had been born after the major footings of reform had been poured. But as the Gregorys were coming to prominence, several reactions to radical change began to make themselves felt. In the imperial palace itself, Emperor Julian had been reared a Christian but was passionately dedicated to reforming and reviving paganism and old Greco-Roman virtues. In the years 361-63 he made no secret of his dislike for Christianity but dared not persecute Christians. He could and did, however, favor pagans for all significant government and cultural posts. He also badgered the Christians for their inconsistencies—especially their growing love of classical literature and social position—and he kept them squabbling with each other. Julian was bad enough, but those who served immediately before and after him were only more publicly Christian. They were not more orthodox, nor more moral and ethical.

Thoughtful Christians had begun to wonder if the euphoria of being free to practice their faith and the advantages of being favored by an emperor who called himself Christian had not really become instruments of temptation and betrayal.

In Roman understanding, the emperor embodied in his person the fundamental character of Rome and its empire. In a profound way he *was* the empire. From a Christian point of view, the emperor held a special place between God and the people. He was priestly, but more than priestly. Often churchmen declared the ruler to be among the apostles and also a sort of Christ figure. To come into the emperor's court was to come into an anteroom of the heavenly kingdom itself.

In a very deep and subtle way, this was a Christianizing of the ancient Roman practice of venerating the emperor. It led both rulers and people to place a higher value on the maintenance of the Roman imperial system than earlier generations of believers would have wanted to do. It also opened the door for a later insistence that to be truly Christian, one must be truly Roman. These tendencies did not go unnoted by thoughtful Christian writers.

The emperors' tendency to play politics with theology and with the structure of the Church had become a scandal to many by the 350s, and so it would be for most of the remainder of the Cappadocians' lives. So bad did it get that at one point Athanasius, the exceptionally influential bishop of Alexandria, called Emperor Constantius II (regnant 337-61) the "forerunner of the Antichrist." This scandal in turn impelled Christians to give much thought to the nature of the kingdom of God and its relationship to earthly kingdoms. More narrowly, many thoughtful Christians raised questions about the nature of the Church as the earthly manifestation of the heavenly kingdom. Behind these questions was the very basic issue of the nature of the Christian life itself, especially as that life must be lived in an obviously flawed Church and an obviously fallen world.

A very popular response was monasticism. At this time, few conceived of monasticism as escapist. Rather, the population at large looked upon the monks as models. Their virtues belonged to the whole Body of Christ, and their privations, prayers, and meditations were undertaken for the sake of all believers. Few looked upon the monastic way of life as a means of saving oneself alone; it was a means of saving the Church.

Even as early as the 320s but reaching a rather widespread consensus by about the 360s, many seem to have felt that the better pattern for monks was that they live in groups, not as hermits.

In groups they could develop ways and means of prayer and meditation that would be free of the vagaries of solitude. They could also build model colonies of the kingdom of heaven. Basil and Gregory Nazianzus were among those who spent time as more or less isolated ascetics. Basil, however, was later to write a manual for monastic communities that remains basic to monastic life in Eastern Orthodoxy to this day.

Gregory of Nyssa certainly held monastics in high regard. But as a man of affairs, his response to the question of the nature of the Christian life, especially as it must be lived in less than ideal circumstances, was very different from those that characterized monasticism. Especially noteworthy is his conviction that the fundamental human problem is not simply being human. Monasticism in his day presented a near caricature of this pessimistic point of view that blamed our sinfulness on our fleshliness.

Gregory insisted that the basic problem is not one of matter versus spirit, but one of willful opposition to the will of God. In this he resembled Christians of the first two centuries more than he did those of his own time. Further, he said, all reality comes from God, and God is a Creator, not an impersonal source that somehow emits or sloshes over its own boundaries various degrees of being. So the world we know is certainly not simply a microcosm of all that is, as the Stoics wanted folks to believe. But neither is the world a shadow or mere spark of reality, as the Platonists taught. The world we know, says Gregory, is a sector of reality, and all the qualities of our world are intelligible, spiritual qualities.

The human being, then, continually makes spiritual choices in a physical world; in a physical body the human being yearns to see God. Here, then, is the marvel of the Christian faith—grace is given so we might put the body to spiritual service, altogether spiritual service, in this life. That service is absolute love to God and neighbor. And when this body is laid aside in death, we put on resurrected bodies and continue the service begun on earth. Neither in heaven nor on earth, says Gregory, is it possible to be a Christian without a body. It is precisely in the body that we triumph over "happenstance," over the tyranny of sense impressions.

Many Christians, feeling hopelessly caught in webs of circumstances, believed that human freedom was an illusion. Gregory responded that Christ is the Model here. Christ's earthly sojourn began with a free decision and came to its climax not in the

Crucifixion, in which all freedom appeared to be lost, but in the Resurrection. In the Resurrection true freedom, the freedom from death, was restored. And its power is available to all for this life.

In all this personal emphasis, Gregory did not ignore the essentially communal character of Christianity. Of critical importance to him was the petition the Lord taught His disciples to pray: "Thy kingdom come. Thy will be done in earth" (Matt. 6:10, KJV). In the background of all he says stands the heavenly kingdom and its earthly manifestation, the Church—however battered. But he places in the foreground the question of the spirituality of the individual believer.

Gregory emphasizes the developmental character of the Christian life. One cannot read his works without sensing a demand that we move ahead spiritually. But ahead to what? What is the goal or aim of the Christian life? And where and when may it be attained?

Gregory responds to these questions by asserting that our goal is complete conformity to the will of God—or, to put it far more personally, the Christian's aim is to be conformed to the image of Christ. Gregory's conviction is that such conformity is possible, through the operations of the Holy Spirit, in this life (especially through the means of grace offered by the Church), insofar as the individual is capable of it. Of course, its full realization comes when we take on our resurrected body in the fully realized heavenly kingdom. Ethical or spiritual perfection, for Gregory, is a term related not to an external standard, but to capabilities and purposes, to the end for which something was made. So the perfection to which he urges Christians is clearly not a matter of skills and sheer intellectual prowess, but a relationship to God and to others.

One more thing needs to be said in a general introduction to Gregory's writings. Newton Flew and others have insisted that Gregory's basic presuppositions are Platonic or Neoplatonic. If so, Gregory would have believed that essential reality is an independent realm of unchanging essences, ideas, and forms. What we would call the created world he would have believed to be a sort of overflow of that independent realm. He would have said that what we call reality is the overflow trapped in matter. The reality of the human being, then, would lie in the human soul. The body would be unnecessary at best, a prison house at worst. The only true reality would be God.

This Platonic reading of Gregory arises out of a conviction that beginning with the apostle Paul, Christianity had increasingly explained itself in terms provided by the dominant philosophy of the day. So, it was held, Christian ethics were barely concealed Stoicism. Also Christian understandings of the nature of being (metaphysics) were barely concealed Platonism or, later, Neoplatonism.

To be fair, some of the early Christian writers did indeed adopt and adapt classical philosophies in their attempts to explain the faith. But the case has been overdrawn, and in no instance has it been more overdrawn by the scholars than in their interpretation of the teachings of Gregory of Nyssa. Research since World War II has clearly demonstrated that Gregory freely utilizes Platonic and Neoplatonic language. But his basic presuppositions call on the thoughtful reader to realize that he is transforming that language. Gregory begins not with Plato nor Plotinus nor their followers, but the Hebrew Bible, or the Septuagint, and the collection of first-century writings that would come to be called the New Testament. And he begins reflection with the worship of the Church.

The work quoted here bears the alternate title *Concerning What a Christian Must Be*. It contains Gregory's extended thoughts on what it means to call oneself Christian. In a short letter traditionally said to be addressed to one Harmonius, Gregory had said that to be a Christian is simply to imitate the divine nature. Now he will go on, in terms supplied by the various names and descriptions given to Christ by the apostle Paul. He here says that the ground of our imitation of the divine nature is the fact that we were made in the divine image. We will truly imitate, says Gregory, as we perfect our own natures through lives of perfect virtue.

At first glance, Gregory seems to be inviting us to engage in some ambitious program of self-sanctification. But what must be kept in mind always in reading this tract is Gregory's basic understanding, made abundantly clear elsewhere. He teaches that our redemption, far from being up to us, could be accomplished only by One who was fully human and fully divine—and that the application of that accomplishment comes only through the ministrations of the Holy Spirit in the Church.

On Perfection

Your zeal to know how one may, by a life of moral excellence, become perfect and so attain blamelessness in every way squares with your purpose in life. I might have thought it to be important that you find in my life models for all that you are contending for, so that I might provide you with the education you seek through deeds rather than words. In that way, my coaching in the direction of what is good would have merited belief because my life harmonized with my words. But though I do pray that one day this harmony may be reality, I do not yet see myself as one whose life can be offered to you as an example. Instead, I can only offer an essay. So, in order that I may not seem to be of no use at all and unable to contribute to your aim, I have decided to lay before you a meticulous description of the life toward which we must move. Here, then, I begin my essay.

SEEK TO BECOME CHRISTLIKE

We do not receive our name from anyone connected with us. Rather, our good Master, Jesus Christ, endowed us with companionship in His beloved name. It makes no difference whether one be rich or highborn, or of humble origins and poor, or of some social standing because of occupation or position: the sole authoritative name for those believing in Him is "Christian."

And since this grace was allotted to us from above, we must first of all understand the magnificence of the gift, so that we can worthily thank the God who has given it to us. Then we must demonstrate in our lives that we ourselves are what the power of this great name demands that we be. The magnificence of the gift, of which we are deemed worthy through companionship with the Master, becomes clear to us when we acknowledge the true significance of the name of Christ. This means that when, in our prayers, we call upon the Lord of all by this name, we may grasp the meaning of the intellectual object that we are receiving into our souls. Then, too, we must reverently recognize that we imply who He is when He is called upon by this name. As a consequence of recognizing this and as a result of our zeal for His way of life and our use of His name as the Teacher and Guide for our lives, we shall also clearly ascertain the kinds of persons we shall be shown to be.

Hence, when we take St. Paul as our leader in these two tasks, we have the most sure guide to the simple truth of that which we are seeking; for he, more than anyone else, knew what Christ is. Paul showed by what he did what kind of person is named after Christ. He imitated Him so brilliantly that he revealed his Master in himself. And through his meticulous imitation of his prototype, his own soul was transformed. Paul no longer seemed to be living and talking, but Christ himself seemed to be living in him. If a discriminating moral analyzer asks, "Are you seeking proof of the Christ who speaks in me?" Paul answers, "It is now no longer I that live, but Christ lives in me."

This man knew the significance of the name of Christ for us. He said that Christ is "the power of God and the wisdom of God." He called Him "peace" and "light inaccessible" in whom God dwells. He called Christ "sanctification and redemption," "great high priest," "passover," and "a propitiation" for souls. For Paul, Christ was "the brightness of glory and the image of substance," also "maker of the world." He was "spiritual food," "spiritual drink, and spiritual rock," "water," "foundation" of faith, and "cornerstone." Christ was the "image of the invisible God," the "great God," and "head of the body, the Church." He was "the firstborn of every creature," "firstfruits of those who have fallen asleep," "firstborn from the dead," and "firstborn of many brethren." Christ was the "mediator between God and men," the "only begotten Son," "crowned with glory and honor." He was "Lord of glory" and the "beginning" of being. Christ was "king of justice and king of peace." He was the "ineffable king of all, having the power of the kingdom" and many other such things not easily counted.

When all of these are put side by side, each makes its own contribution to the revelation of what it is to be named after Christ, and each lends a certain emphasis. To the degree that we take these intellectual objects into our souls, they are all clues to the unutterable greatness of the gift that is ours. However, it is by the title of King that Christ is magisterially and primarily

CHRIST IS KING, AND HIS REIGN IS TO BE SEEN IN US

identified, because kingship is the underlying rank of all value and power and rule. As we learn from the history books, the anointing of kingship takes place first, and the validity and privileges of the other titles depend on those of royalty. So it is that the one who is cognizant of the nature of the individual elements also is cognizant of the power that encompasses them. Thus kingship itself asserts the meaning of the title that we have from Christ.

Therefore, since we are . . . honored by the name of Christ, being called Christians, thanks to our good Master, all of the connections of this name must also be seen in us. Our lives must be a testimony of it, so that the title not be a misnomer when applied to us. Being does not come from naming. Whatever the underlying nature of something happens to be is discovered through the meaning attached to the name. I mean this: if someone calls man a tree or a rock, does that make man a plant or a stone? Of course not! First of all, he must be a man, and then he must be treated as a man, in keeping with his nature. Titles based on similarities, as if one could say that a man is a statue or an imitation horse, are false. When something is validly and not falsely named, its nature fully manifests the truth of the form of address. . . .

So, those naming themselves after Christ must first of all become **BE WHAT YOUR NAME IMPLIES** what the name implies and then adapt themselves to the title. We mark off a man himself from what may be considered a good likeness of him in a picture by pointing out characteristic differences. We call the man a logical, thinking creature; his picture is an inanimate piece of wood [or paper] that has assumed human form through imitation. So also shall we differentiate . . . the true Christian from one who only seems to be Christian. The characteristics of the true Christian are all of those that we see in relation to Christ. We imitate Christ's characteristics for which we have capacity; we reverence and worship those that our nature does not come close to by imitation. Either by imitation or by worship, the Christian life must exemplify all of the figures of speech that signify Christ if "the man of God is to be perfect," as the apostle says. And this perfection must never be deformed by evil.

There are persons who devise mythical creatures in their speeches and writings. They mold bull-headed horses or serpent-footed monsters or other such mixtures of species. . . . So, irrationally they take liberties with nature and devise something other than the human being—manufacturing that which in nature is impossible. We would not say that what they have fabricated . . . is a human being, even if some parts of the figure happen to resemble certain parts of the human body. In the same way, one cannot accurately be called a Christian if he does not assent to the faith with his mind, even if he conforms to it in other ways. Nor can he accurately be called a Christian if his mind assents but his body does not harmonize with his declared way of life—if he exhibits the anger of dragons or the bestiality of snakes, or if he puts together with his human character the horse's lust for females. In cases like this, one becomes double-natured, a centaur [a fabled half man and half horse] composed of reason and passion. One can easily see many such people about. Either they resemble the Minotaur [half man and half bull]—bull-headed in this belief in idolatry though appearing to lead a good life—or they make themselves centaurs and dragons by joining a Christian countenance to a bestial body.

But the Christian should be recognized in his integrity, as should be the case with the human body, so it is appropriate that the charac-

BE FULLY CHRISTIAN

teristics of his life speak in behalf of all of the good qualities connected with Christ. To be in part what the name Christian implies, but in other ways inclined to its contradiction, is to divide oneself into a battleground where there are two factions, good and evil. Thus one comes to be without truth and inconsistent. So says the apostle: "What fellowship has light with darkness?"

Because there is an obvious and irreconcilable contradiction between light and darkness, anyone participating in both has a share in neither; the two are drawn up in simultaneous opposition to each other in his mixed life. His faith lights a part of his life, but his dark habits put out the lamp of reason. Because it is impossible, not to say inconsistent, for light and darkness to be in partnership, the person in whom dwells each of these opposites becomes his own enemy. Divided two ways, between virtue and evil, he sets up a line of belligerence within himself—a battle line. And, just as it is impossible for both of two enemies to be victors over each other, the victory of one causing the death of the other, so also in this civil war caused by the confusion in [the believer's life], the stronger element cannot win without completely destroying the other.

Now, when the wicked phalanx attacks it, how will the army of reverence be stronger than evil? If the stronger is to win, the enemy

THE ENEMY MUST BE COMPLETELY DESTROYED

must be completely done away with. So it is that virtue will gain the victory over evil only when the entire enemy, all of those unsound elements, collapses before an alliance of the reasonable elements. Then that which was spoken from the mouth of God through prophecy will be fulfilled: "It is I who bring both life and death." It simply is not possible for the good to dwell in me unless it is made to live through the death of my enemy. As long as we continue to cling to opposites with each hand, there cannot be participation in one being only, for both elements cannot participate in the same being. If we hang on to evil, we lose the ability to take hold of virtue.

Now, let us take up the original discussion—namely, that the sole road to the pure and divine life for lovers of virtue is knowing what the name of Christ means and conforming our lives to that knowledge. We attune our lives to virtue also by giving high priority to the other terms from the holy voice of Paul. Putting these before us with all due zeal, we shall make them the surest guide for a life of virtue—imitating some of these traits, as we said in the first part, and revering and worshiping others. Let the marshaling of these serve as a battle line for us.

Let us begin with the first of them: it says, "Christ is the power of God and the wisdom of God." From this descrip-

CHRIST GIVES POWER AND WISDOM tion of Christ, we acquire ideas appropriate for the Divine that make the name an object of reverence for us. All creation came into existence through Him and is united with Him, both that which is known through perception and that which lies beyond observation. From this perspective of Christ as the Maker of all things, wisdom is necessarily entwined with power. . . . The great and indescribable marvels of creation would not exist were it not that wisdom had conceived their coming into being; and had power, through which thoughts become deeds.

The meaning of the name of Christ is rightly divided into this twofold emphasis on wisdom and power, so that when we see the magnitude of that which constitutes being itself, we may recognize His unutterable power by way of what we comprehend. It is also divided this way so that when we figure out how all that did not exist earlier came into being, . . . we will then worship the unfathomable wisdom of the One who thought of these things.

Also, it is not purposeless or without benefit to us to believe in the power and wisdom of Christ from the perspective of the possession of the good. For when one prays, he attracts to himself through prayer that which he is invoking and gazing upon

PRAYER BRINGS PERFECTION OF LIFE with the eye of his soul. So it is that the person looking toward power (Christ is Power) "is strengthened with power in the inner man," as the apostle says. And the person who calls upon the wisdom that the Lord has always had comes to be wise. . . . In fact, one whose name is that of Christ, who is himself Power and Wisdom, will also himself exhibit wisdom through a wise use of the power of choice. When wisdom and power are shown in us, the one choosing what is just and the other confirming that choice, we attain to a perfection of life that is intertwined with both of these qualities.

In recognizing Christ as Peace, we shall authentically manifest the title Christian through the peace in our lives. For, as the apostle

**ENMITY MUST
BE DESTROYED**
says, the One "has slain enmity." So then, let us not bring enmity to life in ourselves but, rather, demonstrate through our lives that it is dead. Let us not raise up through ire and backbiting against each other that which God has duly mortified for the sake of our salvation. Such a raising up would destroy our souls and cause an evil resurrecting of that which is justly dead. But if we have Christ, who is Peace, let us also mortify hatred in ourselves in order to attain that which we believe is in Him, because He "has broken down the dividing wall of the enclosure." Out of the two elements of wisdom and power in himself, He has created "one new person" and made peace.

**BANISH CIVIL WAR
IN OUR NATURE**
Therefore, let us also reconcile not only those fighting against us externally but also our own internal elements that are at variance, in order that flesh may no longer "lust against the spirit, nor the spirit against the flesh." Making the spirit and the flesh subject to the divine law, let us live peacefully, having passed on into the new and peaceful person and having become one from two, for the definition of peace is "the harmony of dissonant parts." Once the civil war in our nature is banished, then we also become peace, being at peace within ourselves, and we make it manifest that we have truly and authentically taken on the name of Christ.

In knowing Christ to be the "true light," which is "inaccessible" to falsehood, we learn that it is necessary for our lives, too, to be lit by the rays of the true Light. Now, the beams of "the Sun of Righteousness," which stream forth for our illumination, are virtues. Through these, we "lay aside the works of darkness," so as to "walk becomingly as in the day." And "we renounce those things that shame conceals." By doing all things in the light, we become the light itself, so that it shines before others. This is the unique quality of light. And

**THE POWER OF
HIS SANCTIFICATION**
if we recognize Christ as "sanctification," the One in whom every action is faithful and pure, let us prove by our lives that we ourselves stand separate, being true partakers of His name; that our lives conform in deed, not only in word, to the power of His sanctification.

Learning that Christ is "redemption," because He gave himself as an atoning sacrifice on our behalf, we are taught this: when He provided us with immortality as our unique possession, as if He were bestowing a particular honor on each soul, He ransomed us from death with His own life. If then we become slaves of the One who redeemed us, we seek to become like our Master alone, on the basis that we no longer live for ourselves, but for the One who owns us because He gave His life for us.

We are no longer self-governing but possessions of Him who, having purchased us, is Master of His own. Indeed, the Master's will shall be the law of our lives. And as "the law of sin" ruled us when death was dominant, so, now that we have become the property of life, we must comply with the government in power. Therefore, let us never deviate from the will of life nor desert through sinfulness to the wicked and ancient tyrant of souls—I am referring to [spiritual] death.

We are also conformed to Christ if we hear from Paul that He is the "passover" and "high priest," for Christ was indeed sacrificed as the paschal Victim for our sakes. And the priest is none other than Christ himself when He brings the sacrifice to God. As it is said: "He delivered himself up for us, an offering and a sacrifice." By way of these words we learn this: the person who looks toward that One presents himself as an offering and a sacrifice, and a passover, and will manifest himself to God as a living sacrifice, "holy, pleasing to God," as becomes a "reasonable worship." And the directive for this holy office is: "Do not be conformed to this world, but be transformed by the renewing of your mind, in order that you may discern what is the good and the acceptable and the perfect will of God."

PRESENT YOURSELVES A LIVING SACRIFICE TO GOD

If the flesh lives and is not sacrificed according to the law of the Spirit, then it is not possible for the will of God to be made manifest in it: "For the wisdom of the flesh is hostile to God and is not subject to the law of God." As long as the flesh lives from which passions spring . . . it is impossible for the pleasing and perfect will of God to be promptly attained to in the lives of the faithful.

Further, Christ, who is known as "a propitiation through his own blood," teaches each one who considers this to become a propitiation himself, sanctifying his soul by the mortification of his members. And when Christ is spoken of as "the brightness of his glory and the image of his substance," the words convey to us the idea of His greatness in the act of being worshiped. Paul was truly inspired by God and taught by God. He examined the unclear and obscure aspects of the divine mysteries "in the depth of the riches of the wisdom and of the knowledge of God." Paul revealed the illuminations that came to him from God concerning the understanding of what is incomprehensible and unsearchable. He did this in word pictures because the tongue cannot measure up to the thought. According to the account of those who heard his explication of mystery, he spoke in this way with due regard for reasonableness, in the interests of thought. So it was that while he comprehended as much as human powers are able to do concerning the divine nature, he revealed the unapproachable and incomprehensible Logos of substantial being in human terms. . . .

But back to Paul's phrase—he also means that God "upholds all things by the word of his power." In this way he resolves the difficulty posed by those with an intellectual itch who **GOD IS ABLE TO DO WHAT HE HAS PROMISED** look for the undiscoverable. They look for an account of matter without any check on their curiosity, asking how the material is experienced by the immaterial, quantity by that which has no quantity itself, form by that which is formless, color by that which is invisible, and the finite by the infinite. He also resolves it when they ask how matter is interwoven with the simple and unformed when there is no quality involved in it. He resolves all such questions by saying that the Word "upholds all things by the word of his power."

All things—from nonexistence to existence. For all things, as many as exist in relation to matter and as many as have received an immaterial nature, all things have one cause of their substance. That one cause is "the Word of Unspeakable Power." From the words "upholds all things by the word of his power," we learn to look to Christ as the Source of being. If we come into being from that Source, and if we have our existence in Him, there is every necessity to believe that there is nothing outside of the One in whom we exist and from whom we come into being and back to whom we return. It is along this line of thought that we see the foundation for the **BLAMELESS BEFORE CHRIST** blamelessness of our lives. Who is that person who believes that he lives "from Him and through Him and unto Him"? Will he be so insolent as to . . . live a life that does not reflect Him?

In calling the Lord "spiritual food and drink," the holy apostle also indicates that he knows that human nature is not simple. There is an intelligible part mixed with a sensual part, and a particular kind of nurture is needed for each of the elements in us. We need material food to strengthen our bodies and spiritual food for the well-being of our souls. In the case of the body, that which is meaty and that which is fluid, by intermingling, preserve our nature through the digestive process. So, by analogy, Paul differentiates with respect to the nurture of the intelligible part, utilizing the same terms—food and drink—and adapting them appropriately to the needs of those who assimilate them. To the exhausted and fainting, bread comes, strengthening such a person's heart; to those who are fatigued by reason of the misery of their lives and thirsty because of it as well, wine comes with merriment for the heart.

Now, it is necessary to know, from what has been said, the power of the Word by which the soul is nourished according to its need. . . . The prophet clearly indicates the relief that comes to the weary from the Word "in green pastures and in still waters." If someone taking a look at this mystery should say that the Lord is correctly called "spiritual food and drink," he is not far from the truth. For His "flesh is food indeed," and His "blood is drink indeed." But with respect to that thought, there is participation in such nourishment for all, because the Word, who becomes food and drink, is received and taken in without distinction by those seeking Him.

On the other hand, to broach another idea, participation in this food and drink is not thoughtless or indiscriminate, for the apostle puts a limit on it in this way: "Let a man examine himself, and so let him eat of that bread and drink of that cup; for he who eats and drinks unworthily eats and drinks judgment to himself." . . . So, the command of the apostle . . . to all is to receive the Holy Body with a pure conscience. If there is a stain from sin anywhere, we must cleanse it away with the water of our tears.

When Christ is called "a rock," the term helps us with resoluteness and perseverance in our life of virtue. That is to say, it helps us to be steadfast in our endurance of suffering.

5

MACARIUS THE EGYPTIAN

Biographical Note

Homily 26 (Collection 3) 7:1—8:2
Filled with All the Fullness of God

Homily 44 (Collection 2—Fifty Spiritual Homilies)
In Christ He Is a New Creature

Homily 19 (Collection 2—Fifty Spiritual Homilies)
Filled with the Holy Spirit

Homily 15 (Collection 2—
Fifty Spiritual Homilies): 13-15
A Further Work of Grace

5

Macarius the Egyptian

Biographical Note

John Wesley read continually throughout a long life. And he read broadly—anything that would help him love God and neighbor, understand creation more intelligently, and rejoice more wholeheartedly in the Creator. Of course, for him, loving meant serving. So he did his reading in the context of serving.

Especially important to Wesley was the reading of those writers who could fire his devotion. So for him, reading was entry into conversation with the author. And, as in any conversation, he found in his reading both trash and treasure.

Wesley also took delight in conversing and writing about what he had read. Some of his letters are really book reviews. Also, in his other works one finds comments and even printed responses to this or that author's ideas, even abstruse ideas. There is in Wesley a sort of fearlessness about considering ideas, even abstruse ideas or those that run counter to some of his cherished notions. And it is an aggressive fearlessness. Wesley sails into waters that he knows are turbulent or uncharted. He has little time for leisure reading, so we do not find novels or other fiction on his list. But we do find thorough acquaintance with the political writers of his day, thorough acquaintance with the scientific literature, and thorough acquaintance as well with then-modern Roman Catholic literature.

So valuable did Wesley deem reading that he decided to create a set of inexpensive editions of more modern works that would acquaint his followers with the rich devotional resources of the church catholic and thus provide them a means of deepening their piety. So it was that he published his *Christian Library*.

Wesley edited rather severely some of the works he included

in this *Christian Library*. But except for extracting what he sometimes called poison, his principles for editing were not theologically defensive. He was not usually trying to protect his followers
from ideas that might be troublesome to him as leader or to them
as followers. Rather, he intended to introduce them to as much of
those rich resources as he could, so he edited chiefly for efficient
reading. He certainly did not approve everything he reprinted. He
says that himself, time and again. He wants to encourage intelli-
gent reflection, not risk-free absorption.

That is how we must understand the inclusion of *The Fifty
Spiritual Homilies* of Macarius the Egyptian in the very first volume of the *Christian Library*, published in 1749. Wesley had read
the homilies during his stay in Savannah, Georgia (1735-38), and
had apparently referred to them on a number of later occasions.
Now he decided that they were a good introduction to the purposes and content of his anthology. This raises the immediate questions "Who is Macarius?" and "What makes his homilies so attractive that Wesley publishes them for his followers?"

Two monks named Macarius, both of whom held some importance as spiritual guides, lived in fourth-century Egypt and died in
the 390s at very advanced ages. Only one of them, however, is
called Macarius the Egyptian. The other is usually called Macarius
of Alexandria. Wesley believed he was editing and printing the
works of Macarius the Egyptian.

It is quite possible, however, that Macarius the Egyptian did
not write the homilies and the "Great Letter," which are attributed
to him, though they probably were written during his lifetime. The
best guess seems to be that these works came from the pen of a
monk in Syria or Asia Minor or even Mesopotamia who had
learned much of what he knew about spirituality from hearing or
reading Basil of Caesarea and Gregory of Nyssa.

The homilies attracted Wesley because they spoke to a religious situation very much like Wesley's. Macarius wrote to instruct
the Christian monks of his day. Both Macarius's audience and
Wesley's wanted to believe that baptism resolved the question of
one's sin and sinning for all time. High claims had been made for
baptism by the great teachers of the Church even as early as the
second century. But pious popular imagination was willing to carry
some of the biblical language, the teachers' thoughts, and the
words and actions of the baptismal liturgies to unintended lengths.

Early Christians reflected, for instance, on Paul's statement in Gal. 3:27—"For all of you who were baptized into Christ have clothed yourselves with Christ" (NIV). They put it together with thoughts from such persons as Irenaeus: "Baptism is the seal of eternal life and is rebirth unto God, in order that we be no more children of mortal men, but children of the eternal and everlasting God." From the language and actions of baptism, which bespoke and symbolized new life, purification, and regeneration, they came to what seemed to them obvious conclusions.

Such powerful language and symbols convinced many that they themselves had no need to live a holy life. Some, in fact, argued that one should continue to sin freely and grandly so that it might be clear that salvation is by the gracious application of Christ's righteousness to the believer and not by the believer's works. Others were more restrained, but they still thought that through baptism they had been saved once and for all and that Christ's righteousness was imputed to them. Therefore, they thought little of developing disciplined lives. In fact, many had taken as a spiritual and theological truth an old saying—"Off with the old coat, on with the new." They understood this to mean that the person in the new coat had not himself or herself really changed. There was no change of character—only a change of "coats."

Still, many thoughtful and observant persons believed very firmly that the sinfulness of many of the baptized was disgraceful and a sacrilege. They came to believe that there had to be more to the Christian life than baptism followed by life on a moral-spiritual roller coaster. They had no desire to downgrade baptism. But they did want to clarify its meaning and to strengthen its spiritual significance as the source of authentic holiness among believers.

This raised a number of difficult questions: In the Bible and in the liturgy, baptism is called "renewal" and "rebirth"; why are we not completely transformed by it? In the Bible it is implied, at least, and in the liturgy it is said that baptism breaks the power of sin over us. Why then do baptized persons continue to sin as if powerless to do anything else? The Bible and the liturgy say that baptism is a once-only divine act. If we claim, then, that there is more spirituality to come after baptism, are we not deprecating baptism and making its claims questionable?

Macarius responds to these questions by talking about our life in Christ and the way in which we really grow in grace. Along the way, he makes several very critical points that we must briefly note. First, we do indeed receive what he calls "the life of the Spirit" at baptism. Baptism does away with sinning by choice. But it does not vaccinate us against willingly and wilfully taking sin on board again. We allow our own thoughts and reflections to work on the impressions we receive from the world around us in ways that lead us into sin and sinning. We do not have to do this; we simply do it. And it really is an abuse of the freedom God has given us.

When we are baptized, says Macarius, we are as newborn babies: we have all the limbs we will ever have, and so we are complete, but we still must mature. And that maturation comes about precisely because of the spiritual tensions in us. In the language of his time and place, Macarius says that both sin and grace dwell in us, neither of them completely driving the other out.

The way in which Macarius concentrates on the problems of those who yearn for perfection has led some to think that he sees the life of tension between remaining sin and holiness as the normal Christian life. It is indeed "normal," in Macarius, if by "normal" one means "common" or "usual" or "typical." But if by "normal" one means "standard" or "according to the norm," one finds that Macarius explicitly rejects such a view. The usual spiritual schizophrenia, as it were, is not the norm. This is not as far as we can go spiritually in this life. Macarius wanted to help the monks cope with the tension only as part of the process of getting rid of it. Thus his message is not one of suppression of sin, but of grace-given freedom from it.

GRACE-GIVEN FREEDOM FROM SIN

Macarius believed that God can free us from all sinfulness in this life and will do so if we demonstrate a genuine desire for Him to do it. "Unspeakable perfection" is precisely our goal, even in this life. It is that and no less that God wants to give us by His Spirit. But here Macarius warns believers against two tendencies: first, the tendency to try to attain to that perfection by their own efforts; second, the tendency to despair of ever reaching it because of the power and pervasiveness of sin in their lives.

Macarius directs his homilies, many of which are really discussions, not monologues, toward believers who are seeking that perfection. Thus he concentrates attention on spiritual tensions

SIN REMAINING IN THE BELIEVER that arise because of remaining sin in the believers' hearts and lives. He seeks to help them use those tensions as instruments in growing spiritually, but he is far from those who would see such tensions as good in themselves—as the best that can be done for us in this life. Such tensions help the believer to see both the depth of his or her own sin and the magnificent holiness of God. They also help the believer see the futility of his or her own efforts at sanctification and the blessedness of the divine and gracious gift of perfection. Most significantly of all, they help the believer to see clearly that there is only one medicine that can cure his or her double-mindedness and to yearn for release.

It is doubtful that John Wesley would have taken his evident interest in Macarius if Macarius's concern had been mere coping and suppression of sin without hope of release until death. Both **GOD'S NORM FOR BELIEVERS** men hold victory over sin in this life to be God's norm for believers. We present here, then, several cuttings from Macarius that demonstrate the point.

Remember in all these readings that Macarius is addressing monks, persons who already understand themselves to be believers. They would almost certainly have been baptized and would be asking their questions with that in mind.

The first extract does not appear in the collection of homilies that Wesley reprinted. It comes from a group of 43 *logoi*, discourses or homilies, that have gained the title *Collection 3*.[1]

Our first selection here is a clear expression of Macarius's understanding of the possibilities of grace in this life. The New Testament and patristic idea of "perfection" was usually expressed by words related to the verb *teleō.* They had to do with completion or fulfillment, but almost always with the idea of "fitness" or "suitability" behind them. So, for instance, a boy does not become a perfect boy by becoming a man; rather, he becomes a perfect boy when he is most boylike, given his age and circumstance.

---

1. The reader who peruses the major edition of *Collection 3* will be surprised to find only 21 *logoi* there. That is because the new edition omits those of the 43 that were represented by abstracts in the edition that has come to us as the *Fifty Spiritual Homilies* and is more technically known now as *Collection 2*. Further, another 8 of the 43 *logoi* in the known manuscripts of *Collection 3* are simply duplicates found also in the 62 *logoi* and two letters known as *Collection 1*. The reader needs to know that there is a long manuscript history of each of these collections that influences the ways in which we may interpret Macarius, though the details of that history need not detain us here.

When Macarius talks of our restoration in Christ, he has in mind what happens to us in the great resurrection of the dead, but

IN THIS LIFE he also has in mind our complete restoration in this life—a restoration absolutely as complete as it can be under the circumstances. The standard is not our restoration in the great resurrection; the standard is all that we can be by grace in this life. So in the passage that follows, Macarius is not looking beyond the grave. He is looking at the application of the promises of new creation here and now.

Homily 26 (Collection 3) 7:1—8:2

Filled with All the Fullness of God

1. Here is what the apostle says: ". . . finally, that you may be able to comprehend with all of the saints what is the breadth and length, the depth and height, and to know the love of Christ which surpasses all knowing, in order that you may be filled with all of the fullness of God." Contemplate the inexpressible mysteries of the *psychē* [human spirit] that the Lord extricated from the darkness that was overlaying it: how He freed it from its pretense and revealed it to itself, and how much He enlarged and extended the concepts in its understanding of the breadths, the lengths, the depths, and the heights of all creation, visible and invisible.

2. The *psychē* is, then, a great work, admirable and divine. And as it would seem, God created it before molding the body itself in

GOD, OUR CREATOR that it is said, "Let us make man according to our image and likeness." God created it and thus, taking some dust of the earth, He molded the body and breathed, by the Spirit, into the *psychē* that He had created. In this act of producing, He made it this way: He did not place in its nature any malice; its nature was unaware of evil; rather, God made it according to the image of the virtues of the Spirit. He placed in it the laws of virtue, discernment, knowledge, wisdom, faith, love *(agapē)*, and the other virtues according to the image of the Spirit.

3. And now, then, Adam or *psychē* is provided with knowledge, with wisdom, with love, and with faith, and the Lord makes himself known to it. He has placed in it an understanding, some concepts, the will, the intellect which is the guide of the *psychē*. He has also put there one other great subtlety—He has made it nimble, winged, untiring, in order that it would come to serve Him by its thoughts, in-

stantly, at the moment that the Spirit desires it. In a word, He has created it so that it might be His spouse, capable of uniting itself to Him, in order that He might join forces with it and that it might become one spirit with Him, as it is written: "The one who joins himself to the Spirit becomes one spirit with him."

8.1. Neither the sages through their wisdom, nor the learned by their understanding have been able to comprehend the subtlety of the *psyche*, nor even to say what it is; the comprehension and exact understanding of the *psyche* are entrusted only to those to whom they are revealed by the Spirit. But that very thing, mind you, reflects and gives evidence of understanding by listening: He is God, the *psyche* is not God; He is Lord, it is a slave; He is the Creator, it is a creature; He is the Artisan, it is the work of art. The two natures have nothing in common; but in His love and infinite mercy, inexpressible and incomprehensible, God has resolved to produce this work of art and this intelligence-endowed creature, precious and chosen from among them all, as the Scripture says: "In order that we might be, as it were, the firstfruits of his creatures." In order that we be united to Him and associated with Him; in order that we be His own dwelling place; in order that we be His Bride, noble and pure.

8.2. Seeing that such blessings are proposed for us, seeing that such promises have been made to us, seeing that God has had such a love for us, let us then banish, children, all carelessness
SEEKING GOD'S BEST and all sloth from our dash to eternal life and in all of our zeal to please the Lord. Let us beg of the Lord that by the power of His own divinity He would deliver us from the dark prison of dishonoring passions. Let us pray that He would claim again His own image and the work that He has molded and make it to shine again, restoring the *psyche* intact and pure. Then, having obtained and merited communion with His Spirit, we may be judged worthy of endlessly enjoying His presence, forever and ever. Amen.

Homily 44 (Collection 2—Fifty Spiritual Homilies)

In Christ He Is a New Creature

As we read this homily, we should keep in mind two important facts: it is addressed to monks who believe the Christian life is a life of great hope, but also a life of continual struggle with the pull and power of inward sin. As we have noted, the monks already accounted themselves believers. In all probability they had

THE PULL AND POWER OF INWARD SIN
been baptized. But they understood that not even the grace of God could sufficiently change us so that in this life we could be free from sin.

For that sort of victory, they believed, we would have to be re-created. And, in fact, they believed the Christian was indeed re-created or born again in baptism. But their experience told them this re-creation or new birth was only an earnest of the real thing. And they believed we must wait until death or until the resurrection of the dead for the real thing to occur. So they saw the normal Christian life as one in which we take three steps forward and two steps backward.

Macarius here invites them to rethink their understanding of re-creation. There is an unspeakably marvelous new life that will be granted at the resurrection, but the new life that we may have now is a genuine re-creation that entails genuine freedom from sin.

1. The person who comes to God yearning to be a true sharer in Christ's throne should come with this purpose in mind: to be changed and re-formed in character and in conduct, **CHRISTLIKENESS** to be made a good and new man, who carries about him nothing of the old man. As it is said: "If anyone be in Christ, he is a new creature." This is precisely why our Lord Jesus Christ came—to change and re-form and renew nature that has been upended by passions and to re-create this soul by mingling it with His own Spirit, the Spirit of the Godhead. New mind and new soul and new eyes and new ears and a new spiritual tongue, in short, an altogether new person—this is what He came to make of those who believe Him. Or, to talk in terms of new wineskins, the re-created soul is anointed with Christ's very own luminous knowledge in order to change its old wine into new, which is His Spirit, for, as He says, "New wine must be put into new bottles."

2. The enemy subjected man, re-created him for himself, enwrapping him in a lusting for wickedness and anointing him with the spirit of evil, and poured into him the wine of all iniquity and evil teaching. But the Lord, having delivered him from the enemy, re-created him, anointing him with His own Spirit and poured into him the wine of life, the new teaching of the Spirit. God changed the natural qualities of the five loaves into the natural qualities of the multitude and gave a voice to the reasonless ass. God converted the whore

GOD CAN DO IT to chastity and arranged for the naturally burning fire to moisten those in the furnace. God who tamed the nature of savage lions for Daniel is able to change the wasted and savage soul from sin into His own goodness and loving-kindness and peace by the holy and good Spirit of promise.

3. Just as the shepherd knows how to cure the mangy sheep and how to protect it from wolves, so Christ the True Shepherd, when He came, was the only One who could cure and convert man, a lost and mangy sheep, from the mange and leprosy of sin. Earlier, neither the priests, nor the Levites, nor the teachers, by offering gifts and sacrifices nor by their sprinklings of blood, could cure the soul; in fact, none of this could they do even for themselves. For Scripture says: "It is not possible that the blood of bulls and goats should take away sin."

So, making manifest the impotence of the physicians of that time, the Lord said: "You will surely quote to me this parable, 'Physician, heal thyself.'" It was as if He had said, "I am not like them, those who cannot so much as heal themselves. I am the true Physician and the Good Shepherd. I lay down My life for the sheep, and I am able to heal all kinds of sickness and disease of the soul. I am the spotless Sheep that was offered up once, and I am able to heal those **LOVE WITH THE WHOLE HEART** who come to Me." True healing of the soul comes from the Lord alone. It says: "Behold the Lamb of God, who takes away the sin of the world." And this He is to the soul that has believed Him and loves Him with a whole heart.

4. So, the Good Shepherd heals the mangy sheep. Sheep cannot heal sheep. And, unless the human being, the rational sheep, be healed, he or she has no entry into the Lord's heavenly Church. This is said even in the law in shadow and image. For instance, the Spirit speaks figuratively about the leper and the person with a blemish: "A leper or a person with a blemish shall not enter into the assembly of the Lord"; and then the leper is commanded to go to the priest and to implore the priest to take him to the house of his tabernacle and to ask him to lay his hands upon the leprous spot and to heal it.

And the meaning is this: this is the way in which Christ, who is the true High Priest of good things to come, bending over souls afflicted with sin's leprosy, enters into the tabernacle of their body and heals and cures their disorders. So it is that the soul will be enabled to enter into the heavenly Church of the saints of the true Israel. On the other hand, any soul bearing the leprosy of the sin of the passions, who has not come to the true High Priest and been healed now in the camp of the saints, cannot enter into the heavenly Church. The blemishless, pure Church seeks souls that are without blemish and pure. As Scripture says, "Blessed are the pure in heart, for they shall see God."

5. The soul that really believes Christ shall be changed and re-formed—from its present iniquitous condition to a new condition that is good, from its present lowly nature into the divine nature—made new by the power of the Holy Ghost. In this way it can be fit for the heavenly kingdom. We can obtain these things by believing and loving Him in truth and by obeying all of His holy commandments. If the casting of light wood upon the water brought up heavy iron in Elisha's day, how much more will the Lord send forth His light, buoyant, good, heavenly Spirit in our day, and through Him bring forth the soul sunk in the water of iniquity and make it light, and wing it to heaven's heights and re-form and change its very nature.

BY THE POWER OF THE HOLY SPIRIT

6. In the visible world, no one can cross the sea by himself unless he has a buoyant wooden ship that can walk over the waters. If a man walks on the sea, he drowns and perishes. In the same way, no soul can cross to the other side of the bitter sea of sin, the perilous deep of the wicked powers of the darkness of the passions, unless he receives the buoyant, heavenly, winged Spirit of Christ, which walks over all wickedness and passes on. Through this, the soul shall be enabled to arrive at the heavenly haven of rest, at the city of the kingdom, by a straight, true course.

And, just as those on board ship do not draw from the sea to drink of it nor take their clothing or food from it, but instead bring these things aboard, so the souls of Christians do not take from this world; rather, they receive from above, from out of heaven, heavenly sustenance and spiritual clothing. And living off of these things while embarked on the ship of the good, life-giving Spirit, they sail beyond the adverse evil powers of principalities and dominions. And just as all ships, the means by which people go across the bitter sea, are built of one substance, wood, so from a single Godhead's heavenly light, shining from the diverse gifts of the one Spirit, all Christian souls receive power and fly high above all iniquity.

LIVING ABOVE SIN

7. But because the vessel also needs a pilot and a gentle, fair

breeze in order to make a good passage, the Lord himself becomes all of these in the faithful soul, lifting it above the fierce storms and the wild waves of wickedness and the violent gusts of sin. Powerfully, artfully, expertly, He breaks up their tempestuousness, as He knows how to do. Without Christ, the heavenly Pilot, none can come through the wicked sea of the powers of darkness or the gusts of bitter temptations. As it is said: "They rose up to the heavens, they went down to the depths." And Christ, walking over the tossing waves, has all of the knowledge of a pilot, knowledge of tumults and temptations. As it says: "For since he himself was tempted, he is able to aid and comfort those who are tempted."

8. So our souls must be remade and changed from their present condition to another condition—a divine nature—and be made new instead of old; made good and kind and faithful instead of bitter and faithless. And being made fit like this, they may be restored to the heavenly kingdom.

GOD'S PURPOSE
FOR US

So Paul writes of his own change and of the apprehension with which the Lord apprehended him: "I press on in order that I may lay hold of that for which also I was laid hold of by Christ." Just how was he laid hold of by God? It was as if some usurper were to seize and carry off a band of captives and were then laid hold of or caught by the true sovereign.

So when Paul was under the influence of the usurping spirit of sin, he persecuted the Church and made havoc of it. But because he did what he did out of zeal for God, though ignorantly supposing that he was contending for the truth, he was not overlooked. The Lord laid hold of him and shone about him in an indescribable way. The heavenly King, the true King, condescending to speak in His own voice to the man, saw him as a slave and set him free. Behold the Master's goodness and power to change, how He can change souls that were enwrapped in sin and had gone back to the desert. In a moment of time He can convert them to His own goodness and peace.

9. With God, all things are possible. This is proven in the case of the thief on the cross. In just a moment he was changed, through faith, and restored to paradise. This is why the Lord came: to remake our souls, to re-create them, to make them "partakers of the divine nature," as it is written. He came to give our soul a heavenly soul, the Spirit of the Godhead, which leads us into all virtue, so that we might live a life eternal.

May we, with all our hearts, believe His inexpressible promises.

THE PROMISE OF THE SPIRIT

After all, "He is true who promised." We must love the Lord and be diligent in exercising the virtues in all that we do, asking persistently and continually to receive in fullness and perfection the promise of His Spirit, so that our souls may be brought to life while we are still in the flesh. For if the soul does not receive the hallowing of the Spirit in this life, through much faith and prayer, and if it be not "made partaker of the divine nature" by being mingled with the grace by which it shall be able to fulfill blamelessly and purely every commandment, it is not made for the kingdom of heaven. The good that one gains here will, in the day of the Lord, be of the very essence of life, through the Father and the Son and the Holy Spirit, forever. Amen.

Homily 19 (Collection 2—Fifty Spiritual Homilies)

Filled with the Holy Spirit

In discussing the doctrine of entire sanctification in the Early Church, we looked briefly at the relationship between the baptismal liturgy and theology. What was said there becomes important again here. Macarius almost takes baptism for granted as the way in which one enters into the kingdom of heaven. And then, in his discourses to his monks, he appeals especially to the meaning of two specific symbols in the baptismal ritual: the vesting of the baptizand in a clean, white garment as he or she came out of the water of baptism, and an anointing with oil. The vesting symbolized the baptizand's being clothed now with "the divine and heavenly raiment, which is the power of the Holy Spirit." The anointing with oil symbolized the filling with the Holy Spirit. It was the liturgical moment of entire sanctification.

Macarius, as some other Christians of his era, seems to have understood that in baptism was the Christian's essential perfecting and entire sanctification. But he wrestles as others do with the spiritual, moral, and ethical distance between what seems to have been done for Christians in baptism and the usual level of Christian life around him. Unlike others, however, he does not take the usual as the inevitable.

He insists that what is symbolized in the anointing with oil, while it is the beginning of sanctification and of Christian perfection, is an earnest of an experience yet to come in the life of the Christian. It is an experience that comes in consequence of maturity in self-understanding and discipline. That experience, which is an experience in and for this life, enables the believer "to do all of the Lord's commandments in truth. Really it is a matter of the Lord doing His own commandments, without coercion or struggle, now bringing forth in purity the fruits of the Spirit" (19:2). For Macarius, then, entire sanctification is a work of grace distinct from justification and subsequent to it—but in no way independent of it. Again, remember that he is addressing his remarks to persons already baptized. And it is probably an all-male audience.

1. Does a person yearn to come to the Lord, to be found worthy of life eternal, to become the dwelling place of Christ, and to be filled with the Holy Spirit in order to produce the fruits of the Spirit and execute Christ's commandments purely and faultlessly? He must begin by first trusting the Lord resolutely and by devoting himself entirely to the very words of His commandments. He must renounce the world altogether, so that his entire character is free of preoccupation with anything merely worldly. And that person should persist in prayer, continually waiting expectantly, in faith, for the visitation and succor of the Lord, always setting his mind on this.

FILLED WITH THE HOLY SPIRIT

Then, because of the sin present with him, he should force himself to do every good work and all of the Lord's commandments. For example, as it is written in the gospel, let him force himself to be humble of mind in the sight of all and to consider himself of lower estate and worse than they, not looking for esteem nor praise nor human repute from anyone. Rather, always having only the Lord and the Lord's commandments before his eyes and yearning in meekness of heart to please Him alone, let him, as the Lord says, "Learn of me, for I am meek and lowly in heart, and you shall find rest for your souls."

2. Likewise, let that person habituate himself to being merciful, kind, compassionate, and good, to the limit of his power. As the Lord says, "Be merciful, just as your Father is merciful." And, as He also says, "If you love me, keep my commandments." And again, be violent, "for the violent take the kingdom of heaven by force." And, "Strive to enter by the straight gate." Above all, let that person constantly remember to keep the humility and comportment of the Lord, His meekness and behavior, as his model. Let him persevere in

prayer, always begging and believing that the Lord may come and dwell in him, may perfect and strengthen him in all His commandment, and may himself become the dwelling place of his soul.

So it is that one day, that which he now does by compulsion, with a grudging heart, he may do willingly, habituating himself continually to that which is good, being always mindful of the Lord, and waiting for Him in the Holy Spirit with much love. Then the Lord—seeing such purpose and diligence in that person as he forces himself to active remembrance of the Lord, ever compelling his heart to that which is good, whether it wishes it or not, and to hu-

DELIVERED FROM INDWELLING SIN mility and meekness and love, guiding it by force to the best of his ability—manifests mercy on him and

delivers him from his enemies and from indwelling sin, filling him with the Holy Ghost. And so it is that afterward, without coercion or struggle, he truly keeps all of the commandments of the Lord, or rather, the Lord in him keeps the Lord's own commandments, now bringing forth in purity the fruits of the Spirit.

3. But before this, in coming to the Lord, he must force himself to that which is good, even against the inclination of his heart. He must continually expect the Lord's mercy with a faith free of doubt. He must force himself to love when he has no love; he must force himself to meekness when he has no meekness; he must force himself to pity and to have a merciful heart; he must force himself, when looked down upon, to bear it patiently, and when made light of or put to shame, not to be angry—as it is said, "Beloved, avenge not yourselves." He must even force himself to pray when his prayers are not spiritual. And so it is that God, seeing that person struggling and coercing himself, in spite of an unwilling heart, grants him the true prayer of the Spirit, grants him true love, true meekness, a truly compassionate heart, and true kindness. In short, the Lord fills that person with the fruits of the Spirit.

4. But if one forces himself to prayer when one has no prayer only in order to obtain the grace of prayer, and will not force himself to meekness and humility and love and the rest of the Lord's commandments, and takes no pains, goes to no trouble, and does not strive to go as far as resolve and free will can go in order to succeed in

MORE THAN RESOLVE AND FREE WILL these, sometimes something of the grace of prayer is given him, along with reviving and gladness from the Spirit, as he asked. But, in charac-

ter, he is as he was. He has no meekness because he took no pains to seek it, nor did he prepare himself ahead of time to become meek. He has no humility because he did not ask for it nor force himself to it. He lacks love for others because he was unconcerned about it and strove not for it by asking in prayer. And in the accomplishment of his work, he has no faith and trust in God because he did not know himself and did not discover that he was without it. He did not take the trouble, whatever it might have cost him, to seek to obtain from the Lord a firm faith toward Him and a genuine trust in Him.

5. In the same way that everyone forces and drives himself to prayer in spite of a reluctant heart, everyone ought to

BUT RESOLVE IS NECESSARY force himself to trust and humility, to love and to meekness, to sincerity, simplicity, and "all patience and long-suffering," as it is written, "with joyfulness." So also everyone ought to force himself to thinking little of himself, esteeming himself to be poor and last; and thus not to engage in idle prattle but to meditate constantly and to speak the things of God with mouth and heart. Everyone ought also to force himself not to be angry or clamorous, as it is said, "Let all bitterness and anger and clamor be put away from you, along with all malice."

In sum, everyone ought to force himself to walk in all of the ways of the Lord, to total practice of virtue and of good and high-minded living, to consistent goodness, to total humility and meekness; not to being proud, high-minded, or puffed up, nor to speaking against anyone.

6. The person who desires to approve himself to Christ and please Him must force himself to do all of these things, so that the Lord, seeing that person's earnestness and purpose in compelling himself thus to all goodness and simplicity, and kindness and humility, love and prayer, and driving himself to them by force, may give

GOD REWARDS THE EARNEST SEEKER him His entire self. Then the Lord himself will do in that person, purely and without struggle or coercion, all these things that the person could not do even by coercion because of the sin that was within. And in like manner, all of the practices of virtue will come to that person. For from that time forward, the Lord coming and dwelling in him, and he in the Lord, the Lord himself performs in him His own commandments, without effort, filling that person with the fruits of the Spirit.

But if one forces himself only to prayer until he receives a gift of it from God but does not in the same way force and compel and accustom himself to these other things, he cannot truly perform them purely and faultlessly. One should prepare himself in this way to do to the best of his power that which is good, for sometimes the divine grace comes while one is asking and praying. God is good and kind, and to those who ask Him He gives what they ask. But if one has not the things of which we have spoken and has not accustomed or adapted himself to them in advance, even if one should receive grace, he will lose it. He will fall through pride, or at least will make no progress, and will not mature in the grace that came to him, since he does not give himself over to the commandments of the Lord with a good will. After all, the dwelling place and repose of the Spirit is humility, love, and meekness, and the other commandments of the Lord.

7. One who truly desires to please God and to receive from Him the heavenly grace of the Spirit, and to grow and be perfected in the Holy Spirit, should, therefore, force himself to keep all of the commandments of God and to subdue his heart, however unwilling it may be, according to this word: "Therefore I account as right all of thy precepts, which touch all things. I hate every false way." As one forces and compels himself to perseverance in prayer, succeeding in it, so he must bend his will to force and compel himself to exercise all of the practices of virtue and form a good habit. In this way, always asking of the Lord, praying to Him, obtaining one's petition, receiving a taste of God, and becoming partaker in the Holy Spirit, one causes the gift that was bestowed on him to grow and thrive, resting in his humility, in love and meekness.

PERFECTED IN THE HOLY SPIRIT

8. The Spirit himself bestows these things upon that person and teaches him true prayer, true love, true meekness. Those things to which he earlier forced himself, things that he sought and tended and meditated upon, are given to him. And having thus matured and been perfected in God, he is permitted to become an heir of the Kingdom. The humble person never falls. Indeed, how could he fall, being lower than anyone else? A proud mind is a great humiliation; a humble mind is a great exaltation and honor and dignity. Let us, therefore, force and compel ourselves to humility, though our heart may dislike it, and to meekness and to love. Let us do this, incessantly praying and beseeching God in faith, hope, and love, with such expectancy and sense of purpose that

MATURED AND PERFECTED IN GOD

SEEK EXPECTING TO RECEIVE

He will send His Spirit into our hearts, so that we may pray and worship God in spirit and in truth.

9. Let us do this so that the Spirit himself may pray in us, that the Spirit himself may teach us true prayer, the prayer that we do not now have, though we force ourselves to it. Let us do this so that the Spirit may teach us true humility, the humility that we cannot now attain, even by force; and that the Spirit may teach us truly to produce a heart of compassion, kindness, and all of the commandments of the Lord, without pain or coercion. The Spirit himself knows how to fill us with His fruits. And so it will be that the Spirit will present our souls pure and faultless, like fair brides, to Christ. For the Lord's commandments will have been fulfilled by us through His Spirit, who alone knows the will of the Lord, and who, when once we are cleansed from every defilement and spot of sin, has perfected us in himself and himself in us.

THE SPIRIT FILLS US WITH HIS FRUITS

Thus presented, we rest in God and His kingdom, and God rests in us world without end. Glory to His compassions and to His mercy and love, that He has condescended to give such honor and glory to mankind, that He has condescended to make them children of the Heavenly Father, and has called them His own brothers. To Him be glory forever. Amen.

Homily 15 (Collection 2—Fifty Spiritual Homilies) 13-15

A Further Work of Grace

As we might expect, Macarius has to respond to a number of serious questions from those interested in the victorious spiritual life of which he has spoken but who are doubtful that such an experience is truly available in this life. The following section shows Macarius dealing with the issue of sinless perfection. "Some say that evil enters us from outside of ourselves and that if we please, we need not admit it entrance but we can send it off" (see 15:13). The issue involved is this: If one has truly been cleansed and freed from all sin, it would seem that such a person would never again sin. How is it that one filled with the divine presence ever falls back into sin? Macarius proposes a response that denies sinless perfection but at the same time offers assurance to those with many scruples who might be tempted to despair because they do not always seem to themselves to be victorious.

We must remember that the question and the response arose in a context in which many believed that baptism completely cleansed from sin and sinfulness. The question asked here, then, is asked against the backdrop of the way in which some persons have come to explain how it is that baptized persons sin. They reason that because of baptism there is no sin within, so sin must approach them from outside themselves, and they simply do not turn it away. According to this way of thinking, any sinning that a baptized person does is strictly an act of the will—it is voluntary transgression.

Macarius's message and point of view, then, would puzzle such persons. First, they would be puzzled because he seems to believe that sin remains even in the baptized. Second, he seems to believe that the exercise of true righteousness requires more than baptism and a good will. From the standpoint of experience, they can understand him perfectly, but they have the grassroots understanding of the total efficacy of baptism to deal with, and they also have to square his point of view with the traditional Christian optimism concerning victory over sin in this life.

On the surface, it would appear that Macarius's view yields to a pessimism, because it denies, or seems to deny, the validity of two beliefs on which grassroots Christians had come to rest their optimism: the belief that baptism cleanses from all sin, including original sin, and the belief that resisting sin is essentially a matter of exercising the will.

In reality, as we have seen in the previous excerpts, Macarius's point of view is both more pessimistic and more optimistic than the grassroots view. Its optimism lies in its conviction that beyond the efficacy of baptism is the efficacy of a further work of grace. Baptism does indeed set us on the path of attempting to produce the fruit of the Spirit, says Macarius, but we discover that the path is arduous, and we either give up and settle for doing no more than we must in order to get by, or we devote ourselves to the struggle whether we really want to or not.

It is fidelity to this task that the Lord honors by sending the Spirit in fullness, so that, as we read in the previous extract, "The Lord himself will do in that person, purely and without struggle or coercion, all these things that the person could not do even by coercion because of the sin that was within. And in like manner, all of the practices of virtue will come to that person. For from that time for-

THE LORD COMING AND DWELLING IN HIM

ward, the Lord coming and dwelling in him, and he in the Lord, the Lord himself performs in him His own commandments, without ef-

fort, filling that person with the fruits of the Spirit" (*Fifty Spiritual Homilies* 19.6).

13. Question: Is it true, as some say, that evil enters us from outside of ourselves and that if we please, we need not admit it entrance but we can send it off?

Response: To this day, as in the case of Eve and because of her compliance when the serpent spoke, sin, which is external to us, gains admission through human compliance. Sin does have power and liberty to enter into the heart. But our thoughts are not external to us. They come from within, from the heart. The apostle says, "I want the men to pray, without wrath and dissension." As the Gospel says, there

SEARCH YOUR HEART

are "thoughts that proceed out of the heart." So, go to prayer, examining your heart and mind, and determine to send your prayer up to God in puri-

ty. Look carefully within to make sure that there is nothing there to hinder that prayer, to make sure that it is pure. Examine yourself to be sure that your mind is giving its whole attention to the Lord. . . . Examine yourself to make sure that you aren't bending your knees to prayer while allowing other matters to divert your thoughts.

14. Now, you say, "The Lord came and condemned sin by the Cross, and it is no longer within." Suppose a soldier parks his chariot at someone's house: he is free to go in and out of that house as he pleases. It's in this way that sin is free to make its case in the heart. As it is written: "Satan entered into the heart of Judas." But, you say, "By Christ's coming sin was condemned, and after baptism, evil is no longer free to argue in the heart." You do know, don't you, that from the coming of the Lord to the present day all that have been baptized have, at times, had bad thoughts? Have not some of the baptized turned to vainglory, or to fornication, or to gluttony? All of those worldly folk who dwell within the pale of the church—are their hearts spotless and pure? Do we not rather find that many sins are committed after baptism, and that many even live in sin? Clearly, even after baptism the thief is free to enter and to do as he pleases.

15. It is written, "Thou shalt love the Lord thy God with all thy heart." But you say, "I do love, and I have the Holy Spirit." Do you

hold the Lord in constant remembrance? Have you passionate affection and burning ardor for Him? Are you persever-
DO I LOVE CHRIST
ABOVE ALL ELSE? ing in them day and night? If your love is like that,
you are pure. But if it is not like that, keep examin-
ing yourself to see whether you really have no inclination to earthly
preoccupation or dirty and evil thoughts when they come your way,
whether your soul really is continually drawn to love and yearning for
God. Worldly thoughts drag the mind down to the earthly and corruptible and do not allow it to love God or to remember the Lord.
On the other hand, the unlettered man often goes to prayer, bending
the knee, and his mind enters into rest. The barrier of evil that would
resist him crumbles, and he enters into vision and wisdom. He goes
where even the powerful and the wise and the well-spoken cannot
penetrate. . . . So, Christians hate earthly glories and account them
but dung in comparison with the magnificence of the divine mysteries. And that magnificence works effectually in them.

6

AUGUSTINE OF HIPPO (354—430)

Biographical Note

On the Perfection of the Righteous Man

6

Augustine of Hippo
(354—430)

Biographical Note

Next to the biblical writers themselves, no one has exercised more theological influence and authority in Western Christianity than Augustine of Hippo. But no one has created more difficulty for the Wesleyan understanding of sanctification and Christian perfection than he. Roman Catholics have always placed Augustine in the very front rank of theological and spiritual authorities. But in practice they have often rejected his point of view. Classical Protestants, including Wesleyans, rather than placing him with others, have tended to grant him a niche superior to all others.

Augustine of Hippo

So for Roman Catholics, his is a dominant voice tempered by other voices—one or two of them, such as Thomas Aquinas, as important as his own. For classical Protestants, including Wesleyans, Augustine tends to be the normative voice outside of the Bible. Further, Protestants, again including Wesleyans, have tended to accept as normative Augustine's understanding of the nature

161

and role of the Bible and much of his interpretation of the Bible, especially of Paul's writings. Of course, most of the time the majority of Christians are unaware that it is Augustine who has a large role in shaping their points of view.

Augustine did not seek such influence and authority. He simply told the story of his spiritual life in a compelling, not to say easy to identify with, way. He responded with clarity and depth to several very serious issues that became perennial in the Church, and he went about his tasks as a bishop with such extraordinary skill and in such an attractive spirit that his own and succeeding generations found his work eminently useful.

Augustine's genius lay in his ability to see the deepest and broadest implications of what others were saying and to respond to those implications from a clearly and consistently Christian point of view. Almost never does he write about abstractions. He wrestles with real life, often using his own experience as his chief illustration. But he wrestles with life at the level of Christian principles, not simply practical solutions. This is what makes his work so enduring. Nonetheless, he is as much a child of his own time and place as most are. That is why, as authoritative as he is, he should not have either the first or the last word.

Augustine tells us quite plainly that he believes God found him and redeemed him while he was in the process of running away from Him—running away, and yet running after precisely what he was running from: "Thou hast made us for Thyself, and our hearts are restless 'til they find their rest in Thee" (*Confessions* I.1). As he sees it, God must have decided to save him in spite of himself. It was none of his own doing; it was all of grace—sovereign grace. And that becomes his theme: the sovereign grace of God and the sovereign God of grace. It becomes the filter through which he reads Scripture and history, thinks about the nature and role of the Church, and understands Christian life in general. Augustine is convinced that sovereign grace is the absolute bedrock of Christian faith.

Few persons in Augustine's day had his ability to grasp a fundamental principle so tenaciously and apply it so pervasively. Yet in those tumultuous times in that part of the Roman Empire—especially in Rome itself—many who could see but dimly what Augustine saw clearly found his perspective comforting. Rome had not known the sole of a conqueror's foot for a thousand years until Alaric and his Visigothic brigands sacked the city in A.D. 410. They had not come to lay Rome in ruins nor to wreak havoc upon its population. They meant only pillage. And they were not pagans, but Christians—Arian Christians. Apparently they did little physical damage, but the psychological effect was enormous. It added to the load of depression that had grown in Rome for the two generations since the government had moved to Constantinople. Many, even among the Christians, who were the majority in town, had apparently developed a fatalism with its attendant ethic. They believed themselves to be mere pawns in the hand of God, unable to control either their present or their future.

So while Augustine had developed his doctrine of salvation by sovereign grace with great joy and as an expression of spiritual confidence, many Roman Christians heard it as counsel for the despairing. They heard Augustine say that we can do little or nothing about sin, personal or societal—original sin has destroyed any freedom, including freedom of the will, that we had before the Fall. They heard him say that in this world, in our own persons, sin will carry the day much of the time. Baptism (usually infant baptism by then) washes away original sin but not our sinful nature. But they thought they heard Augustine say we may be redeemed anyway, by God's divine and gracious election. And we have the Church to provide us the means of grace by which that calling and election are made sure, beginning with baptism. All is in God's hands, and He usually works through the Church.

The ethical consequences of such thinking were abominable. That is what Pelagius thought as he went about Rome in those early years of the fifth century. He was probably a monastic of some sort and was almost certainly from Britain, where Christians seem to have taken ascetics to be the best examples of their faith. He found the Roman Christian ethic far too careless—a denial, in fact, of our moral responsibility. So he and his companions diligently preached and taught that all are indeed sinful but that they are not born that way. One becomes a sinner deliberately, said Pelagius, by willful disobedience of God's law. And against the assertion that even Christians cannot avoid sinning, he said God would not give us a commandment that we would be constitutionally incapable of obeying.

And now the battle was joined: Pelagius arguing that, aided by God's grace, we can always choose the good and be saved; Augustine arguing that *only* by grace can we ever choose the good, and that grace alone, not our choice, saves us. Theologically, Augustine won. Across the centuries, scholar after scholar and council after council have declared that Augustine had it right. Practically, Pelagius won. Across the centuries, Christians have insisted that they themselves have played a decisive part in their own salvation.

Some have thought that the full truth lies somewhere between the two positions. Wesleyan-Holiness theology has sometimes taken this path. But Wesley himself, and most of his theological progeny, have gone first to the Bible and then to Augustine and found him to be of two minds; Augustine let the struggle with the Pelagians lead him into some exaggerations, they say, but he is basically sound. Our free wills are a gift of grace, not an item in our natural equipment; it is grace that makes moral (or immoral) choice possible; and it is thus grace, and grace alone, that saves. By grace, then, we can keep the law of God, which is to love God with heart and soul, mind and strength, and neighbor as self.

In the selection from Augustine printed here, we catch Pelagius's disciple, Coelestius, being insufficiently guarded in the way in which he puts his questions (assuming that he is being reported fairly). And we catch Augustine responding too literally and not qualifying his answers with his usual caution. But such was the nature of the debate in about A.D. 419, and so it has come down to us, even at the end of the 20th century.

Read the selection, then, as a debating piece. But understand too that for many, though not for Wesleyan-Holiness people, it is a summary of the last word on the possibilities of grace in this life.

We shall see that Augustine and those who follow him support Wesleyan-Holiness teaching—up to a point. Augustine follows the Scriptures in affirming that sin is not God's purpose for man. By God's grace it is possible to live above sin. A sinless life is God's goal for all His people. Every Christian should earnestly seek His help to reach this goal, because such perfection may be obtained. But here Augustine stops short of the view of Wesleyans and others. He insists that this work of grace is fulfilled only "after the battle with death is exhausted."

On the Perfection of the Righteous Man

Augustine, to his holy brothers and fellow bishops Eutropius and Paulus:

Your love, so conspicuous in both of you, and so constraining as to make one smile even as it issues orders, obliges me to answer some propositions that your attached note says are supposed to come from Coelestius. I take it that since he is clearly said not to be in Sicily, your note does not refer so much to him as to those who brought report from there, where many brag about holding opinions like his—those who, to quote the apostle, "are themselves deceived and lead others astray."

On the other hand, we can well imagine that what you have sent us is in line with his teaching, or that of his sectaries. The brief definitions, or rather resolutions for debate, do not differ in any way from his general point of view, as I have seen it expressed in another work of which he is undoubtedly the author. So I think there is good reason for the report of the brethren who brought this news to us of what they heard in Sicily— that Coelestius taught such notions and committed them to writing.

Insofar as it may be possible, I would like to meet the obligation which your fraternal kindness lays on me by contriving responses that are as brief as this fellow's debating points. Yet, at the same time, I must also put forward the presuppositions behind my responses; otherwise, who could form a judgment of the value of my confutation? Still, to the best of my ability, assisted as God may mercifully permit by your prayers, I want to conduct the discussion so as to keep it from running to an unnecessary length.

Chapter 2.1—Coelestius's First Brief

"First of all," says Coelestius, "we must ask any who deny that human beings are able to live without sin what sort of sin they are talking about. Are they talking about something that can be avoided or about something unavoidable? If it is unavoidable, then it is not sin; if it can be avoided, then one can live without it simply because it can be avoided. No right nor rule allows us to designate as sin that which cannot in any way be avoided."

I answer: sin can be avoided if our corrupt nature be healed by God's grace, through the Lord Jesus Christ. Insofar as it is unhealthy, it either

CORRUPT NATURE HEALED BY GOD'S GRACE fails to see, through blindness, or fails to accomplish, through infirmity, that which it ought to do. "The flesh lusts against the spirit and the spirit against the flesh," so that one cannot do what one wills to do.

Chapter 2.2—Coelestius's Second Brief

"Next [says Coelestius], we must ask whether sin arises from choice or from necessity. If from necessity, it is not sin; if from choice, it can be avoided."

I answer as I already have answered. And, so that, having sinned, we may be healed, we pray. We pray to Him to whom this petition is addressed in the psalm (cf. 25:17, Vulgate): "Lead me out of my necessities."

Chapter 2.3—Coelestius's Third Brief

Coelestius goes on: "Again, we must ask what sin is: Is it natural? Or is it accidental? If it is natural, it is not sin; if it is accidental, it can drop away. If it can drop away, it can be avoided, and one can very well dispense with that which can be avoided."

The answer goes like this: sin is not natural; in fact, nature (especially nature in that corrupt condition from which we **SIN IS NOT** have become "by nature children of wrath") has too little **NATURAL** willpower to avoid sin unless it be aided and healed by God's grace through our Lord Jesus Christ.

Chapter 2.4—Coelestius's Fourth Brief

"Again [says Coelestius], we must ask what sin is: Is it a real something, or is it only an act? If sin be a reality, then it must, of course, have a creator; and if it be admitted that it has a creator, someone other than God obviously has to be introduced as the author of such a reality. But it is impious to admit anything like this, so we are driven to the conclusion that every sin is an act, not a real something. Now, if it is an act, it is by this very fact capable of being avoided."

My response is that sin is doubtless called an action, and it is an action, not a thing. But then, by the same token, physical lameness is an act, not a thing. The real thing, in this case, is the foot itself, or the body, or the human being. Still, one who is lame cannot avoid lameness unless one's foot be healed. The same change may occur in the inward person—by God's grace through our Lord Jesus Christ. The defect that itself causes one's lameness is not the foot, nor the body, nor even the lameness itself when one is not walking, even though, whenever there is an attempt to walk, there is an inherent defect that causes lameness.

Now, one may ask what we should call this defect, this deformed act: a thing? an act? a disordered something in the thing itself? In the **CARNALITY IS A SCUTTLED** inward person, that which really exists is the **CONDITION OF THE SOUL** soul; a theft is an act, and what influences the soul toward evil is its scuttled condition or character, with its yen for dishonesty. This condition obtains even when the soul is doing nothing to gratify immediately its inclination to avarice, even when it hears the prohibition, "Thou shalt not covet," and censures its own covetousness. Even then, it still holds on to its evil affection.

However, by faith, the soul receives renewal. That is to say, it receives a healing remedy and applies it day by day. But this comes about only by God's grace through our Lord Jesus Christ.

Chapter 3.5—Coelestius's Fifth Brief

[Coelestius says,] "We must next ask whether one ought to be without sin? No doubt one ought. If one ought, one is able; if one is not able, he ought not, for the very reason that he is not able. Now, if one ought not to be without sin, it follows that he ought to be with sin, which then ceases to be sin at all if it be so clearly entailed. However, since it is silly even to put such a statement into words, we are under obligation to confess that one ought to be without sin. And it is clear that one is under no more obligation than one's ability to meet that obligation."

Let me set my answer up with the same illustration that I used in the previous reply. When we see a cripple who has an opportunity to be cured, we have a right to say, "That person ought not to be lame," of course. After all, that person can now take leave of lameness. And yet, the ability to take leave of

WE BECOME RESPONSIBLE WHEN A CURE IS OFFERED lameness does not ensue whenever the cripple wishes. That happens only when the resource for remedy has aided his will and the remedy has been applied and the therapy completed. Such is the case in the inward person in relation to sin—our inner crippling—by the grace of Him "who came not to call the righteous, but sinners." Such is the case, since "the whole need not the physician, but only they that be sick."

Chapter 3.6—Coelestius's Sixth Brief

[Coelestius says,] "Again, we have to ask whether one is commanded to be without sin; for either one is not able and there is no such commandment, or, if there is such a commandment, one is able. For why should that be commanded to be done that there is not ability at all to do?"

The answer here is obvious. One is most wisely commanded to walk aright so that when one discovers one's inability to do even this, one may seek the remedy for the lameness of sin provided for the inward person—that is, the grace of God through our Lord Jesus Christ.

Chapter 3.7—Coelestius's Seventh Brief

[Coelestius says,] "Our next question is whether God wills that the human being be without sin. No doubt God does will it; and no doubt human beings are able to be without sin. Really, who would be so inane as to dither about whether it is possible for us to do that which we have no doubt God wills to be done?"

Here is my response: if God had not willed that the human being should be without sin, He would not have sent His sinless Son to heal humans of their sins. This healing takes place in believers, who

THIS HEALING TAKES PLACE IN BELIEVERS

are being renewed day by day until their righteousness becomes perfected, like fully restored health.

Chapter 3.8—Coelestius's Eighth Brief

[Coelestius continues,] "Now, we must ask this question: How would God have a human being live, with sin or without sin? Surely, He would not have humans live with sin. Just think how great a blasphemy it would be to say that humans had it within their power to live with sin, which God does not want, and to deny that humans have it within their power to live without sin, which God does want! It is as if God had created anyone for this result: that one should be capable of being what God would not have one to be and incapable of being what God would have one to be; or that one should lead a life contrary to God's will rather than one in accord with God's will."

In fact, I have already answered this one, but I see that I must make one more comment: "We are saved by hope; but hope that is seen is not hope; for why should one hope for what one already sees? But if we hope for what we do not see, then with patience we wait for it." Perfect righteousness, therefore, will be reached only when full

PERFECT RIGHTEOUSNESS IS FULLNESS OF LOVE

health is attained; full health shall be attained when love is absolute (for "love is the fulfilling of the law"); and this fullness of love shall come when "we shall see him even as he is." When faith reaches fruition in sight, no addition to love will be possible.

Chapter 4.9—Coelestius's Ninth Brief

[Coelestius then says,] "The next question for which we require a response is this: How is it that the human being exists with sin? Is it by natural necessity or by choice of will? If it is by natural necessity, humans are blameless; if it is by way of willing choice, the question of the source of the freedom of that will is raised. Of course, the answer to the last question is that freedom of the will comes from God. Ah, and that which God bestows is certainly good. (Who would gainsay that?) Now, on what principle do we prove that something is good if it is more prone to evil than to good? (After all, this is the situation if it be true that it is impossible for one to live without sin.)"

Here is my answer: It happens that it is by the exercise of free will that human beings associated themselves with sin; and on the tail of that there followed corruption (the penalty of that association)—a corruption that produced necessity from liberty. Hence the cry of faith to God: "Lead me out of my necessities!" (Old Latin Version—necessitatibus). With these necessities besetting us, we are either unable to understand what we want, or we are not strong enough to bring about what we have come to understand.

DELIVERANCE PROMISED TO BELIEVERS But the Deliverer promises genuine liberty to believers. He says: "If the Son shall make you free, you shall be free indeed." That is to say, nature has lost its liberty; it is vanquished by the sin into which it fell by means of the inclination of its will. So another scripture passage says, "One is slave to whoever overmastered him."

Now, since "only the sick, not everyone, need a physician," so it is not the free but the enslaved who need the Deliverer. This is so because true freedom is also true sanity. This condition would never have been lost if humans' will had remained good. But because the will turned to sinning, the harsh necessity of holding on to sin stalked the sinner. And it will continue to stalk the sinner until the infirmity be entirely remedied—and until the sinner regains the kind of freedom that allows for a permanent will to live happily, on the one hand; and a voluntary and happy necessity of living **ALWAYS AVOIDING SIN** virtuously and always avoiding sin, on the other hand.

Chapter 4.10—Coelestius's Tenth Brief

[Coelestius says:] "How ungodly it is to insist that the human being is evil when the human being was neither made that way nor taught to act that way! And to deny the human being the capability of being good when the human being was both made good and commanded to do good! It is God himself who made the human being good, and, further, commanded that being to do good."

I answer this way: It is indeed God himself who makes humans good and not they themselves; and it is also God, and not humans themselves, who, as they will and believe in and **GOD HIMSELF REMAKES** call for such a delivering, remakes human be-**HUMAN BEINGS GOOD** ings to be good. And all of this is brought about by the day-to-day renewing of the inward man, by the grace of God through our Lord Jesus Christ—the end of it all being the resurrection of the outward man to an eternity of life, instead of punishment, at the last day.

Chapter 5.11—Coelestius's Eleventh Brief

(The general prohibition in Scripture is "Thou shalt not covet"; the general precept is "Thou shalt love." The role of the law.)

[Coelestius says:] "The next question that we must put is this: In how many ways does all sin make itself known? Two, if I'm not mistaken: the doing of things forbidden, and the leaving undone of things bidden.

"Now it is equally certain that we can avoid all that is forbidden and that we can do all that is commanded, for it would be vain either to forbid or to enjoin that which can be neither defended against nor done. So just how can we deny the possibility of one's living without sin when we are compelled to admit that one can just as well avoid all that is forbidden as do all that is commanded?"

My answer is this. There are in the Holy Scriptures many divine precepts (it would be too laborious to mention them all). Now, the Lord, who consummated and also abridged His Word on earth, expressly declared that the law and the prophets hang on two commandments. This He did so that we might understand that whatever else He has enjoined upon us is summed up in these two commandments and must be referred to them: "Thou shalt love the Lord thy **LOVE TO GOD AND** God with all thy heart, and with all thy soul, and **LOVE TO NEIGHBOR** with all thy mind"; and, "Thou shalt love thy neighbor as thyself." "On these two commandments," Christ says, "hang all of the law and the prophets." So, whatever is forbidden to us by God's law, and whatever is bidden, is forbidden and bidden with the direct aim of fulfilling these two commandments.

Probably the general prohibition is "Thou shalt not covet"; and the general precept, "Thou shalt love." So it is that in one particular text, the apostle Paul briefly took up and expressed the two—the prohibition with "Do not be conformed to this world"; the command with "But be ye transformed by the renewing of your mind." The former falls under the negative precept, not to covet; the latter falls under the positive commandment to love. One refers to self-restraint; the other to righteousness. One enjoins avoidance of evil; the other, the pursuit of good. By abhorring covetousness, we put off the old man; by manifesting love, we put on the new.

But no one can be restrained unless God endows him with the gift; nor do we ourselves shed abroad God's love in our hearts, rather, this is done by the Holy Spirit that is given to us. And this takes place

GOD'S LOVE IN OUR HEARTS IS GIVEN TO US BY THE HOLY SPIRIT

day to day in those who mature—by willing and believing and praying—and who, "forgetting those things that are behind, reach forth unto those things that are before." For the reason that the law instills all these precepts is not that one may swell with pride and exalt oneself in fulfilling them, but rather, in failing to fulfill them, in his exhaustion, may hie himself to grace. This is how the law fulfills its role as "schoolmaster." It so terrifies one as to "lead him to Christ," that Christ may give him His love.

Chapter 6.12—Coelestius's Twelfth Brief

(The lust of the flesh is nothing other than the desire for sin.)

[Coelestius says:] "Again the question comes up, how is it that the human being is unable to live without sin—by will or by nature? [If I cannot live without sin because God created my nature that way], it is not sin; if by will, will can very easily, willfully, be changed."

I would answer by reminding him that he ought to reflect on the extreme presumption of saying that it is "very easy" for will to be changed at will. Not simply that it is possible, for this is undeniable, when God's grace comes to aid, but that it is "very easy," considering that the apostle says, "The flesh lusts against the Spirit, and the Spirit against the flesh; and these are contrary the one to the other; so that you do not do the things that you would." He does not say, "These

HUMAN WILL CHOOSES RIGHT ONLY BY THE HELP OF GOD

are contrary the one to the other, so that you will not do the things that you can," but, "so that you do not do the things that you would."

The lust of the flesh is, of course, culpable and vicious and nothing other than desire for sin. Thus the same apostle instructs us not to let it "reign in our mortal body," by these words indicating quite plainly that there is something existing in our mortal body that must not be allowed to dominate it. How is it that this lust of the flesh has not been changed by the will—whose existence the apostle clearly implies by saying, "So that you do not do the things that you would [or will]"—if the will can so easily be changed at will? Our argument here does not throw the blame upon the nature of either the soul or the body, which God created: it is wholly good. But we do say that our nature has been perverted by the human's own will and cannot be made whole without the grace of God.

Chapter 6.13—Coelestius's Thirteenth Brief

[Coelestius continues:] "Our next question is this: If the human being cannot exist without sin, whose fault is it? Is it one's own or the fault of someone else? If it is one's own, in what way is one to blame for not being what one is unable to be?"

My answer is: The human being is to blame for not being without sin wholly on this account—by the **THE WEAKNESS OF HUMAN WILL RESULTS FROM SINFUL HUMAN CHOICES** human will alone have humans come into such compulsiveness as cannot be overcome by human will alone.

Chapter 6.14—Coelestius's Fourteenth Brief

(Why the law is said to be "the strength of sin.")

[Coelestius says:] "Again, the question must be asked, In what way can human nature be said to be good (as none but Marcion and Manichaeus venture to deny) if it is impossible for it to be free from evil? For who can possibly say of sin that it is not evil?"

I answer this way: human nature is both good and able to be free from evil. So it is that we pray, "Deliver us from evil." But this deliverance is not fully accomplished as long **HUMAN NATURE IS BOTH GOOD AND ABLE TO BE FREE FROM EVIL** as the soul is oppressed by the body, which is hanging on to corruption. Still, this process is being effected by grace through faith, so that eventually it may be said, "O Death, where is your **BY GRACE THROUGH FAITH** struggle? Where is your sting, O Death? The sting of death is sin, and the strength of sin is the law." This is said because the law only increases the desire for sin by proscribing it, unless the Holy Spirit spreads abroad that love that shall at last be full and perfect when we shall see face-to-face.

Chapter 6.15—Coelestius's Fifteenth Brief

[Coelestius goes on:] "This has already been said: 'It cannot be denied that God is surely righteous.' But God imputes every sin to the human being. I suppose that it must be granted that whatever is not imputed as sin is not sin. Now, how can God be said to be righteous if there be any sin that is unavoidable and yet He imputes it as sin to any committing it?"

I answer: Long ago, in contradiction of the proud it was declared, "Blessed is the person to whom the Lord does not impute sin." He does not impute it to those who say to Him in faith, "Forgive us our debts, as we forgive our debtors." So quite rightly does He

FORGIVEN SIN IS NOT HELD AGAINST US

withhold this imputation, for He says, in righteousness, "With what measure you mete, it shall be measured to you again."

Sin, however, is that in which there is not the love that ought to be there. Or where there is less love than there ought to be, whether, in terms of the human will, or a deficiency [that could have been corrected]. This holds because on

WE ARE ACCOUNTABLE FOR KNOWN SIN AND FOR ACCEPTING GOD'S HELP

those occasions in which the lack or deficiency was avoidable (at least insofar as a humble will may be assisted), one acted according to one's present will (in self-praise, proud of such a will) and did that which was avoidable.

Chapter 7.16—Coelestius's Sixteenth Brief

After all of these quibbles, their author (Coelestius) introduces himself as one arguing with another. He represents himself as one being examined, to whom the examiner has put the questions: "Show me the person who is without sin." He responds: "I show you one who might be without sin. . . ."

Our answer to all of this ongoing argument is this: no controversy should have been raised between Coelestius as examinee and his interrogator on these points, because Coelestius nowhere tries to affirm that anyone—himself or anyone else—is without sin. He merely said

ONE COULD LIVE WITHOUT SIN

in reply that one could be—a position that we do not ourselves deny. But a question does arise: When does this possibility come about, and through whom? If it occurs in the present, then no faithful soul that is enclosed in the "body of this death" need offer the following prayer or speak such words as these: "Forgive us our debts, as we forgive our debtors." For in holy baptism all past debts have already been forgiven.

But whoever tries to persuade us that such a prayer is improper for faithful members of Christ in fact acknowledges that he is not himself a Christian. Again, if one were able to live without sin from one's own resources, Christ died in vain. But "Christ is not dead in vain." So no one can be without sin, even if one wished it, unless one be assisted by the grace of God through our Lord Jesus Christ.

NONE CAN LIVE WITHOUT SIN UNLESS ASSISTED BY THE GRACE OF GOD

This perfection may be attained. To that purpose growing Christians are even now undergoing discipline. And there will by all means be a completion of the process—after the battle with death is exhausted; and love, now cherished by the operation of faith and hope, shall be perfected in the fruition of sight and possession.

7

JOHN CHRYSOSTOM
(ca. 347—407)

Biographical Note

Commentary on St. John the Apostle and Evangelist
Homily 10, John 1:11-13
His Own Received Him Not

Homily 76, John 14:31—15:10
The True Vine

7

John Chrysostom
(ca. 347—407)

John Chrysostom. Mosaic (10th century) from
the nave of Hagia Sophia, Istanbul, Turkey.

Biographical Note

Chrysostom was really John's nickname. His surname is now
lost to us. "Chrysostom" means "golden-mouthed," and the large
collection of his sermons that has come down to us tells us that it
was an accurate title. Later generations accounted him as the
greatest preacher in the Early Church.

John was born in Antioch, Syria, into the home of an educated, wealthy government official. We know almost nothing of his father's religion, but we know that his mother nurtured her own

Christian faith carefully. His father died while John was still quite young, but he had provided well for his family, so John was able to retain the privileges of the upper class—acquaintance with the movers and shakers of society, and a good education.

John was an exceptional student and seemed destined for the civil service or for a career in law. But at age 20 or 21, he accepted baptism and began to prepare for the Christian ministry. He took his time. First he studied Scripture under his own bishop, Melitius; then he went to the desert for a time and lived the life of an ascetic. This was not to be his chosen lifestyle, but he always retained a deep respect for those who chose it. In 381 John was ordained a deacon, and at last, in 386, nearing 40 years of age, he was ordained a presbyter or priest.

For 10 years after his ordination, John served the people of Antioch, preaching in several of the city's churches to very attentive crowds. In 398, much against his wishes, he went to the capital of the Roman Empire, Constantinople, as patriarch.

Most of the sermons that we have from Chrysostom, including the homilies printed here, come from his ministry in Antioch. What the reader notes very quickly about these sermons is their plainness of speech and their forcefulness. Chrysostom feared only the wrath of God. So he often named the sinner with the sin, and he simply would not let an enemy of the faith go unanswered. Social position—his own or that of others—mattered little to him. He did not hesitate to denounce the morality of the Roman emperor or the court, nor did he back away from the destitution into which his forthrightness landed him on several occasions.

Chrysostom was surely a prophet, but on some topics he was a prig. In his earlier ministry, for instance, he regularly deprecated marriage. Chaste asceticism is God's will, he argued; marriage is a divine concession, not a divine preference. Only later did he admit that asceticism might not be everyone's way to spirituality and that it certainly is not the sole way approved by God.

It was his plainspoken piety and his zeal for reform that ended his career. First he let his zeal for reform get ahead of his authority as patriarch, deposing some bishops at Ephesus, over whom he had no direct authority. Then in a sermon he unmistakably referred to his erstwhile friend, the empress Eudoxia, as "Jezebel." These zealous acts opened the door for some ecclesiastical enemies—most notably Theophilus, patriarch (archbishop) of

Alexandria—to see to his deposition from the bishopric at Constantinople. However, he was soon reinstated, because people could see that his trial was rigged.

But Eudoxia was not to be placated, and she had him deposed again and exiled. This time the deposition held in spite of the fact that expressions of support for Chrysostom poured into the imperial court from all around the empire, including strong statements from the bishop of Rome. Chrysostom spent the latter part of this exile in a village on the Black Sea, and there he died in September 407. He died in exile, but the people of Constantinople did not forget him. In 437 his body was brought back to Constantinople and reburied there with rites befitting a saintly patriarch.

John Chrysostom was a leader among leaders. He helped shape Christian doctrine in one of Christianity's most critical hours—the period in which the Church was seeking to define precisely just what it means to say that Jesus Christ is both God and man. The tradition that now goes under the broad title of Eastern Orthodoxy especially remembers and honors his name and work. The Western Christian tradition—Roman Catholic and Protestant—does not know him well. Outside of Anglicanism, Western Christians have hardly known him at all. Even in Anglicanism he has been known but feebly. Still, John's understanding of what it is to be Christian, and of the aims and possibilities of grace in this life, have stayed alive, fitfully, in Anglicanism. There the Wesleys absorbed it and left it to their spiritual progeny, especially in their doctrine of Christian perfection.

At the heart of Chrysostom's understanding of Christianity is a very simple proposition: God became man in order that man might become God. Chrysostom did not invent the proposition. In the late second century, Irenaeus (see chap. 2, pp 62-67) first put this point succinctly.

But Irenaeus was hardly venturing a new thought even then. The collection of Christian writings that circulated in Irenaeus's day and would later be known as the New Testament was full of the idea. The First Epistle of John expresses it as a hope: "When he shall appear, we shall be like him; for we shall see him as he is" (3:2, KJV). And it expresses it as a reality in this life: "As he is, so are we in this world" (4:17, RSV). Paul's way of putting it was to talk of being "in Christ"—"If any man be in Christ, he is a new creature" (2 Cor. 5:17, KJV). (This verse can also be translated: "If anyone is in Christ, there is a new creation" [NRSV].) And, of course, the Gospels nowhere teach that for the believer anything less than a genuine moral transformation of character takes place in this life. "You must be born again" (John 3:7, NASB). "Be perfect, as your heavenly Father is perfect" (Matt. 5:48, NASB). "You and I are one even as the Father and I are one" (cf. John 17:21).

Latin-speaking Christianity, with its inherent tendency to think in legal terms, was uneasy with this kind of description of the Christian.[1] When Western Christians were asked, "Who is God?" they tended to answer as if the question had been, "What is God like?" And they did the same with the question "Who is the human being?" So they talked of God in terms of the divine perfections, and they talked of the human being in terms of human limitations.

When Latin-speaking Christians talked of the human being's having been made in the image and likeness of God, they emphasized the difference in quality between an "image" or a "likeness" and the real thing. They dwelt upon the Fall and the fact that it had distorted (some said destroyed) even the image of God in us. Only in Jesus Christ, fully God and fully human, was there no qualitative difference between image and reality and no distortion (or destruction) of the image.

When Latin-speaking Christians thought of Jesus Christ, they reflected especially on His suffering and death; here atonement was made for the Fall and its effects, and full forgiveness was offered. However, full restoration of all of the damage done, both cosmic and personal, would come only with "a new heaven and a new earth" (Rev. 21:1, RSV). The history of salvation begins with the Fall and ends with the Cross, though, of course, Christ will return to judge the living and the dead and to establish His everlasting kingdom on earth. What has happened since Calvary is the repetition of the Fall and of Calvary. Calvary is repeated whenever the mass is said: Christ is again offered as a sacrifice for sin. And this will continue until He returns.

Greek-speaking Christianity, on the other hand, tended to think in terms of how everything is related to everything else. So when they were asked, "Who is God?" they turned immediately to

---

1. I am writing in very broad strokes here, in sweeping generalizations, for every one of which exceptions abound. But the generalizations still hold true as generalizations.

the Trinity and to the work of the Trinity in the world—creating, redeeming, sustaining. If one were to ask Greek-speaking Christianity, "Who is the human being?" they answered in terms of the human being's relationship to God, to other humans, and to the world. When Greek-speaking Christians talked of the human being's having been made in the image and likeness of God, they emphasized the positive relationship between the image and likeness and the real thing, the Trinity. It is the incarnation of God in Jesus of Nazareth that makes possible the restoration of that image and likeness. The very fact that the Incarnation took place in this world makes possible the restoration of that image in us, in our world.

Jesus Christ is one of us, and He is the "express image of" the "[divine] nature" (Heb. 1:3, KJV, NASB): God of very God becomes man of very man. He is the New Creation, the new declaration concerning the true purposes of the old creation. The history of salvation begins at the Creation, is reaffirmed with the Incarnation, and will end with the final perfecting of all things, including the full restoration of the believing human being, in Christ. In the meantime, our essential re-creation is already accomplished. The very work that God the Father wrought in raising Jesus from the dead in absolute newness of life and showing His glory in Him in this life is the work He does in us for Christ's sake. When we celebrate Eucharist, say Eastern Christians, we receive Christ in the elements, we receive that new life, we are re-created in Christ's likeness, and we celebrate the heavenly banquet on earth.

Especially noteworthy in this Eastern perspective are two points you will see over and over, in either explication or implication: godliness is a gift of grace, not the product of or reward for works; and the form of godliness is Christlikeness, essential Christlikeness, which is to say, it is perfect love.

Commentary on St. John the Apostle and Evangelist
Homily 10, John 1:11-13

His Own Received Him Not

He came unto his own, and his own received him not (John 1:11).

Because God is merciful, loving, and inclined to doing good, everything that He does and all that He plans is directed toward making us shine with virtue. But while He wants us to be virtuous, He tries to persuade us to virtue rather than constraining or forcing anyone to it. And, by granting benefits, He draws all of those who want to be drawn, He attracts them to himself.

This is the reason some received Him when He came, while others did not. He does not want any to be His servants who do not
TO BE HOLY, WE MUST CHOOSE HOLINESS want to be or who feel constrained to be. He wants everyone to be His servant willingly and freely, grateful to Him for the privilege of serving Him.

When men have the kinds of positions that include servants, they coerce even the unwilling to live under the law of slavery. But God, who lacks nothing and who needs nothing we might have—the God who does everything that He does for the sake of our salvation—grants us full freedom in this matter. He brings to bear neither compulsion nor necessity on any who are unwilling. In fact, He sees only our gain. To take up this service unwillingly is the same thing as not serving at all.

So, you say, "Then why does He punish those who do not want to listen to Him? Why did He threaten punishment in hell for those who do not heed His commands?" The reason is that He is deeply concerned about us—so good is He—and is not aloof from us even when we turn and run away, even though we do not obey. On the other hand, if we are not willing to walk along the path of persuasion and kindness, if we have scorned the path of His goodness, then He interposes the other way, the way of punishment and torture. It is indeed grievous, but therapeutic. When one scorns the former way, the latter is necessarily interposed.

Now, [human] lawgivers set up many harsh penalties for lawbreakers, but we are not their enemies because of it. Rather, we even honor the [lawgivers] for establishing the sanctions because they thought about the good order in our lives. They did this by prescribing honor for those who live virtuous lives, and, through punishments, restraining the unruly and those who would disturb the peace of others.

Now, since we esteem and love [such human benefactors], should we not all the more marvel at God and love Him in return for
GOD'S GREAT LOVE His care for us? Of course we should! The difference between their care for us and His is immeasurable. His bountiful goodness is truly inexpressible—and beyond exaggerating. But look! "He came unto his own." He did not do this

to meet His own needs, for, as I have noted, the Deity lacks nothing. Rather, He did it because His own would benefit from it. Yet His own did not receive Him when He came to them in this way, for their benefit. Rather, they even drove Him off. Not only drove Him off, but threw Him out of the vineyard and slew Him.

Still, not even for this reason did He decree repentance closed to them. Even after such great transgression, He gave them the right to have their sins cleansed away by faith in Him if they were willing. And He gave them the right to be made equal to those who had not done any such evil, to those who especially loved Him. What's more, it is not just I saying these things to you, or saying them merely to persuade you. Everything that happened in the life of the blessed Paul proclaims this fact loudly.

When Paul, who after the Crucifixion tracked down followers of Christ and stoned His martyr Stephen, had repented and renounced his previous sins and had become a follower of Him who had been hunted, God immediately accounted him among His friends. Even among those holding preeminence. Though he had been a "blasphemer, persecutor, and violent aggressor," God commissioned him a messenger and a teacher of the whole world. Even so, Paul himself, glorying in God's mercy, reported these facts unashamed. He even wrote, as if on a monument, of the deeds that he had dared to commit earlier. He called everyone's attention to them in order to make manifest the greatness of God's gift—rather than shying away from saying anything at all about them and covering up God's inexpressible, indescribable mercy.

So he recounted in detail his persecutions of the Church and his plots and struggles against it. On the one hand, he would say, "I am not worthy to be called an apostle because I persecuted the Church of God"; on the other, he would say, "Jesus came to save sinners, of whom I am chief"; and then again, "You have heard of my former way of life in Judaism; how beyond all measure I persecuted the Church of God and ravaged it."

Paul clearly told what kind of person he had been, and what an adversary and foe Christ had saved. The apostle frankly revealed the battle that, eaten up with zeal, he had waged against Christ. This, in order to give some kind of return to Christ, as it were. And because of this, he offered good hope, even to those who had despaired of themselves. He even went so far as to say that Christ had pardoned him for this reason: that in him, first of all, God "might show forth all patience" and the exceeding riches of His goodness "as an example to those who shall believe in Him for the attainment of life everlasting." I say this because the evangelist's words, "He came unto his own, and his own received him not," would seem to refer to impudent deeds too great for any forgiveness.

He who fills all things and is everywhere present: where does He come from? He who holds all things in His hand and rules them: what kind of place did He leave bereft of His presence? In fact, He has not left any place to go to another, yet He has done just that by His coming down to us. It is like this: though He was in the world, He did not seem to be here because He was not yet known; but later, He revealed himself and chose to put on our flesh. The evangelist called this revelation and descent "a coming." It is surprising that the disciple was not ashamed of this humbling of his Master. He even wrote freely of it—no small proof of the honesty of his character.

Moreover, should anyone feel ashamed, he should be ashamed for those who revile, not for the One humiliated. In fact, the One humiliated has shone forth more brilliantly because He was reviled, for even after the insult He manifests great concern for those who reviled. What is more, they have been shown up everywhere as ingrates and corrupt because they have expelled as an enemy and a foe Him who came loaded with great benefits. So they were hurt in two ways: in the way noted and by their not getting what those get who receive

POWER TO BECOME SONS OF GOD Him. And what do these latter obtain? "To as many as received him, to them gave he power to become the sons of God." That is what the evangelist said.

But why, blessed evangelist, do you not also mention to us the punishment received by those who do not receive Him? Why do you merely say that they were His own and did not receive Him when He came unto His own? Why did you not add that they will suffer for this? And why did you say what sort of punishment they will undergo? After all, by doing so, you would have scared them very much; and by such a threat you would have mitigated the harshness of their perversity. So why were you silent? And the evangelist answers: "Think! What other penalty could be greater than deliberately depriving themselves of noble lineage and honor and not becoming sons of God when the power of becoming such is available?"

On the other hand, the evangelist revealed more clearly as he went on that their punishment will not be limited to that of failing to receive this benefit. Rather, the unquenchable fire also awaits them. And meanwhile, he noted the indescribable rewards of those who received Him. He set them forth briefly in these words: "To as many as received him, to them gave he power to become the sons of God." Whether slaves or freemen, whether Greeks or barbarians or Scythians, whether foolish or wise, whether children or old men, whether honorable or without honor, whether rich or poor, whether rulers or private citizens, he meant that all would deserve the same honor. Faith and the grace of the Holy Spirit have molded all to the same form; they have pressed upon them the one royal stamp; they have expunged any difference arising from worldly circumstances.

What could possibly compare to this loving-kindness? An [earthly] king, made of the same clay as we, believes it improper to enroll slaves in the royal army, though they are his fellowmen and share the same human nature with him, and though they often have a better character than he. But the only begotten Son of God has not considered it improper to enroll in His family tax collectors and charlatans and slaves, and persons even less honorable than any of these, and even many who are unsound in body and bear innumerable infirmities.

Such is the power of faith in Him! Such is the greatness of His grace! As the fire comes in contact with ores from the mines and forthwith makes true gold of the ore, so also, and even more so, does baptism make golden instead of earthy those who have been washed **THE FIRE OF** in it. This is because, at that time, the Spirit falls like **THE SPIRIT** fire on our souls. It burns away the "likeness to the earthy" and restores the "likeness of the heavenly." Restores it newly formed and shimmering, glistening as if from the smelter.

But why then did he not say, "He made them sons of God," instead of "He gave them power to become the sons of God"? It is to demonstrate that we must put forth much effort so that the image of sonship, stamped on us in baptism, may remain wholly untarnished and intact. At the same time, it is to indicate that no one will be able to deprive us of this power—unless we, of our own accord, deprive ourselves.

Now, if those who have received authority along certain lines from human beings have almost as much power as those granting authority to them, much more shall we, who have gotten this honor from God, be most powerful of all—provided we do nothing unworthy of this power—because He who bestowed this power upon us is the greatest and noblest of all.

Also the apostle wanted to emphasize the point that grace does not come to us randomly. It comes only to those who want it and struggle for it. In fact, it is precisely within the power of those who want it and struggle for it to become children. **WE MUST EARNESTLY DESIRE THE GIFT** Unless they first yearn for it, the gift does not come, nor does it do anything in them.

Now then, having everywhere else set aside the notion of force and emphasized voluntary choice and free will, he has also spoken of these in this text. He did it because, in the case of these mystical gifts, it is God's part to give grace, man's to provide faith; but even when these things have been done, we still must put forward much earnest effort. If one would preserve purity of life, it does not suffice simply to be baptized and to believe. If we mean to delight in this radiance forever, we must make our life worthy of it. God has made this dependent upon our will. Through baptism, we experience a mystical birth, and we are purified from all of the sins that we committed prior to it. But to remain pure after this—to acquire no taint subsequently—depends upon our will and our effort.

So he has reminded us of how we were born and has shown the superiority of this birth by comparing it with human birth pangs: "Who were born, not of blood nor of the will of the flesh nor of the will of man, but of God." Furthermore, he did this so that we, pondering the paltriness and the fragility of the former birth—that "of blood" and "the will of the flesh"—and recognizing the value and nobility of the latter, which is of grace, should thus hold it in high esteem (an esteem worthy of its character as a gift bestowed), and thus from thenceforward exercise much zeal.

It is no small thing to fear that, having dirtied this beautiful vesture by our subsequent carelessness and sins, we may be thrown out of the inner room and the bridal chamber like those five virgins—the foolish ones—or like the one who did not **RESPONSIBLE TO ACCEPT GOD'S PROVISION** have the wedding garment. The latter was one of the banqueters, for he was invited like the rest; but he, after being invited and after being so honored, insulted his host. Take heed to the sort of punishment he suffered. How pathetic and lamentable! He came to share in that magnificent banquet; but not only was he excluded from the feast, but also he was tied up hand and foot, driven into the outer darkness, and subjected to continual and endless wailing and gnashing of teeth.

Beloved, let us not then think that faith suffices for our salvation. If we do not give evidence of purity of life, but rather come forward in a garment unworthy of this blessed invitation,

STRIVE FOR PURITY OF LIFE nothing will stop us from undergoing the same sufferings as that miserable man. It is ridiculous that while He who is both God and Sovereign is not ashamed to invite the worthless and beggars and good-for-nothings, even bringing them in from the wide places in the road to His banquet, we show such indifference as not to improve ourselves because of such an honor. Instead, even after the invitation, we continue in the same evil, giving offense to the ineffable mercy of our Host.

This is not the reason that He called us to this spiritual and venerable participation in the mysteries: that we should come dressed in our earlier wickedness. Rather that, doffing the shameful vesture, we might change into the clothing that guests in the palace ought to wear. And should we not want to act as befits that invitation, such behavior is not to the loss of Him who has honored us but to ourselves. He does not throw us out of the splendid gathering of invited guests; we throw ourselves out.

Indeed, He has done all that He should have done. Here is why I say this: He has made the marriage banquet, prepared the table, and sent messengers to invite us;

GOD'S BANQUET IS FOR THE RIGHTEOUS He received us when we got here and has honored us in every other way. We, on the other hand, have acted scornfully toward Him, toward everyone else present, and toward the wedding—by our soiled clothing, by our impure activities. So it is that we deserve to be thrown out. He drives away the brassy and the sassy because He honors the wedding and the other guests. Were He to permit those clad in such vesture to stay, He would himself seem to be insulting the rest. Oh, may it be that no one, neither we nor anyone else, may meet with such treatment from Him who has called us.

You see, all of these things have been described in writing before they happen so that, having been castigated by the menace of the written word, we might not allow this degradation and punishment to come to life in deed; that we might make it remain only in words; and that we might answer that invitation, each in a shining garment. May we all delight in this blessing through the grace and mercy of our Lord Jesus Christ, through whom glory, power, and honor be to the Father, together with the Holy Spirit, now, and always, and forever and ever. Amen.

Homily 76, John 14:31—15:10

The following homily reminds the editor of the embarrassment of riches found in the works of John Chrysostom. Reproduced here is *Homily 76* from Chrysostom's *Commentary on St. John the Apostle and Evangelist.* But it is set in an especially rich series of 13 homilies covering John 13:1 to 17:26 *(Homilies 70-82).*[2]

The True Vine

Arise, let us go from here. I am the true vine, and my Father is the vinedresser (John 14:31—15:1).

Want of spiritual understanding makes the soul feeble and base, just as being well taught in heavenly doctrine makes it strong and noble. If the soul does not profit from the teaching given, it is weak, not naturally, but by choice. The qualities inherent in one's nature are invariable; so when I see the once bold human being becoming timorous, I contend that this conduct is not an inherent flaw. Or, when I see those who were timorous a moment ago becoming suddenly bold, I draw the same conclusion. I credit everything to their free choice.

The disciples were craven before they were accounted worthy of the gift of the Spirit and attained the spiritual understanding that

COWARDLY BEFORE THE GIFT OF THE SPIRIT they needed. However, later, they became bolder than lions. Peter could not take the teasings of a little serving girl, but later he did not hold his tongue, though he was scourged and exposed to countless perils. No, he spoke up, and he endured his sufferings as if they were but a dream—but not before the Crucifixion. So Christ said, "Arise, let us go from here."

You say, "May I ask why He said that? Did He simply not know when Judas would come? Or was He afraid that Judas would come right there and arrest them—that those plotting against Him would come before He had completed that most noble of His teachings?"

I say, "Perish the thought! Such ideas are far beneath His dignity!"

You say, "Well, if He was not afraid, why in the world did He take them away from there? Why not finish the talk and then con-

---

2. The editor devoutly hopes that you will be led from here to read the surrounding homilies. They support and form the context for each other. You may find them in almost any of the great collections of classical Christian literature such as *The Fathers of the Church* or *The Nicene, Post-Nicene Fathers (Series One).* 5210.

duct them to the garden, known so well by Judas? Moreover, even if Judas had been there, could Christ not have blinded His opponents as He had already done once, though absent? Why did He leave the room in which they ate?"

He was giving His disciples a rest. He was doing this because it was likely that both the time and the place made them fearful and anxious. They were in a place easy for their enemies to get into, and it was the dead of night. They couldn't even give heed to what He was saying. Their thoughts about those coming to get them could only distract them. And this was all the more true because that which the Master was telling them made them expect the worst. He said, "I will not converse much more with you, for the ruler of the world is coming."

Hearing things like this, they became distraught, thinking that they were going to be caught right away. So He led them to another place in order that they would think that they were safe and finally listen to Him without gnawing fear. This was necessary because they were about to hear instructions of signal importance. That, then, is why He said, "Arise, let us go from here." And then He went on to say, "I am the vine, you are the branches."

You say, "What was He wanting to imply through the parable?"

Just this: that no one can have life if he does not give heed to Christ's words, and that the miracles that would later occur would be done through the power of Christ.

You go on to say: "He says, 'My Father is the vinedresser.' Does this mean that the Son needs help?"

Hardly! This illustration does not mean that. Look how carefully He developed the parable. He did not talk of how the root profits by the vinedresser's care, but of how the branches do. Moreover, in this setting He took no note of the Root other than that they should learn that nothing can be done apart from His power and that they must be joined to Him by faith, as the branch is to the vine.

He says, "Every branch in me that bears no fruit the Father will take away." By implication, He is here referring to behavior. He is showing that it is impossible to be in Him without works. He says, "And he will purge every branch that bears fruit." That is to say, He will give it the benefit of much care. In reality, roots need care before branches do—to be dug around and dressed; but He said nothing at all of that here. He spoke only of the branches. He was indicating that He was self-sufficient, while His disciples needed much help from the Vinedresser, even if they had excellent character. That is why He said, "He will purge the one that bears fruit."

Indeed, one cannot be in the Vine without bearing fruit; and the one that bears fruit is made more fruitful. Now one might say that Jesus made this statement in the light of the persecutions that were about to come upon them, for the words "He will purge it" mean "he will prune it" (purging makes the branch more productive), showing in this way that their trials would strengthen them.

Then, so that they might not dig around the implications of these statements, and lest He throw them into anxiety, He assured them: "You are already clean because of the word that I have spoken unto you."

Do you see how He called their attention to the fact that He takes care of the vines? Here is what He meant: "I **IT IS CHRIST** have cleansed you," though in fact He had earlier said **WHO CLEANSES** that the Father does this. There is no difference (here) between the work of the Father and the Son.

"Now," He says, "you must do your part in this." Then, showing that He really had no need of their cooperation, but that, to the contrary, it was for their benefit that He urged this, He went on to say, "As the branch cannot bear fruit of itself, so neither can he who does not abide in Me." So it is that, lest they, being fearful, become estranged from Him, He fortified their souls, which were being demoralized by fear. He tied them closely to himself and held out to them bright hope for the future. After all, it is the root that remains; it is the lot of branches either to be taken away or to remain. So, after constraining us from both motives, both reward and punishment, He specially emphasized the need of our cooperation.

"He who abides in me, and I in him," He says. Now do you see that the Son contributes no less than the Father does to caring for the disciples? To be sure, the Father purges them; but the Son keeps them abiding in himself. Well, abiding in the Root makes the branches bear fruit. Even if the branch is not pruned, if it abides in the Root, it bears fruit—though not as much as it ought. On the other hand, the branch that does not abide in the Root bears no fruit whatever. Still, it is clear that the purging of the branch is the work of the Son as well as being the work of the Father. Likewise, abiding in the Root is ascribable to the Father who begat the Root.

Do you see that everything here has a common origin—both the purging of the branch and the return accrued from the power gained through association with the Root? But the loss, too, is great—the inability to do anything. And this is not all there is to the punishment. He made the word mean more. He said that [he who does not abide in the Vine] "shall be cast out." That person will not enjoy the cultivation of the Vinedresser. "He will wither." That is to say, if he was at all in the Root, he is extricated; if he had any grace, it is stripped away, and he is bereft of all nurture and life from that Source. And the final step? "He will be cast into the fire."

GRACE CAN BE FORFEITED

Quite different, however, is the condition of one who abides in Him. For He then showed what it means to abide in Him in saying, "If my words abide in you." Do you see now how much sense it made to say earlier that He looks for the proof of our words in deeds? After saying, "Whatever you ask I will do," He said, "If you love me, keep my commandments." Again, "If you abide in me, and if my words abide in you, ask what you will, and it shall be done to you." Moreover, He said this to show that those who conspired against Him were the branches that would burn, while the disciples would bring forth fruit.

So, after dispelling the fear that they felt with regard to His enemies, and after showing them they would themselves be unconquerable, He declared, "In this is my Father glorified, that you may become my disciples, and may bear much fruit." With this, He made His declarations credible. For, if bringing forth fruit redounds to the glory of the Father, He will not overlook His own glory.

He says, "May become my disciples." Do you see that the one who bears fruit is His disciple? And about the meaning of His word, "In this is my Father glorified": He is saying, "The Father rejoices when you abide in Me; when you bear fruit."

He goes on to say, "As my Father has loved me, I also have loved you." He here spoke from a human perspective at length. And what is said in this way has an effectiveness of its own. Indeed, He chose to go so far as to die for us. And though we were slaves, and opponents, and enemies, He accounted us worthy of such high honor as even to bring us up to heaven. In this we must admit that He manifested an immense measure of love. And it is out of this that He says, "If I love you, take heart; if the glory of the Father lies in your bearing fruit, you must not suspect that something has gone awry."

Then look how, in order not to cause the disciples to be downcast, He encouraged them again: "Abide in my love, for you are in control of this." But how? He says, "If you keep my commandments, as I also have kept my Father's commandments." Again, He speaks from a human point of view, for, of course, the Lawgiver would not be subject to commandments. Do you see that on this occasion, as I've often said of other passages, He spoke this way because of the incapacity of His hearers? He often spoke to the fears of the disciples and showed them that they were safe. It was their foes who would

EVIDENCE OF A PURE LIFE

perish. They themselves had gotten everything that they had from the Son, and if they would give evidence of a pure life, not a one of them would ever perish.

What's more, notice how authoritatively He addressed them. He did not say, "Abide in the love of the Father." Rather, "Abide in my love." Then, lest they should say, "Just when You have made us despised by all, You abandon us and go away!" He made it clear that He was not abandoning them. Rather, He said that He remained as closely united to them as the branch does to the vine. Still, on the other hand, to keep them from becoming slothful through overconfidence, He made it clear that virtue could be lost if it were not practiced.

Then, lest He dispose them to fall away by seeming to make the matter depend on Him alone, He said, "In this is my Father glorified." In fact, everywhere, He showed them both His own love and that of the Father. So it was not merely the ventures of the Jews that constituted the Father's glory, but those things that the disciples were going to receive.

Then, lest they might say, "We have fallen out of the Father's good graces, we have been abandoned, deserted, stripped of everything," He said, "Look at Me! I am loved by My Father; nonetheless, I shall endure the sufferings that lie ahead of Me; and so I am not forsaking you nor leaving you because I do not love you. And if I am

ABIDE IN MY LOVE

slain, do not look upon this as a proof that the Father does not love Me. You ought not to be perturbed. In proportion to your love, these evils will be powerless to harm you—if you abide in My love."

8

SYMEON (SIMON) THE NEW THEOLOGIAN (949—1022)

Biographical Note

Catecheses
Discourse 8: Perfect Love—How It Works
Discourse 10: Perfect Holiness
Discourse 33: Partaking of the Holy Spirit

8

Symeon (Simon) the New Theologian (949—1022)

Biographical Note

Symeon (Simon) the New Theologian lived in the eastern continuation of the old Roman Empire in a period of renewal. Emperor Basil II (who ruled 976—1025) accomplished at least fitful unity and prosperity and territorial expansion. At the same time, what had been the western sector of the empire began to end 500 years of fragmentation. What had been hundreds of practically independent duchies began to regroup into what would become the independent nations of western Europe. Both East and West thought of themselves as Christian, and most people expected the Christian church to be the spiritual director of their culture.

In the West, monastic reform was leavening the life of the church almost everywhere. Beginning in about 910, various communities of monks and nuns began again to make communal worship the center of monastic life, and they vigorously revived the ideals of poverty, chastity, and obedience. In the East, too, in this period, monks took up again their ancient role as model Christians, living in model Christian communities, interceding for themselves and for the rest of the church.

But in both East and West, the monastic leaven had to work in a context in which the aristocracy held rather firm control over the appointment or election of bishops and other ecclesiastical officials. Sometimes this made for splendid piety; more often it fed foulest corruption. However, by the end of this period, about 1050, the papacy had begun to reawaken to its moral and spiritual responsibilities. It joined forces with monasticism to bring about at least modest reform, especially at the point of the aristocratic lay control of the church.

In the East, civil government had held close control over the church since the days of Constantine (337 and beyond). And there the church had developed a theology that actually affirmed the authority of the emperor over its own bishops. Now, in Symeon's time, under the Macedonian dynasty, the civil government had become concerned that monasteries controlled far too much land for the good of the government and society; they were becoming too rich for their own good. (Obviously, the government's motives were mixed.) The monks did not usually gain land by setting out to do so. They gained land because their reputation for piety encouraged people who coveted their prayers and coveted the icons (holy pictures) that their pious hands had made. In return, the people gave the monks gifts, among which the gift of land—especially a farm or an orchard—was the most valued.

About a decade before Symeon was born, Emperor Romanus I Lecapenus had placed limits on monastic accumulations of land, believing that wealth could only corrupt the monks. And he also sought to protect the small freeholder, whose livelihood would be threatened by the development of large estates. The legislation of Romanus I was not very strong, and the government lacked the will to enforce it strictly. But in 964, Emperor Nicephoras Phocas, seeing that Romanus's policy had fallen to disuse, acted decisively.

Nicephoras was himself very pious and vigorously supported monasticism and monastic ideas. In fact, he even wore a hair shirt—the garb of the perpetually penitent—and had some thoughts about retiring to the monastic life. He acted out of his concern lest the monks lose their ideals.

Casting an eye on the enormous landholdings of the monks, Nicephoras, in the notorious Novel (constitutional law) of 964, forbade the founding of any new monasteries or other "sacred institutions." He also prohibited the monastics from collecting the income from endowments or receiving donations toward the maintenance of older monasteries, hospitals, or hostelries. Nor could the monasteries accept gifts for the benefit of bishops or metropolitans (archbishops).

The monks and nuns upon whom the Novel of 964 fell were popular with the public. These same clerics had learned much in the way of public relations in the long, long, earlier struggle with imperial policy concerning the use of icons—which they had won. At first the monks turned the Novel to their advantage. They convinced many that in forbidding them to establish new monastic houses or to receive gifts, the government intended to persecute them and had little interest in the piety of the masses.

Then, with great public support, they convinced Emperor Basil II to abrogate the law. They did this by playing on Basil's own sincere conviction that a number of his political and social problems were divine punishments for support of the Novel. Once again, the monks and nuns were open to the corruption of wealth. And three other sources of spiritual corruption tempted them as well: flattery of the politicians; its corollary, political manipulation (Basil II also used it as a means of pacifying the masses and keeping political unity); and third, ritualism.

Symeon knew firsthand the dangers of self-seeking flattery. The government and the church saw in him the promise of high leadership and took upon themselves the responsibility of educating him at the imperial court. From age 14 to about age 20, he assiduously took up the studies and duties intended to place him on the path to preferment. Then, from about age 20 to 27, having refused to go on to advanced studies under court sponsorship, he apparently served in several managerial posts and rose perhaps to be a diplomat and senator. However, in those same years, insofar as it was possible, he kept a monastic regimen, though (he confesses) he was otherwise quite worldly. And, at about age 27, he left government service altogether and entered the monastery of Studion.

From the time he entered the court to the time he entered Studion, Symeon had become a lay monk. His spiritual father was Symeon the Studite (i.e., a monk of Studion). The older Symeon retained that role even as the younger entered the life of a monastic novice. But Studion dissatisfied the younger Symeon. It was famous and rich and of splendid reputation in court circles. But as the converted Symeon saw it, Studion was all too worldly, and its piety tended toward the merely formal.

Symeon's personal austerities, sometimes his words, and his demands upon the piety of Abbot Petros and the other monks stood as rebukes to the community at Studion. Within a few months he was invited to leave. Then Symeon the elder suggested to him that he enter the physically and morally decrepit monastery of St. Mamas. The younger obeyed and within three years found himself made a monk, ordained a priest, and consecrated as abbot of St. Mamas, where he would serve for the next quarter century.

The reputation of St. Mamas and its new abbot drew significant numbers of men into the monastic life. It also drew large numbers of people, including many of the elite, to hear Symeon's discourses on Scripture and the early fathers. Here was no mere formalism, but religion of the heart; no mere ritualism or legalism, but a call to holiness in every aspect of life.

Sooner or later the ecclesiastical superiors of one so influential must fight the temptation to jealousy. Sergius II, the patriarch (archbishop) of Constantinople (999—1019), yielded to it and in 1009 sent Symeon into exile on the east side of the Bosporus, to the village of Paloukiton. There Symeon and some monks who went into exile with him built a small monastery around the chapel of St. Marina, which they rebuilt. Eventually Sergius himself lifted the exile. He even offered Symeon an archbishopric, but Symeon freely remained in Paloukiton to counsel and to write.

Thanks to Symeon's disciple Nicetas Stethatos, we have contemporary editions of 58 of Symeon's hymns and 34 of the discourses he gave to the monks of St. Mamas. These show clearly why people sought Symeon's spiritual counsel. And they also show why his monks from time to time rebelled against him and his ecclesiastical superiors sometimes found him troublesome. He unceasingly insists on the traditional graces and virtues. Negatively, they are renunciation, detachment, repentance, obliviousness to the pull of the senses *(apatheia)*, remembrance of mortality, and remorse for sin. Positively, they are faith, the practice of the divine commandments, and contemplation. But beyond these that are enabled by the grace of baptism by water, Symeon insisted that there lay the grace of the baptism with the Holy Spirit. Under the conditions of this baptism, Symeon taught, the Christian moves to a direct experience of the fullness of the Holy Spirit in this life and becomes aware of union with the Trinity. This teaching is what got him into trouble.

The times were not suited to such a vision of the Christian life, even though Symeon easily demonstrated that he taught nothing but what the accredited teachers of the Church had taught from the beginning. In general, the church in the East sought reform, but it tended to believe that reform had to do with the hierarchy's keeping its doctrinal and liturgical houses in order. It made only the most modest spiritual and ethical demands upon believers, condemning only blatant disregard for the teachings of Scripture. The church required only various forms of penance for serious sin or disrespect for itself.

Salvation lay in trusting the church—understood as the sacrament-celebrating institution run by the hierarchy. The people were to trust the church to know and to teach that which was needed for salvation and to guide in right worship. Specifically, one was to believe that he or she was saved if he or she had been baptized and occasionally attended celebrations of the Eucharist.

The church did not expect the ordinary believer to be theologically knowledgeable, only to believe that the church was. To worship with the church was to confess this attitude. The church certainly did not preach the need for a conversion experience, nor the need for any continuing personal seeking of the will of God. Needless to say, understanding faith in this way, the believer became highly dependent upon the church. It was believed that the church had preserved the words and deeds of the fathers of the primitive Church. It would, therefore, guard and adjudge the appropriateness of various expressions of the faith. And, of course, the church governed worship.

Symeon's perspective subverted all of this. It subverted religion as it was usually practiced, whether monastic or otherwise. Yet many believed that something about that perspective rang true. After all, he grounded his understanding in Scripture and the fathers, and he gave personal witness to it in word and in a holy life. As we have noted, Symeon insisted that beyond water baptism the believer should seek what he calls "the baptism with the Holy Spirit." The idea was not new. Most adherents of the Christianity of his day and place believed that this baptism and the holy life that followed from it were typical of the Early Church. They simply believed that the Early Church was special in that regard.

But Symeon was sure that this gift awaited all Christians of whatever era. He was so sure that he declared that the biblical "blasphemy against the Holy Spirit" (Matt. 12:31) is precisely the denial that the Spirit can purify and empower believers in an experience of conscious union with the Trinity in this life. He understood it to be a habitual experience, not simply an occasional or an extraordinary experience.

The church in the East had long since developed the terms for considering and professing such an experience. Principal among these was the term *theosis*, denoting the process of becoming godly.

The Eastern fathers had quite consistently insisted that when we think about salvation, we begin by thinking about what God through grace originally created us to be. And they understood that His original intention still stands in spite of the Fall. Christ came, they said, to give witness to that intention and to make possible its fulfillment. God became man in order that humans might become God. And just as God became man in the kind of life we now know, so it is His intention that humans become God in this life.

Of course, they understood the problems their language presented, and they warned again and again that we think of godliness in terms of our familial or filial relationship to God rather than in terms of some metaphysical relationship to Him. We should think of Him in terms of *love,* the word Scripture uses to sum up who God is, rather than in terms of attributes that He has. We should think in terms of the incarnated One, rather than in terms of pure Spirit.

In the West, most Christians insisted that when we think about human nature and salvation together, we begin by thinking about the ruination brought upon us by the Fall and our subsequent need for pardon and justification. God became man in order to atone for human sin; and in the Eucharist we continue to offer Christ up as our Sacrifice for sin—not literally, of course, but spiritually.

There was thus a great difference between the points at which East and West said we should begin to think about human nature and salvation. This made for great differences in what they believed we could become here on earth. Nevertheless, both East and West said (and say) the same creeds except for one phrase. In the Nicene Creed, the West adds the words "and the Son" after the phrase "and I believe in the Holy Spirit, . . . who proceeds from the Father."

There is some debate as to why Symeon has long been called "the New Theologian." He certainly is not a theologian in the usual

Western sense of being the constructor or conveyor of a system of Christian doctrine. Nor does he teach anything not heard before in the Christian Church.

To refer to the original meaning of the word "theology," Symeon is one to whom *Theos* (God) has given a living *Logos* (Word). And we would probably best understand the term "new" by thinking about renewal, because the temperament of Eastern Christianity rejects out of hand anything new in spirituality. "New" as it relates to Symeon's teaching has to do with the revival or renewal of the religion of the heart among Eastern Christians.

It also has to do with the revival of the understanding of the continuing, active role of the Holy Spirit in the sanctification of believers in this life. Symeon had no new word about God; he only revived an old word—that Christians have to do not simply with a doctrinally correct and liturgically proper church, but with the living God, who wills to give himself to them that they might be like Him—nothing less.

Symeon's special word in all of this lies in his insistence that good works will issue from the sanctified life. Works do not sanctify, but the believer will not be sanctified apart from them. Symeon would have approved Luther's oft-repeated and famous dictum: "Good works do not make a good man, but a good man does good works." But Luther tends to understand good works to be rather natural responses to justifying grace. In contrast, Symeon explicitly understands them to be both effects of and responses to sanctifying grace.

Catecheses

Discourse 8: Perfect Love—How It Works

Concerning the impossibility of being believers, Christians, or of becoming sons, children, of God, unless we zealously become partakers of the Holy Spirit even in this life.

1. **Unmasking those who pretend to be virtuous brothers and fathers**

He who [only] feigns virtue, fooling and destroying many, is truly wretched. And he is liable to the condemnation and hatred of both God and men. . . . The devil took on the roles of serpent and counselor and really brought death. He deprived man of all the fruits of paradise while pretending to be good and useful. So it was that he showed himself to be an enemy of God and a killer. . . .

But this work [of unmasking others who only pretend to be virtuous] is only for those whose sensitivities are not caught up in this worldly atmosphere nor in the sensuality of the world and all that pertains to it. It is for those whose minds are not affected by things visible; it is for those who have left behind the lowliness of physicality. I am talking about those who are equal to angels, those perfectly united to God, those who have wholly possessed Christ in themselves through action and experience, through perception, knowledge, and contemplation.

2. Loving correction of one's brothers

Surely it is wicked to eavesdrop on the conversations or to spy on the activities of one's neighbor meaning to criticize or vilify him, to slander him, or, when it suits one, to tell the world what one has seen or heard. However, it is not wicked to eavesdrop or to observe another's activities if it is done in order to put one's neighbor back on the right road and done with compassion, wisdom, and prudence—and with tearful prayers from the depths of one's own soul.

I have myself observed a man who exerted much effort and took great pains to ensure that nothing that his companions did or said got by him. Far from doing this to harm them, he did it **SPEAKING THE TRUTH IN LOVE** that he might talk them out of doing or thinking evil.

He dissuaded one by words, another by gifts, and still another in some other way. And, truth to tell, I have seen this man at times weeping over one and groaning over another; he would sometimes hit his own face or beat his own chest for someone else. Himself taking the place of one who had sinned and looking upon himself as if he were the evildoer, he would confess to God and prostrate himself before Him in bitter sorrow.

And I have watched the great rejoicing of one man in those who struggled and won; he applauded their progress as if he, instead of they, were to receive the reward of their virtues and efforts. And in the case of those who fell in word or deed, or of those who kept on doing that which is evil, he mourned bitterly and lamented as if he himself were the one really responsible for all of those things and had to give account for them and suffer their punishment.

And I have seen yet another who was so zealous and full of yearning for the salvation of brethren that he often begged God, who loves the human race, with all of his soul and with warm tears either to save them or to condemn him with them. He was like Moses—

even like God himself—insofar as he in no way wanted to be saved alone. He was spiritually so bound to them by holy love in the Holy Spirit that he did not care to enter even the kingdom of heaven if it meant that he would be cut off from them. O holy bond! O unspeakable power! O celestially-minded soul, or, rather, soul born of God and much perfected in love of God and neighbor!

3. True love

Now, one who has not yet attained to this love nor seen a hint of it in his own soul nor in any way sensed its presence is still earthly-minded and surrounded by earthiness. Really, his

LOVE DIVINE, ALL LOVES EXCELLING

nature is to burrow into the earth like the so-called blind rat because he is blind just like that and able to hear only earthly voices. How tragic that we who have been born of God and become immortal and are partakers of the heavenly calling, we who are "heirs of God and fellow-heirs with Christ," who are citizens of heaven, have not yet sensed such great blessings in reality!

We are without feeling, as it were, like iron that is tossed into the fire or like a lifeless pelt that cannot feel the scarlet dye into which it is dipped. We retain this attitude, even though we find ourselves surrounded by such great blessings from God. We confess that we do not have any inward sense of it. We brag as if we were already saved and counted among the saints; we pretend and bedeck ourselves with an artificial sanctity. We are like those whose lives are spent in misery as performers in a concert hall or a theater; like clowns and whores who, without natural beauty, vainly scheme to beautify themselves with makeup and unnatural colors. How different are the features of the saints, who have "been born from above."

4. No one can be a Christian without love

When a newborn emerges from its mother's womb, it unwittingly feels the air and is spontaneously stimulated to cry and bawl. So it is that we know that when one is "born from above," he comes out from this world as if it were a dark womb and enters into the intellectual and heavenly light. And as he peeks a bit inside it, as it were, he is instantaneously filled with joy unspeakable. As he thinks in a natural way about that from which he has been delivered, he sheds tears without pain. It is in this way that one begins to be counted among Christians.

But tell me how those can in any way be called Christian who have not come into the knowledge and contemplation of such beauty,

NOT YET MADE PERFECT IN LOVE those who have not sought it with much patience, with groaning and with tears, so that they might be cleansed by these practices and thus come to it and be perfectly united with it and have communion with it? They are not truly Christians! If "that which is born of the flesh is flesh and that which is born of the Spirit is spirit," how can one who has become human through human birth but has never thought nor believed that one must be born spiritually, one who has never struggled for this, ever come to be spiritual and count himself to be among spiritual men?

He might sneak in and be like one who wears dirty clothes. But as he joins the brightly robed saints at the royal feast, he will be cast out, "bound hand and foot." Because he is not a son of light but of flesh and blood, he will be sent away to the everlasting fire, "which is prepared for the devil and his angels." And how will that person not be separated from all of the faithful and be condemned with unbelievers and with the very devil? [He will be separated, even though he once] received the "power to become a son of God" and an heir of the kingdom of heaven and eternal blessings. He who has learned in many ways what are the deeds and the commandments by means of which he is to be elevated to such honor and glory [may yet be lost—lost from God because he] has despised all of this and preferred earthly and perishable things, choosing a porcine life and considering transient glory better than eternal.

Discourse 10: Perfect Holiness

Concerning partaking of the Holy Spirit and concerning holiness and the perfect absence of sensual yearning. That the person who loves human praise will gain no benefit from the other virtues, though he may excel in all of them.

1. Terrestrial and celestial glory, brothers and fathers

Do you see how those who wait on an earthly sovereign think of it as a great glory? They are proud of it, and worldlings make them objects of envy. This being the case in matters vain and passing, how much more should we who have enlisted in the army of the heavenly

THE PURE IN HEART SHALL SEE GOD King rejoice and be glad that we have been found worthy of reception into His service and called upon to render homage to His name. Moreover, think

how far beyond any congratulation for that earthly kind of blessedness it would be to be accounted worthy to see Him face-to-face,
numbered among those who stand before Him.

Indeed, what human mind, what human tongue, could describe
the greatness of the glory and honor of being numbered among His
special servants and friends, of being accounted worthy to hear the very
words and voice of the Master? And more, if that "which no eye has
seen, nor ear heard, nor the heart of man conceived, which God has
prepared for those who love him," is above human comprehension and
above all human blessings, how much beyond even that is God himself
who prepared them! Not only is He above them, but so also are those
who are accounted worthy to see Him and to stand before Him and
communicate with Him, those who have become partakers and sharers
in His deity and His glory. They have become altogether superior to
the good things that God has prepared for them, for they have received
as their inheritance the very Lord who had prepared these good things.

That human beings have reached such heights in this life, not
merely after death, and continue to do so even in these days, even
HOLY while living this present life, is something that all of the
IN THIS LIFE inspired Scripture teaches. All of the saints confirm this
[biblical] testimony by way of their own lives, among
them our blessed father Symeon the Studite [the New Theologian's
mentor], whose memory we celebrate today. And it is confirmed as
well by those who praise the saints.

Our most holy father, Symeon, of whose life and conduct (so
pleasing to God) we have read, lived an ascetic life. And he manifested in the loftiness of his virtues and by superhuman achievements the
kind of life that we have noted. In both the city and a most illustrious
monastery, he surpassed not only those who shone in his own generation but even many of the earlier fathers. Therefore, insofar as we are
able, we praise him and call him blessed and eulogize him, for he has
shown himself to merit much praise and commendation.

2. Criteria for holiness and blessedness

All of the praise and blessedness of the saints consists of these two
elements: their orthodox faith with its praiseworthy life and the gift of
THE GIFT OF the Holy Spirit with His spiritual gifts. A third point fol-
THE SPIRIT lows these: when one lives aright as a friend of God in orthodox faith, and when God confers His gifts on him and
glorifies him through the gift of the Spirit, the praise of the entire

Church, the faithful and all of their teachers, ensues, with pronouncement of his blessedness. But if the foundation of faith and works be not laid without fail, it is impossible for anyone ever to enjoy the presence of the adorable and divine Spirit and to receive His gift. Unless the Spirit be present in a person, and be known to abide in him, it makes no sense to call him spiritual. If he hasn't become spiritual, how shall he be holy? If he hasn't become holy, for what work or activity might he be reckoned as blessed—seeing that God is blessedness?

How can one consider a person to be blessed who has no past in God, or, rather, who does not have Him entirely within himself? It is **BE HOLY, FOR I AM HOLY** impossible. If the sun had no light, how could it be called "sun"? If a person does not partake of the all-holy Spirit, how can he be called holy, seeing that the Lord has said, "You shall be holy, for I am holy"? In order to encourage us, as it were, to imitate Him by our deeds, the Compassionate One, coming to us while we are yet in our sins, says: "If you really desire communion with Me, forsake evildoing and practice doing good; pursue every virtue; become holy insofar as it is possible, for I am holy; I am pure and undefiled. This is how I am by nature; it is how you will be if you forbear the corruption of sins by practicing the commandments and partake of Me by the grace of the Holy Spirit." This is what is implied in the term "become."

3. Zeal for good works

A person becomes holy by abstaining from evil and by the practice of good works. But it's not as if one were sanctified simply by **NOT SANCTIFIED BY WORKS** works, for no soul will be justified by the works of the law. Rather, by practicing such deeds, he is brought into communion with the holy God. I am certain that the Lord said this especially to those who had already received the grace of the Spirit in order to urge them not to presume on the gift and, through apathy, return to evil. It is as if He said, "O spiritual man, you who have received the grace of the Holy Spirit and in that way received Me, do not give yourself over to idleness, for idleness brings forth wickedness, and wickedness gives birth to all kinds of evil. If you yearn for Me to be in you and with you, and that you should be in Me and with Me, become holy by the daily practice of the commandments."

However, it is necessary that the mind should take an interest in the practice of the commandments of God and be eager to do them,

EAGER TO DO GOOD WORKS since it is in continual motion and is incapable of absolute inactivity. So it is that the entire human life is filled with care and concern and cannot be altogether at rest, though many have struggled to make it so. It is beyond their ability and power. But in the beginning, the human being was created with just such a nature. In Eden, Adam was commanded to till and to take care of the place, and we have within us a natural inclination to work, a movement toward the good. Those who give themselves over to idleness and apathy cast themselves into an unnatural subjection to passions, even though they may be spiritual and holy.

4. How love of glory ruins the practice of virtues

When a constantly flowing fountain stops flowing even for just a bit, it disappears. It becomes a pool instead of a fountain. So it is with one who constantly cleanses himself by practicing the commandments and is cleansed and sanctified by God—if **CONSTANTLY CLEANSED** he were even briefly to cease practicing them, he would cease from holiness. He who knowingly lets himself be led astray by even one single sin completely falls away from purity, just as a waterpot is totally polluted by a little dung.

What I am calling sin is not simply that which is done by the body; it is those inner passions that we invisibly satisfy. Brethren, don't greet what I am saying with skepticism! Instead, rest assured that even if we practice every virtue and perform miracles and omit nothing either great or small from the commandment but still yearn only for the praise that comes from human beings, and, however tentatively, seek it by what we do, and rush to receive it, we shall be bereft of the reward for all else. For **DANGERS OF PRIDE** if we receive the praise that comes from humans rather than preferring that which comes from God, we are adjudged as idolaters, for we worship the creature rather than the Creator. And the one who, when it is proffered, accepts earthly praise with delight and joy and prides himself upon it and rejoices over it in his heart, is judged as a fornicator. He is like one who chooses to live a celibate life and to avoid the companionship of women, not resorting to them nor desiring to live with them, but who immediately receives with pleasure a woman who comes to him and sexually sates himself.

5. How passion and holiness are incompatible

It is this way with all other desires and passions too. Anyone who willingly gives himself over to envy, greed, jealousy, quarreling, or any other evil will not obtain the crown of righteousness. God is righteous, so He cannot tolerate companionship with the unrighteous. He is pure, so He will not defile himself with the impure. He is without passions, so He does not dwell with the passionate. He is holy, so He does not enter the defiled and wicked soul. A wicked person is one who takes the seed of the wicked sower into his heart and grows thorns and thistles as fruit for the devil. As the Lord's Word says, these, in turn, are fuel for the eternal fire—envy, hatred, quarrelsomeness, jealousy, competitiveness, presumption, vainglory, pride, guile, idle curiosity, slander, and any other abominable passion that the soul takes pleasure in fulfilling and that defiles us inwardly.

Far be it from us, brothers, ever to bear the fruit of such weeds, or because of carelessness to take the seed of the evil one into our hearts. Instead, for Christ's sake, let us bear fruit, 30-, 60-, and 100-fold of that which the Spirit has cultivated within us—love, joy, peace, kindness, goodness, long-suffering, faith, meekness, self-control. And let us do it so that we may be fed with the bread of knowledge and grow in virtues and attain to the perfect man, to the measure of the stature of the fullness of Christ, to whom all glory is due forever. Amen.

ATTAIN TO THE PERFECT MAN

Discourse 33: Partaking of the Holy Spirit

That it is impossible for meritorious deeds to manifest themselves except in the coming of the Holy Spirit, without whom no one can attain to virtue or be of use to others or receive assurance. How the three Persons in the Godhead are in all respects equal and identical in essence.

1. The need to kindle the lamp of the soul

Brethren and fathers,

God is fire. So the whole Bible calls Him. The soul of each of us is a lamp. But even if it be filled with oil or tow or other flammable material, a lamp is absolutely lightless until it takes fire and is kindled. It is that way with the soul too. Though it may seem to be bedecked with all of the virtues, until it catches fire, that is, until it receives the divine nature and light, it is still unkindled and lightless, and its works are [morally] ambiguous. All must be tested and shown by the light. The one whose soul lamp remains dark, that is, untouched by the divine fire, stands all the more in need of a guide with a bright lantern, one who will scrutinize his activities.

FIND THE LIGHT, WALK IN THE LIGHT

Having mercy on the faults revealed to him in confession, the guide will quickly straighten out any crookedness in those activities. Just as one who walks about at night cannot avoid stumbling, so one who has not yet seen the divine light cannot avoid falling into sin. As Christ says, "If anyone walks in the day, he does not stumble because he sees the light. But if anyone walks in the night, he stumbles because he has no light in him." In saying "in him," He referred to the divine and immaterial light, because one cannot have physical light within.

2. The light of the Holy Spirit and of Christ

Just as it is useless to one walking in darkness to have many very beautiful lamps if they are all out and cannot help him see himself or anyone else, so it is with one who seems to have all of the virtues (as if that were possible) but not the light of the Holy Spirit within. Such a person can neither see his own actions properly nor have any assurance as to whether they please God. Such a person can neither lead

GOD'S LIGHT WITHIN

others nor teach them what God wills. Nor is such a person, even if human beings set him up as a patriarch, fit to listen to the thoughts of others until he has that light shining within him. Christ says, "Walk while you have the light, lest the darkness overtake you; he who walks in darkness does not know whither he goes." And if he does not know where he is going, how will he show the way to others?

And of what use is it for one without a burning, shining fire to put an extinguished lamp on another stand? This is not what he should do! What should he do? That which the God who

LET YOUR LIGHT SHINE

is above all things has decided: [He says] "No one after lighting a lamp puts it in a cellar or under a bushel but on a stand, that those coming in may see the light." Having said this, He adds some words about the characteristics of a lamp that both guides and has the light itself: [He says] "The lamp of the body is the eye." What else does He mean by "the eye" than simply the mind, which will never become simple until it contemplates the simple light? The simple light is Christ, so one who has Christ's light shining in his mind is said to have the mind of Christ. When your light is simple in this way, the entire immaterial content of your soul will be full of light.

But if the mind be evil, that is, darkened and extinguished, then your body will be full of darkness. "Therefore be careful lest the light in you be darkness." So He tells us to "take heed, lest you think that you have what you do not possess." Note how the Master himself addresses us as His own servants when He tells us, "Take heed that you do not deceive yourself and think that you have light within you when it is not light but darkness." Let us see to it that we say the same words as the Master to our fellow servants and do not say anything perverted or false.

So it is that we say: "Brethren, make sure that while we seem to be in God and seem to think we have communion with Him, we are not found excluded and separated from Him, not seeing His light. If that light had lit our lamps, our souls, it would shine brightly within us, just as our God and Lord, Jesus Christ, said: 'If your whole body is full of light, having no part of it dark, it will be wholly bright, as when a lamp gives you light with its rays.' What greater witness than this shall we cite to clarify the issue for you? Tell me, if you disbelieve the Master, how will you believe your fellow servant?"

3. Knowledge, the key

Now what shall I say to those who relish a reputation—to be made priests and prelates and abbots—and want others to confide in them, saying that they are worthy of the work of binding and loosing? When I see that they know nothing about things necessary and divine . . . I am reminded of what Christ says to the Pharisees and scribes: "Woe to you, scribes! You have taken away the key to knowledge. You did not enter yourselves, and you hindered those who were entering." And what is the key of knowledge other than the grace of the Holy

THE HOLY SPIRIT OPENS OUR MINDS

Spirit given by faith? In truth it produces knowledge and understanding through illumination; it opens our closed and veiled mind by way of many parables and symbols as well as by clear truths, just as I told you.

4. The key, the door, and the house

Now, I will tell you again, the door is the Son, for, says He, "I am the door." The door key is the Holy Spirit, for, says He, "Receive

RECEIVE THE HOLY SPIRIT

the Holy Spirit; if you forgive the sins of any, they are forgiven; if you retain the sins of any, they are retained."

The house is the Father, for, "In my Father's house are many rooms." So give careful attention to the spiritual sense of the figure. Unless the key opens the door, it is not opened (as He says, "To him the porter opens"). And if the door is not opened, no one goes into the Father's house. As Christ says, "No one comes to the Father but by me."

5. The key, a symbol of the Holy Spirit

He also said, "When he, the Spirit of truth, comes, who proceeds from the Father, he will bear witness of me, and will guide you into all truth." This is to say that the Holy Spirit first opens our minds and teaches us specifically concerning the Father and the Son. Do you see how the Father and the Son are made known inseparably through or, rather, in the Spirit? Again, He also says, "If I do not go away, the Paraclete will not come to you; but when he comes, he will bring all things to your remembrance." Again: "If you love me, you will keep my commandments; and I will pray to the Father, and he will give you another Paraclete to be with you forever—the Spirit of truth." Somewhat later, He says, "In that day (i.e., when the Holy Spirit comes to you) you will know that I am in the Father, and you in me, and I in you." Again: "John baptized with water, but you shall be baptized with the Holy Spirit." Truly stated, for unless one is baptized with the Holy Spirit, he does not become a child of God or a fellow heir with Christ. . . .

THE HOLY SPIRIT PROMISED

6. God's dwelling

The Holy Spirit is referred to as a key because we are first illuminated in mind through Him and in Him. We are purified and illuminated with the light of knowledge; we are baptized from above and born again and made into children of God. As Paul says, "The Spirit himself intercedes for us with sighs too deep for words." Again: "God has given his Spirit in our hearts, crying, 'Abba! Father!'" This shows us that the door is light. The door shows us that He who lives in the house is unapproachable light himself. He who dwells there is no other than God. His house is nothing other than light. So too, the light of the Godhead and God are not two disparate things. He and the house are one and the same—the house and He who dwells within it—just as the light and God are the same.

GOD IS LIGHT

Theologically, we use the term "house" to refer to the Son, and we use it of the Father as well, for He says, "Thou, O Father, art in me and I in them and they in me, and I, O Father, in thee, that we may be one." In the same vein, the Spirit says, "I will live in them and move among them." "I and the Father will come and make our home with him." He says these things

I WILL LIVE IN THEM

through the Spirit, as Paul says, "Now the Lord is the Spirit." Now, if the Lord is the Spirit and the Father is in Him [the Lord/Spirit] and He [the Lord/Spirit] is in the Father and we are likewise in Him [the Lord/Spirit], then He [the Lord/Spirit] is with God the Father and God is in Him [see 2 Cor. 3:17-18].

7. The Persons of the Trinity

Just in case we need to state anything more precisely: that which the one is, the other two are also. The three are the same in essence and nature and Kingship; they are thought of in this way. If a name be attributed to one, it, by nature, applies to the others, except for the names Father, Son, and Holy Spirit, and the terms "beget," "begotten," and "proceeding." These latter indisputably apply to the Holy Trinity by nature and in a distinctive way. We are forbidden to think or talk about any interchange of names—reversing them or changing them. The terms characterize the three Persons, so we cannot put the Son before the Father nor the Holy Spirit before the Son. We must speak of them together: "Father, Son, and Holy Spirit." And we must do this without the slightest difference in duration between them. The Son is begotten, and the Spirit proceeds simultaneously with the Father's existence.

8. The unity of the divine nature

In every other case, any name or comparison attributed to a Person of the Trinity by himself is attributable to all three together. So, when one speaks of light, each Person is light, and the three together are one light. When one speaks of eternal life, each **THE HOLY SPIRIT IS THE SPIRIT OF GOD** of them is eternal life—the Father, the Son, the Holy Spirit—and the three are one life. So God the Father is Spirit; the Spirit is the Lord; and the Holy Spirit is God. Each Person is God by himself, and together the three are one God. Each one is Lord, and the three are Lord. There is one God who is above all, Creator of all; each one of the Trinity is that by himself, and they are together one God and Maker of all things.

The Old Testament also says, "In the beginning God created heaven and earth. And God said, 'Let there be light,' and there was light." This expression gives us an understanding of the Father. When David says, "By the word of the Lord were the heavens made," we understand that this applies to the Son. The phrase "and all the host of them by the breath of his mouth" we deem to be spoken of the Holy Spirit. John, the "son of thunder," says in the Gospel, "In the beginning was the Word, and the Word was with God (that is, the Father), and the Word (that is, the Son) was God." "All things were made by him, and without him was nothing made that was made."

9. Obtaining true knowledge of God

So I beg you who carry the name "children of God," you who think that you are Christians, learn these things! Do you priests and monks instruct others in vain words and think that you are masters? How phony! Inquire of your elders and archpriests, get yourselves together in the love of God and seek first to learn and really experience these things, and then you will want to see this and through your experience become like God. Yearn not merely to play a role and wear a suitable costume, in that way approximating apostolic prestige. If you rush with your liabilities to rule over others before you gain knowledge of the mysteries of God, you will hear these words: "Woe to those who are wise in their own eyes and shrewd in their own sight! Woe to those who put darkness for light and light for darkness!"

Brothers in Christ, I beg you, first lay a good foundation in humility as you build up virtues. Then, through training in godliness raise up a house of knowledge of the mysteries of God. **HUMILITY A BASIC VIRTUE** Be enlightened in this way by the divine light, and look upon God with the purified eye of the heart, insofar as this is possible for us mortals to do. Then become more completely initiated into the mysteries of the kingdom of heaven. In this way, you will move from this knowledge, given from on high by the Father of lights, to the word of teaching, so that you may teach your neighbors "what is the will of God, what is good and acceptable and perfect."

Thus through our instruction we will bring "a people of his own" to God, who has appointed us teachers of His Church by His Holy Spirit. And we will not be cast out of Christ's wedding feast as contemptuous and without a wedding garment. Rather, as wise stewards who have duly apportioned the word of teaching among our fellow servants and, beyond that, duly disciplined our own lives, may we enter in to Him without obstruction, shining with life and heavenly knowledge. May we be luminous and filled **MAY WE BE FILLED WITH THE HOLY SPIRIT** with the Holy Spirit and reign with Christ as joint heirs with Him of that which belongs to the kingdom of God the Father through the Holy Spirit, the ever living and immortal fountain and life. To Him be all glory, honor, and worship, now and evermore, and to eternity. Amen.

9

BERNARD OF CLAIRVAUX
(1090—1153)

Biographical Note

On Loving God

Prologue for the Letter on Love

9

Bernard of Clairvaux (1090—1153)

Biographical Note

In the year 910 in what is now the French town of Cluny (some 65 miles west of present-day Geneva, Switzerland), William, duke of Aquitaine, chartered a new monastery. The monks would strictly observe the Rule of Benedict of Nursia (d. ca. 543), free of any secular control and free of the control of any bishop save the bishop of far-away Rome. This monastery became one of the centers of a remarkable religious revival that lasted some 300 years.

Statue of
Bernard of Clairvaux.

The Cluniac monks emphasized worship, both private and corporate, but especially public worship in the Benedictine pattern, which placed great value on prayer. This in turn revitalized the use of Scripture, both its private study and public reading.

In time, the piety of Cluny made it a favorite stop for pious tourists—and also made it very wealthy, so that any of the farming and craftwork necessary for sustaining the community were done by hired laypersons. The monastery invested its wealth in a splendidly appointed church building, exceptionally well made service

217

books, and the liturgical education of monks, so that its worship became magnificent. The monks devoted themselves solely to private and corporate worship and to the study necessary to sustain these. Within a century and a half of its founding, worship at Cluny, and the context in which it was done, had become sufficiently magnificent to create several peaceful rebellions. The critics agreed with Cluny's purposes but believed that she had departed from the spirit of Benedict's Rule in achieving them.

Among those rebelling was Bernard, who was to become abbot of the reforming monastic house at Clairvaux, not usually shown on today's maps, lay some 80 miles southeast of Paris and 140 miles north-by-northwest of Cluny. Bernard was his name, Clairvaux the name of the monastery he headed. The point of the reform at Clairvaux was to reestablish evangelical poverty as a mark of Christian perfection. Bernard's monks were to return to a strict observance of Benedict's Rule and to balance manual labor with worship. But manual labor was understood to be a form of prayer no less pious than private or corporate worship. Clairvaux would have nothing to do with the elaborate worship or the ornateness of appointments that marked Cluny—or with its neglect of the salutary effects of physical labor. But Clairvaux did imitate Cluny in its profound commitment to worship grounded in Scripture.

Clairvaux also resisted another form of the peaceful anti-Cluniac rebellion—extreme austerity. This severe piety insisted on a return to a more nearly hermitlike monasticism. Clairvaux clearly retained the Benedictine idea of community but accepted one fundamental point made by the rebellion: that authentic Christian spirituality must be intensely personal.

So Bernard led a monastery in which the emphasis was on personal and corporate prayer deeply grounded in Scripture with manual labor as a form of that prayer. Such worship was to be entered upon by monks deeply committed on a personal basis to being Christlike.

Bernard's understanding of monastic spirituality reflected in part the spirituality of the church at large, at least that branch of it that looked upon the bishop of Rome as Christianity's universal bishop. This was a period in which deepest pessimism concerning human character, even the character of Christians, marched hand in hand with highest optimism about what grace could do in and through Christians and their institutions. Perhaps the majority of

Christians, even those unable to travel, had come to believe that a pilgrimage to some sacred spot was the ideal penance. And these people believed not only that extraordinary grants of grace awaited pilgrims in those holy destinations but also that rewards were proportional to the arduousness of the journey itself.

There was holiness to be had for those who would seek it with all of their heart and soul, mind and strength. The Crusades, especially the first three, were the greatest of all intensifications of this tension between pessimism concerning human character and optimism concerning the spiritual return on pious investments. So Bernard could sponsor, as it were, new quasi-monastic military orders and even write a propaganda piece titled *In Praise of the New Knighthood*. In it he praises the Templars, for they need "lack nothing of Evangelical perfection" (4.7). He faces frankly the anomaly of monastics engaging in physical violence and killing.

Bernard argues that there are circumstances under which Christians may kill other people (infidels, of course) without staining their own souls. He also argues that human nature cannot be trusted to reach proper conclusions when it is confronted by contradictory or inconsistent assertions. It is another expression of his profound optimism of grace and equally profound pessimism about human nature.

Abelard had earlier developed a large following of teenagers and young adults by pitting the words of one Christian thinker against the words of another on many important and complex theological questions. He was confident that the Holy Spirit would so work in his mind and those of his disciples that by following a course of rigorous logical analysis, the truth would come clear for all to accept. In rebuttal, Bernard fully believed that Abelard's method did not take into sufficiently serious account the willingness of even the Christian intellect to follow after what it likes rather than after the truth.

The supreme irony of Bernard's life is that he ruled Europe the way an abbot ruled a severely ascetic monastery in a remote place, where the kinds of power that kings usually covet were abhorred. He ruled spiritually and not politically, of course. But in the Christian commonwealth of medieval Europe, the distinction between kinds of power was not as clear as it has become in our time. Kings had some priestly functions; saints and ecclesiastical authorities had political power. Bernard was recognized as both saint and abbot.

If one were looking for the definition of a medieval Benedictine monk, he or she would look under "Bernard of Clairvaux." He could be very unpleasant and narrow-minded, almost bigoted, as Abelard discovered. He could become a fanatic over causes of dubious value and sometimes seem to advocate that ends justify means, as he did in stirring up support for the Second Crusade. His zeal could outrun his wisdom, as it did in the extreme physical austerities of his youth. But deep within his character lay two traits that really seem to be gifts of divine grace: an unself-conscious humility, and a healthy spirit of self-criticism. Here was one in whom the yearning for Christlikeness shone like the noonday, even when he was dead wrong.

Bernard's way of reflecting on the faith was typically monastic. It headed in the same direction as did most theology of his day—explication of the faith. But as we have already intimated, monastic theology arose out of the daily round of disciplined prayer, out of readings from the Bible, and from the fathers. Reflection upon the readings occurred in the context of a close community who called upon the monastic to reinvest his or her thinking in the common spiritual life. So monastic theological reflection and investigation arose primarily from a devotional or meditational mode rather than from the analytic and objective mode of the bishops' and palace schools.

It should not surprise anyone that Bernard fills his treatises with biblical quotations and allusions. It should not surprise, but it often does—especially Protestants, who are generally unfamiliar with Benedictine spirituality. In any monastery that came close to fidelity to any of the various rules in vogue in the Middle Ages, a monastic would hear more Scripture read and would read more Scripture in a year than the ordinary modern Protestant will hear or read in a long lifetime. Further, even where a priest might have to be imported into a community on a weekly or even monthly basis to say mass, all understood the mass to be the center of devotion and reflection. It was understood that devotion and reflection were to focus on Christ. Obviously, this understanding was often honored in the breach, and it sometimes spawned eccentricities and even foolishness. But such was seldom the case in the monastic reforms that stimulated the founding of Clairvaux, and it was assuredly not the case in the soul of Bernard.

Bernard speaks and writes to believers, almost always monastic believers. That has to be kept in mind in reading his works. Also to be kept in mind is that for at least 600 years, it had been the custom to refer to monastics as *perfecti,* the "perfect." Those practicing Benedict's threefold rule of poverty, chastity, and obedience were said to be "following the counsels of perfection." They understood themselves to have attained and to be walking in the way of "evangelical perfection."

At the same time, writer after writer, including Bernard, makes it clear that perfection has not been attained. How do we reconcile the two types of statements? Almost always, when Bernard, and most others, assert or imply that "perfection is unattainable in this life," they are referring to the *ideal* practice of poverty, chastity, and obedience, with all of the spiritual depth in meaning that monastic spirituality had given to those terms. Almost always, when Bernard, and most others, assert or imply that "perfection" is possible or has even been attained, they are referring to "evangelical perfection."

Evangelical perfection is a grace-given inclination to do the whole will of God out of a heart filled with love of Christ. The divine agent who brings and sustains this inclination is the Holy Spirit, and its norm is Christlikeness. The inclination is not really anything in itself; the active agent is the living presence of the Spirit in His fullness. Here, then, is entire sanctification—that is to say, a complete cleansing of the heart from all that is willfully contrary to the love of God, and a complete immersion in love by the coming of the Spirit.

EVANGELICAL PERFECTION

To express the depth and breadth of Christian experience, Bernard chooses the language of courtship and marriage. However, rather than the usual language of medieval life, he turns toward Scripture, especially the Song of Solomon. This has raised almost endless comment from an age deeply affected by Freud and by a loss of perspective on what it means to say, "I believe in God . . . Creator of heaven and earth." Modern readers of Bernard, then, will find themselves having to accustom themselves to a vocabulary largely unused today in expressing religious ideas. It should be taken as it comes.

The modern reader well versed in Scripture will sometimes wonder at Bernard's biblical quotations. He consistently used either the Old Latin version or Jerome's work itself, the Vulgate. These versions differ substantially from our modern translations in numbers of places. We now have better manuscripts available and better ways of determining which terms are truly better than Jerome or his predecessors had. Also, one small difference lies in the numbering of the Psalms.

A larger difference lies in Bernard's acceptance of apocryphal books as canonical, in accordance with the practice of his day. So one finds quotations from such books as Sirach and Wisdom and allusions to them. These quotations, however, are surprisingly few and almost never introduce ideas foreign to those in the canonical books.

We have chosen to include a large part of one work of Bernard's in this anthology, because it is typical in spirit, though generally superior in content, to much of medieval monasticism's perspective on holiness. In *Liber de diligendo Deo (On Loving God)*, Bernard is at his most lucid. It has been translated a number of times and is here freshly translated, though one must express gratitude to previous translators against whose work this translator's has been checked and sometimes corrected.

Bernard of Clairvaux does not reflect the language of Wesley and his followers as clearly as appears in the preceding excerpts from Symeon (Simon). But the relevant ideas are there. The call to love God supremely parallels Wesley's emphasis on perfect love. Bernard also emphasizes that such love is the gift of God. The sin of human pride and self-centeredness, with the necessity for its removal through grace, is clearly biblical and Wesleyan. The centrality of submitting the human will to the whole will of God is prominent in Bernard. Also in Bernard's work, the yearning to be Christlike is the hunger for righteousness that the Wesleys found in the Scriptures. Bernard, like his Wesleyan successors, stressed the truth that a holy life and character were a part of God's plan for Christians in this life.

As explained in our chapter 1, these were strands of biblical teaching that Wesley and his successors wove together in the biblical doctrines of sin, entire sanctification, and Christian perfection.

On Loving God
(Liber de diligendo Deo)

Prologue
To the illustrious Lord Haimeric, cardinal-deacon and chancellor of the See of Rome, from Bernard, abbot of Clairvaux, desiring that he may live for the Lord and die in Him:

Until now, your custom has been to ask me for my prayers, not for my answers to questions. And I must confess that I am not very capable in either case, although my profession entails prayer, even if my practice falls short of my obligations. To be forthright, I feel I am wanting in diligence and genius, the natural qualities required for such work. Now, I am happy that in return for worldly gifts, you are asking for spiritual services, but you might have requested this of someone who is richer than I. So accept what, in poverty, I do have, lest silence cause me to seem to be a philosopher.

Philosophers, along with the learned and the unlearned, habitually make excuses of this sort. And it is not easy to say—unless it be proven in the accomplishing of the task imposed—whether the excuse is really prompted by ignorance or by modesty. I do not promise to answer all of your questions; only the one you pose about loving God. And even then, my response will be what He condescends to allot me. This topic tastes sweeter to the mind, it is discussed with more sureness, and is heeded with greater profit. So, keep the other questions for brighter minds.

You want me to tell you why and how God ought to be loved. My answer to the "why" is that God is himself the reason that He is to be loved. As for the "how," there is to be no limit to that love. Is this

NO LIMIT TO OUR LOVE FOR GOD sufficient response? Perhaps, but only for a wise person. So, since I am debtor also to the unwise, I will follow custom and add something for them after saying what suffices for the wise. Such being the case, I do not find it toilsome to treat of the same ideas more at length, if not more deeply, for the sake of those who are slow to catch on to concepts.

Hence, I insist that there are two reasons why God should be loved for His own sake: (1) no one can be more justly loved and (2) none with greater return. In fact, when someone asks why God should be loved, the question has two possible meanings. It can be asked whether the question is "For what merit of His should God be loved?" or, whether the question is "For what advantage to us should God be loved?" My response to both questions is certainly the same, for I am able to see no other reason for loving Him than himself. So, let us first see how He merits our love.

How God Is to Be Loved for His Own Sake

1.1. Surely, God is entitled to much from us, for He gave himself to us when we merited it least. Moreover, what could He have given us that was better than himself? So when trying to find out why God should be loved, when anyone asks by what right He must be loved, the answer is that the principal reason for loving Him is that He first loved us. When one ponders who it is that loves and whom He loves and how much He loves, surely He merits being loved in return. Is He not the One whom every spirit confesses, saying, "You are my God, for You need not my possessions"? This divine love is sincere, because it is the love of Him who seeks not His own gain.

To whom is such love manifested? It is written: "While we were yet his foes, he reconciled us to himself." So God loved freely—even enemies. How much did He love? St. John answers: "God so loved the world that he gave his only begotten Son." St. Paul adds: "He did not spare his only Son but delivered him up for us." And the Son said of himself: "No one has greater love than he who lays down his life for his friends." So it is that the Righteous One deserved to be loved by the wicked, and the Highest and Omnipotent One by the weak.

But someone says, "This is true with respect to the human being, but not with respect to the angels." True, because it was not necessary for the angels. He who came to the aid of the human being in the time of need kept the angels from such needs. And He, who because He loved the human being, did not leave the human being in such a condition.

2.2. I think that those to whom this is clear see why God should be loved, that is, why He deserves to be loved. If the unfaithful hide these facts, God can always throw their ungrateful spirits into confusion by the numberless gifts that He clearly places at the disposal of human beings. For who else gives food to all who eat, sight to all who see, and air to all who breathe? It would be foolish to yearn to count them all up. Those things that I have just noted cannot be enumerated. Suffice it to indicate the principal ones: bread,

GOD GIVES UNDESERVED LOVE sun, and air. I call them the principal gifts, not because they are better, but because the body cannot live without them.

The more noted natural qualities of the human being, such as dignity, knowledge, and virtue, are found in the soul, the higher part of the human being. The dignity of the human being is free will, by which the human being is superior to the animals and even dominates them. Knowledge is that by means of which the

VIRTUE MEANS SEEKING GOD human being recognizes that this dignity is within and that it is not of one's own making. Virtue is that by means of which the human being continuously and avidly seeks for its Creator, and when it finds Him, clings to Him with all of its might.

3. Each of these three gifts has two facets. Dignity is not only a natural distinctiveness but also the power to dominate because fear of the human being looms over all of the animals on earth. Knowledge is also twofold, because we understand that this distinction and other natural characteristics are within us, but we do not create them ourselves. Lastly, virtue is seen to be twofold: by it we seek our Creator; and once we find Him, we cling so closely to Him that we become inseparable from Him. Consequently, dignity without knowledge is unprofitable, and without virtue it can be a hindrance. The ensuing rationale explains both of these facts.

What glory is there in having something that you do not know you have? Or to know that you have it for glory here, but to be ignorant of the fact that you do not have it of your own powers nor for glorying yourself before God? The apostle says to the one who glorifies himself: "What have you that you have not received? And since

WE NEED TO RECOGNIZE WHAT GOD HAS GIVEN US you have received it, how can you boast of it as if you had not received it?" He does not simply say, "How can you boast of it," but adds, "as if you had not received it?" He says this in order to show that the guilt lies not in boasting of something but in treating it as if it were not a gift that one had received. This is properly called vainglory because it lacks firm foundation in the truth. St. Paul distinguishes between true and vain glory: "The one who boasts, let that one boast in the Lord." That is to say, in the truth, for the Lord is truth.

4. Lest you decline to boast at all, or (on the other hand) do so vainly, there are two facts that you should know: first, what you are; second, that you are not what you are by your own power. Last, if you do not know yourself, do as it is written: "Go follow the flocks of your associates." Here is what really happens. When a person promoted to high dignity does not value the boon received, he is, be-

RECEIVE HONOR WITH HUMILITY cause of his ignorance, rightly compared to the beasts, with whom he shares his current condition of corruption and mortality.

Further, one comes to pattern conduct after that which one experiences through the senses when one does not esteem the gift of reason and begins to mingle with the herds of dumb animals. Led on by curiosity, one becomes like any other animal, for one does not see that one has received more than they. This being the case, we should dread that ignorance that gives us too low an opinion of ourselves; and, we should dread no less, but rather more, that which causes us to think ourselves to be better than we are. The latter is what occurs when we fool ourselves into thinking that some good is in us of ourselves.

But surely, even more than these two kinds of ignorance, you ought to abhor and avoid the presumption by which, knowingly and purposefully, you seek your glory in boons that are not your own and that you surely know are not yours through your own power. In such behavior, you would not be ashamed to steal another's glory. In fact, while the first kind of ignorance has no glory, and the second kind has glory, but not in the sight of God, the third evil, committed quite knowingly, is a usurpation of divine rights. This arrogance is worse and more perilous than the second kind of ignorance—in which God is ignored, for it causes us to despise Him. If ignorance makes beasts of us, arrogance makes us to be like demons. Pride it is, **PRIDE, THE GREATEST SIN** the greatest of sins, to use gifts as if they were ours by natural right and to usurp the benefactor's glory while receiving benefits.

5. This is why virtue [seeking and finding God] is as necessary as dignity and knowledge (it is the fruit of both). The Creator and Giver of all is sought for and clung to and rightly glorified in all good things by virtue. Contrarily, the person who knows what is good but does not do it will receive many lashes. And why? Because that person "did not wish to know how to do well"; even worse, "while in bed he plotted evil." As would an evil servant, such a person strives to seize, even to steal, the good Lord's glory for characteristics that the gift of knowledge would tell him are surely not from himself.

So it follows that dignity without knowledge is surely unprofitable and that knowledge without virtue is damnable. But the virtuous person, for whom knowledge is not harmful nor dignity useless, lifts up his voice to God and candidly confesses: "Not to us, O Lord, not to us, but to your name give glory," which means, "O Lord, we attribute to ourselves none of our dignity or knowledge. We ascribe it all to Your name, from whence all good comes."

6. But look, we have lost sight of our topic in attempting to show that they who do not know Christ are sufficiently informed by natural law to be obligated to love God for His own sake—natural

law as seen in the perfection of the human mind and body. To summarize what has been said, we repeat: Is there an unfaithful person who does not know that he has received the necessities of life in the body—that by which he lives and sees and breathes—from Him who gives nourishment to all flesh? That we receive all from Him who makes His sun to rise on the good and the evil, and His rain to fall on the just and the unjust?

Or who is able to be sufficiently wicked to think that the author of the human dignity that shines in one's soul could be anyone other than the One who, in the Book of Genesis, says, "Let us make the human being after our own image and likeness"? Who **MADE IN GOD'S IMAGE** is able to think that the One who gives knowledge is someone other than the One who teaches knowledge? Or, who would believe that he has received or hopes to receive the gift of virtue from any source other than the hand of the Lord of virtue? So it is that God is worthy to be loved for His own sake, even by the unfaithful person, who, though ignorant of Christ, still knows himself.

So it is that everyone, including the unfaithful person, who fails to love the Lord his God with all of his heart, all of his soul, and all of his strength, is inexcusable. An innate justice, which is not unknown to reason, declares to him from within that he ought to love with his **LOVE GOD, TO WHOM WE OWE ALL** entire being the One to whom he owes all that he is. Still, it is difficult, if not impossible, for one who has received all things from God to turn entirely to the will of God, of his own free will, instead of turning to his own will and holding on to these gifts as his own, for his **GOD'S WILL, NOT MY WILL** own use. As it is written: "All seek what is their own." And, "The human being's intents and thoughts are inclined to evil."

3.7. On the other hand, the faithful know how absolute is their need of Jesus and Him crucified. So, at the same time that they admire and esteem in Him that love that passes all understanding, they are ashamed of their failure to give the little that they have in return for so great a love and honor. Those who understand that they are loved, the more easily love more: "The one to whom less is given loves less." To be sure, the Jew and the pagan are not at all urged forward by the wound of love such as the Church experiences. . . . The Church envisions King Solomon with the royal crown, which his mother had placed upon his head. She envisions the Father's only Son bearing His cross, the Lord of majesty, beaten and covered with spittle; she sees the Author of life and glory pierced by nails, wounded by a spear, filled with reproach, and finally laying down His precious life for His friends. As she looks upon this, the sword of love impales her soul. . . .

If we desire to have Christ as a frequent guest, we must keep our hearts fortified by the witness of our faith in the mercy of the One who died for us and in the power of the One who rose from the dead. As David said: "I have heard these two things: power belongs to God, and mercy belongs to you, O Lord." The testimonies of both of these are believable: Christ died for our sins and rose again from the dead for our justification. He ascended into heaven for our protection, He

CHRIST SENT THE SPIRIT sent the Spirit for our consolation, and He will someday return for our fulfillment. He surely demonstrated His mercy in dying and His power in rising again. And He showed both of these in the others.

10. Such are the fruits and such are the flowers with which the bride asks to be nourished and strengthened. . . .

She will experience what she had heard: "The flesh profits nothing; the Spirit gives life." What she had read will become real to her: "My Spirit is sweeter than honey, and my inheritance than honey and the honeycomb." And that which follows this—"My remembrance will last for ages to come"—means it will last as long as the present era lasts, one generation arriving as its predecessor passes away.

It means that the elect will not be bereft of the consolation of memory until they are able to indulge in the feast of the presence of God. So it is written: "They will spread abroad the memory of your sweetness." This no doubt refers to those of whom it is said in the preceding phrase: "Generation after generation will praise your works." Thus it is that memory is for the continuing ages and remembrance consoles the present generation throughout its pilgrimage, while presence is for the kingdom of heaven, where the elect are already glorified.

4.11. It is important to indicate which generation it is that finds consolation in remembering God. Surely it is not the stiff-necked and rebellious generation to whom it is said: "Woe to you who are rich, you have your consolation." Rather it is the generation that can say, "My soul refused to be consoled." And we can receive the assertion if one goes on: "I was mindful of the Lord and delighted." It is appropriate that they who find no pleasure in the joys of this life think of those to come, and that they who refuse to be consoled by the abundance of changing things delight in thoughts of eternity. This is the generation of those who seek the Lord, who seek not their own advantage but the face of the God of Jacob.

In the meantime, memory is a delight for those who look and long for the presence of God—not that they are completely satisfied, but that they long the more for Him in order that they might be

YEARNING FOR MORE OF GOD

filled. So it is that He testifies that He is himself food: "Whoever eats me will hunger for more." And whoever is fed by Him says, "I shall be satisfied when your glory appears." Blessed are those who now go hungry and thirst for justice, for they alone will someday be satisfied. . . .

The words of Christ are recalled to our mind every day in the memorial of the Passion: "He who eats my flesh and drinks my blood has everlasting life." That is to say, he who meditates on My death and mortifies his members that belong to this earth, following My example, has eternal life. This means that if you "share in my sufferings, you will partake of my glory."

Many back off at these words and abandon Him. They say by their reactions: "This word is too demanding; who can give ear to it?" The generation that did not put its heart right, whose spirit is not faithful to God, talks like this, and, placing its aspirations in untrustworthy riches, feels oppressed by the message of the Cross and assesses the memory of the Passion to be a burden. How will it ever bear the weight of these words in His presence: "Depart, ye cursed, into everlasting fire, which was prepared for the devil and his angels." This stone will crush the one upon whom it falls. On the other hand, the righteous generation will be blessed, for, like the apostle, whether at

SEEKING TO PLEASE GOD

home or abroad, it seeks to please God. It will hear: "Come, ye blessed of my Father, inherit the kingdom prepared for you since the foundation of the world. . . ."

12. . . . The faithful soul sighs deeply for His presence and rests peacefully when thinking of Him, but must glory in the ignominy of the Cross until it is able to contemplate the glory of the unveiled face

SEEKING TO FIND GOD

of God. . . . There she will be enlightened by rays of wisdom. Now, she may exult and say, "His left hand is under my head, and his right hand embraces me." His left hand symbolizes His matchless love, which caused Him to lay down His life for His friends, while His right hand signifies the beatific vision, which He has promised them, and the joy of His august presence. The vision of God that causes us to bear resemblance to Him and its inestimable satisfaction are accurately figured by the right hand, as the psalmist joyfully sings: "In your right hand are everlasting joys." His love, admirable, memorable, and ever to be recalled, is well placed in the left hand, because the bride reclines on it and rests until evil is past. . . .

13. . . . What more is accomplished by meditating on such great and unmerited mercy, so free and so proven a love, such unexpected obligingness, fearless mildness, and astounding kindness? What more, I say, will all of these diligently pondered qualities accomplish if they **FREED FROM ALL** do not enthrall the mind of the one who, entirely **UNWORTHY LOVE** freed from all unworthy love, ponders them, and attract it deeply in a wonderful way? . . .

Then the bride certainly hastens more eagerly in the scent of her perfumes. She loves ardently, but even as she finds herself deeply in love, she thinks that she loves too little because she is loved so much. Nor is she in error. What can requite such profound love by such a Great Lover? It is as if a minuscule grain of dust were to collect all of its strength to render an equivalent love to the Divine Majesty, who anticipates its affection and is revealed as altogether determined upon saving it. Finally, the words "God so loved the world that he gave his only begotten Son" were doubtless words spoken of the Father; and the words "He gave himself up" were doubtless meant of the Son. Of the Holy Spirit, it is said: "But the Paraclete, the Holy Spirit, whom the Father will send in my name, will teach you all things and will cause you to remember all that I have said to you." So it is: God loves and loves with His entire being, for it is the whole Trinity who loves.

5.14. I believe that whoever ponders this is sufficiently aware why the human being should love God—that is whence God merits love. On the other hand, the unfaithful person has neither the Father nor the Holy Spirit because that person has not the Son. "The one who honors not the Son honors not the Father who sent him." Nor does such a person honor the Holy Spirit, whom the Son sent. Hence, it is no wonder that one loves less the One whom one knows **ALL TO HIM** less. Nonetheless, even such a one is cognizant that one **I OWE** owes Him all whom one knows to be the Creator of all of one's being. What then should He be for me as one who believes my God to be not only the liberal Giver, [but also] the munificent Administrator, the kindest Consoler, and the vigilant Governor of my life? And exceeding that, the most wealthy Redeemer, the eternal Defender who enriches and glorifies, as it is written: "With him is plenteous redemption"; and, "He entered into the sanctuary once and for all, after winning eternal salvation."

The psalmist says of our conversion: "He will not forsake his saints. They will be kept safe forever." Concerning enriching, the Gospel says, "Good measure, pressed down, shaken up, and running over will they pour into your bosom"; and again: "Eye has not seen nor ear heard, nor has it entered the heart of the human being what God has prepared for those who love him." Of our glorification, St. Paul says, "We await our Savior and Lord, Jesus Christ, who will transform our lowly bodies, molding them into the likeness of his glorified body." And again, "The sufferings of this life are not to be compared with the future glory which is to be revealed in us." Better yet: "That which is but passing, light tribulation in this life, produces in us a degree of glory beyond measure for the life to come, as we contemplate the things that are unseen, not those that are seen."

15. What shall I render to the Lord for all of these benefits? Reason and natural justice impel the unfaithful person to surrender

GOD IS WORTHY OF OUR SUPREME LOVE

his whole being to Him from whom he received it and to love Him with all his strength. Assuredly, faith invites me to love all the more the One whom I esteem as so much greater than I, because He not only gives me myself but also gives me himself. The age of faith had not yet arrived, God had not yet appeared in flesh, nor died on the Cross, nor risen from the grave, nor returned to the Father. He had not yet commended His great love to us, about which I have said so much. The human being had not yet been commanded to love the Lord his God with all of his heart, all of his soul, and all of his strength—with all that he is, knows, and can do. . . .

If I owe all for having been created, what can I add for being re-created, and for being re-created in this manner? It was less easy to re-make me than to make me. It is written not only of me but of every created being: "He spoke and they were made." But the One who created me by one word had to speak many words to re-create me, had to work miracles, had to endure distress, and not just distress but maltreatment. "What shall I render to the Lord for all of his benefits to me?" In His first work He gave himself to me, and when He gave himself to me, He returned me to myself. I am indebted to myself twice over, for being given to and for being returned. So what can I give God in return for himself? Even if I could give myself to Him a thousand times, what would that be worth to God?

How God Ought to Be Loved

6.16. To repeat briefly what has so far been said: Think first how it is that God deserves to be loved—that there is to be no boundary to that love, for He first loved us. As lowly as we are and just as we are, so greatly and so willingly did such a One as He love us that we must love Him limitlessly. You will recall that I said earlier, and now finally, I ask: What should be the aim and grade of our love, given the fact that its object is God, who is immeasurable and infinite? . . .

GOD DESERVES ALL OUR LOVE

"I shall love you, O Lord, my fortress, my strength, my refuge, and my deliverer." And I shall love whatever You hold to be desirable and worthy of love for me. O my God, my Help, as much as I am able, I shall love You for Your gift. My love is less than that to which You are entitled, but not less than I can give, for even though I am not able to love You as I ought, I still cannot love You more than I am able to. Only when You give me more shall I be able to love You more, though You will never be able to find my love worthy of You. For: "Your eyes have beheld my flaws, and everything shall be written down in your book," even all who do what they are able to do, even if they are not able to do all that they should do.

GOD GIVES LOVE

As I see it, the degree to which God should be loved is sufficiently clear: He should be loved according to His own merit. I say, "According to His own merit," but to whom is the degree of this merit truly clear? Who is able to say? Who is able to comprehend it?

7.17. Now let us consider how He is to be loved for our benefit. . . . Earlier, when asking why and how God is to be loved, I said that there are two ways to understand the question: It may mean "Through what merit of His does God deserve our love?" or it may mean "What benefit do we get in loving Him?" . . . Having spoken of God's merit according to the gift I have received . . . it remains to me to speak of the benefit insofar as that gift too will be given to me.

God Is Not Loved Without a Reward

God is not loved without a reward, though one should love Him without regard for it. Genuine charity cannot be worthless, yet, since "it seeks not its own advantage," it cannot be said to be mercenary.

Love pertains to the will. It is not a business deal that can acquire or be acquired by a contract. Animating us freely, it makes us uncalculating. True love is content with itself, for it has its reward, its object. You do not truly love whatever you seem to love if you love it because of something other than itself. One should really love the end pursued, not that by means of which it is pursued. Paul does not evangelize in order to eat; he eats in order to evangelize. It is the gospel that he loves, not the food.

True love deserves its reward, but it does not seek it. A prize may be *offered* to one who does not yet love. It is *due* the one who loves. It is *given* the one who perseveres. When we must persuade persons in lesser matters, we coax the reluctant with promises and prizes. But we do not coax the willing. Who would think of offering someone a prize for doing something that he or she wants to do? For instance, no one pays a hungry person to eat, nor pays a thirsty person to drink, nor pays a mother to feed the child of her own womb. Who would even consider imploring someone or offering prizes to someone to remind him to put a fence around his vineyard or to dig around his tree or to build his own home? So much more likely is it

SEEK NO REWARD OTHER THAN GOD that the soul that loves God will seek no reward other than the God whom it loves. Were the soul to insist on anything else, it would surely be a matter of loving that other thing and not God.

18. Every rational creature always naturally wants that which more nearly satisfies the mind and the will. They are never satisfied with anything lacking the qualities that they think it ought to have. . . . What about those promoted to high honors? Do we not behold them striving even more, with unquenchable ambition, to climb still higher? There is no end to all of this because not a single one of these "riches" can be understood to be the highest or the best. So why be surprised when a person cannot be content with that which is lower or worse since one cannot find peace this side of what is highest and best?

Stupidity it is, and madness, always to yearn for that which can neither satisfy nor even decrease yearning. While you enjoy those riches, you strive for that which is wanting, and you are discontented, pining for that which you lack. So it is that, running hither and yon among the delights of this life, the fidgety mind is fatigued but never content. . . .

Who is able to have everything? One grasps the fruits of his labor, small as they may be, never knowing when he will suffer the grief of losing them. Yet, one is sure to lose them someday. . . . If you want to gain what you wish in this way, to get hold of that which leaves

SEEK ONLY THE HIGHEST
nothing more to be desired, why trouble yourself about the rest of it? You are running on crooked roads, and you will die long before you come to the end that you are looking for.

19. So it is that the wicked trudge round in circles. They naturally want whatever will fill their yearnings, yet they foolishly turn down that which would direct them to their true end—an end that lies not in consumption but in consummation. So they vainly wear themselves out instead of completing their lives with a happy ending. . . .

The law of human desire causes one to dwell on what he lacks instead of what he has and to grow tired of what he has, preferring to have what he lacks, once he has gotten and abhorred all else in heaven and on earth. There one will rest, for just as there is no repose this side of eternity, so, on the other side, there will be no restlessness to nag one. Then one will surely say, "It is good for me to stay close to

STAY CLOSE TO GOD
God." One will even go on to say, "Who is there in heaven for me, and whom have I desired upon earth, if it were not you?" And too: "O God of my heart; God, my portion forever." So, as I said, whoever yearns for the greatest good can reach it if he or she can first take possession of all that he or she desires that is short of that good itself.

20. But this is altogether impossible. Life is too short, strength too feeble, competition too keen, people too worn by the long road and hapless efforts. They want to attain all that they desire, but they are unable to come to the end of all their desires. If only they could be happy with attaining everything mentally and not actually. They could easily do that, and it would not be in vain, for the human mind is more comprehensive and more subtle than the human senses.

The mind even anticipates the senses in everything, so that the senses do not risk coming into contact with an object unless the mind has already certified its usefulness. I think that this is what the text alludes to: "Prove all things, and hold to that which is good." The mind looks ahead on behalf of the senses, and the senses ought not to follow after their desires until the mind consents. Otherwise, you do not ascend the mountain of the Lord nor stand in His holy place, for you have gotten your soul, your rational soul, in vain. As you follow your senses like a dumb animal, your drowsy reason puts up no resistance. Those who do not think ahead run off to the side of the road. They do not heed the counsel of the apostle: "Run, then, to win." When will they ever come to Him to whom they do not wish to come until they have experienced all of the rest? The

SEEK FIRST THE KINGDOM yen to experience everything else first is like a vicious circle; it goes on forever.

21. The righteous person is not like that. When he hears of the behavior of the wicked, . . . he is inclined to keep to the royal road, which turns neither to the right nor to the left. As the prophet finally avers: "The path of the just is straight, and level for walking." These are the persons who take the healthful shortcut and avoid the perilous and barren, winding way. They choose the quick and timesaving word, not wanting all that they see but instead selling all that they have and giving it to the poor. Clearly, "The poor are blessed, for theirs is the kingdom of heaven."

Of course, everyone runs, but one must distinguish between runners. Finally, "The Lord knows the way of the just; the way of the wicked will perish." Consequently, "Better is a little to the just than all of the wealth of the wicked." As Wisdom says, and as foolishness learns, money never satisfies those who love it. Instead, "They that

HUNGER AND THIRST FOR RIGHTEOUSNESS hunger and thirst for righteousness shall be filled." Righteousness is the necessary, natural nourishment of the rational soul. . . . What do

material goods mean to the mind? The body cannot live on notions, nor can the mind ever subsist on meat. "Bless the Lord, my soul, who satisfies your desires with good things." He does satisfy with good things, He spurs us on to good, He keeps us in goodness, He anticipates, sustains, and fulfills. He creates our desire; He is what we want.

22. Earlier, I said that God is the reason for loving God. That is correct, for He is the efficient and the final Cause of our love. He proffers opportunity, creates the affection, and consummates the desire. He makes himself lovable, or, rather, He is himself lovable. He hopes to be so happily loved that He will not be loved in vain. His love makes ready and rewards our love. Considerately, He leads the way; reasonably He repays us; He is our dear Hope. He is rich for all who call upon Him, although He is able to give us nothing better than himself. He gave himself as merit for us, He reserves himself to be our Reward, He serves himself as nourishment for holy souls, He sold himself as a ransom for captive souls.

O Lord, You are so good to the soul who seeks You—what must

You be to the one who finds You? Even more wonderful, none can seek You unless he or she has already found You. It is Your wish to be found in order to be sought, and sought in order to be found. You may be
sought and found but not overtaken. Even when we say, "In the
morning my prayer will come before you," we ought to recall that all
prayer becomes tepid unless we first receive divine inspiration.

Now that we have considered where our love ends, let us consider where it begins.

8.23. Love is one of the four natural passions. . . . That is why
the first and greatest commandment is: "You shall love the Lord your
God."

The First Degree of Love:
The Human Being Loves Itself for Its Own Sake

Because nature has gotten more fragile and feeble, necessity
binds the human being to serve it first. This is carnal love, the love by
which one loves himself above all for his own sake. One
is aware only of oneself. As St. Paul says, "First came
animal, then what was spiritual." Love is not imposed
by decree; it is planted in nature. Who hates his own flesh? Now,
should it happen that love become excessive and overflow the banks
of what is needful and flood the fields of delight, like some savage
current, the overflow is immediately halted by the commandment
that says, "You shall love your neighbor as yourself."

It is certainly fair that one who partakes of the same nature not
be deprived of the same benefits, especially the benefit that is grafted
into that nature. If one feels put upon in satisfying not only one's kin-
folk's needs but also their contentments, one must moderate one's
own if one does not wish to be in the wrong. One may be as self-in-
dulgent as one pleases so long as one recalls that one's neighbor has
the same rights. O man, the law of life and or-
der places temperance on you as a restraint so
that you do not pursue your own lusts and per-
ish, so that you do not, through lasciviousness, use the gifts of nature
in the service of the enemy of the soul.

Would it not be more righteous and honorable to share the gifts
of nature with your neighbor, your fellow human, than with your enemy? If you spurn sensual pleasures and rest content with the teaching of the apostle with respect to food and clothing—in fidelity to

Wisdom's advice—you will soon be able to protect your love from "carnal yearnings that embattle the soul." And I think that you will not find it burdensome to share that which you have kept away from the enemy of your soul with those of your own nature. Then, if you do not refuse to give that which your brother needs from the pleasure that you have denied yourself, your love will be serious and righteous. That is how fleshly love becomes social—it is extended to others.

24. But what does one do if, in helping one's neighbor, one finds himself short of life's necessities? What else can you do other than pay in full trust to Him "who gives generously and without reproach, who opens his hand and fills every creature with blessings"? Since He helps us so often in times of plenty, there is no doubt that He will freely help us in time of need. It is written: "Seek first the kingdom of God and his righteousness, and the rest will be added to it." Even without being asked, God vows that He will give that which is necessary to the person who withholds from himself what he does not need and loves his neighbor. This it is to seek the kingdom of God and to beg His help against the tyranny of sin; this it is to prefer the yoke of love and sobriety rather than to allow sin to rule in your mortal body. . . .

SEEK FIRST THE KINGDOM OF GOD

25. Nonetheless, in order to love one's neighbor with perfect righteousness, one must bear God in mind. In other words, how can one have pure love for one's neighbor if one does not love that neighbor in God? Now, it is impossible to love in God without loving God. So, it is necessary to love God first; then one is able to love one's neighbor in God. So it is that God makes himself lovable and creates whatever else is good.

LOVE GOD FIRST

Here is how He does this. He who created nature protects it. . . . The world could not subsist without Him to whom it owes its very existence. According to a profound and salutary principle, the same Creator wills that the human being be disciplined by troubles so that when the human fails and God comes to his aid, the human being, saved by God, will proffer God the honor due Him. This, so that no rational creature may overlook its dependence upon God or dare, through pride, to arrogate to itself benefits due the Creator. It is written: "Call to me in the day of sorrow. I will save you, and you shall honor me." In this way, the human being, who is animal and fleshly and knows how to love only itself, begins to love God for its own benefit. It learns from frequent experience that in God it can do everything that is good for it, and that without God it is able to do nothing good.

The Second Degree of Love: The Human Being Loves God for Its Own Benefit

9.26. Therefore, such a human being loves God, but for its own profit and not yet for God's sake. Nonetheless, prudence would have you know what you can do by yourself and what you can do with the help of God to avoid offending Him who preserves you from sin. So, if a man's troubles come more often and, consequently, he turns to God and is often liberated by God, even if he had a heart of stone in a breast of iron, wouldn't he conclude that it is the grace of God that liberates him? And wouldn't such a person come to love God, not for his own gain but for God's own sake?

The Third Degree of Love: The Human Being Loves Itself for the Sake of God

10.27. Blessed is the person who has reached the third degree of love: such a person no longer loves even himself except for God's sake. "O God, your righteousness is as the mountains of God." This love is a mountain, God's eminent peak. It is indeed the thriving and fertile mountain. "Who shall ascend the mountain of the Lord?" "Who will give me the wings of a dove that I may fly away and find rest?" "This place is made peaceful, an abode in Sion." . . . When will this kind of affection be experienced, so that, drunk with divine love, the mind may forget itself and seems to itself to be as a broken vessel, hurrying toward God and clenching Him, becoming one in spirit with Him, saying, "My flesh and my heart have wasted away, O God of my heart, O God, my portion for eternity."

I would say that the person to whom it is given to experience something like this—so rare is it in this life—even if it happen but once and only for a moment, is blessed and holy. To lose yourself, as if you no longer existed, to cease completely to experience yourself, to reduce yourself to nothing, is not a matter of a human frame of mind but is a divine experience. . . .

TO LOSE YOURSELF IS A DIVINE EXPERIENCE

28. Still, since Scripture says that God created everything for His own ends, the day must come when the worker will devote himself to his Maker and be in accord with Him. So, it is necessary that our souls attain a similar state, a state in which we desire that neither

we nor other beings have existed nor do exist except for His will alone (surely not for our pleasure), just as God willed everything to exist—

I DELIGHT TO DO YOUR WILL, O GOD for himself. The fulfillment of our desires pleases us less than to see His will done in us and for us, as we beg every day in prayer, saying, "Your will be done on earth as it is in heaven."

O pure and holy love! O sweet and agreeable affection! O pure and sinless intention of the will, all the more sinless and pure because it looses us from the moral contagion of self-serving vanity; and all the more sweet and amenable for everything about it is divine. To go through such an experience makes us like God. . . . [For this] it is necessary that . . . all human sentiments melt mysteriously and flow into the will of God. Otherwise, if something human survives in man, how will God be all in all? Of course, the substance remains, but under another form, another glory, another power. When will this happen? Who will see it? Who will possess it? "When shall I come, and when shall I appear in God's presence?" O my Lord, my God, "My heart said to you, 'My face has sought you. Lord, I seek your face.'" Do you think that I shall see Your holy temple?

29. I do not think it can really happen until this is a fact: "You shall love the Lord your God with all of your heart, with all of your soul, and with all of your strength." It cannot really happen until the heart does not have to think about the body; until the soul no longer has to give it life and sensitivity—as it does in this life. Loosed from this aggravation, its strength is firmly set in the power of God. After all, it is impossible to gather all of these together and turn them toward the face of God so long as caring for this feeble and wretched body is such an all-consuming concern. So, it is in a spiritual and immortal body, one serene and pleasant, one subject in all things to the spirit, that the soul hopes to reach the third degree of love—or,

ONLY GOD CAN MAKE US HOLY rather, to be held by it. Yet, the giving of this degree of love is in the hands of God, to give to whomever He desires to give it. It is not obtained by human effort.

This is not to say that one will easily reach the highest degree of love, as he runs with the greatest haste and desire toward the joy of the Lord, when he is no longer restrained by any yearning of the flesh or bothered by troubles. . . . We believe that the holy

MADE HOLY IN THIS LIFE martyrs received this grace, at least in part, while they were still in their victorious bodies. . . . The strength of this love took such total hold on their souls that they were able to expose their bodies to external torments, despising their pain. Surely, the experience of intense pain was only able to subvert their serenity. It could not overcome them. . . .

31. Clearly, the flesh is a good and faithful partner for a good spirit. It helps when [the spirit] is burdened; or it relieves if it does not help. Surely the body benefits and is in no way a burden. . . . Listen to the bridegroom (in the Song of Songs) inviting us to this advance: . . . He calls to those laboring in the body to eat; he bids those who have put aside their bodies to drink; and he urges those who have reassumed their bodies to inebriate themselves, calling them His dearest ones, as if they were filled with love.

There is a difference between those who are simply called friends, who groan under the burden of the flesh, who are held to be **HUMAN LIMITATIONS** dear for their love, and those who are free of the **WHILE IN THE FLESH** bonds of flesh, who are all the more dear because they are more ready and free to love. More pointedly than the other two sorts, these latter persons are called dearest and are, in fact, dearest. Having received a second garment, they are in their reassumed and glorified bodies. Because nothing remains to entice them or retain them, they are all the more freely and willingly carried toward love. Neither of the first two states can lay claim to such a condition because the body is tolerated with distress in the first state, and in the second state the body is hoped for as something that is lacking.

32. Therefore, in the first state, the faithful eats its bread; but, sad to say, it does so by the sweat of its brow. While in the flesh it moves by faith, which necessarily acts by way of love. If it does not act, it dies. What is more, our Savior indicates that this work is food: "My food is to do the will of my Father." Later, having discarded its flesh, the soul no longer feeds on the bread of sorrow; but, having eaten thus, it is permitted to drink more deeply of the wine of love—but not pure wine, for it is written of the bride in the Song of Songs: "I drank my wine mixed with milk." . . .

To bring matters to an end: after finding the only needful thing, what is there to keep the soul from bidding itself farewell and passing **WHEN GOD IS** altogether into God, all the more having done with be**ALL IN ALL** ing like itself as it becomes more and more like God? Only then is the soul allowed to drink the pure wine of wisdom, of which it is said: "How good is my cup, it inebriates me!"

Why be surprised if the soul is inebriated by the riches of the Lord's presence, when it can drink . . . with Christ in His Father's house, free from earthly cares? . . .

This, I think, is nothing other than the Son of God, who, passing by, serves us as He promised: "The righteous are feasting and rejoicing in the sight of God, enjoying their happiness." Here is satiation without excess; here is insatiable curiosity without restiveness; here is eternal, unexplainable desire knowing no want. Finally, here is that sober drunkenness of truth—really burning for God. So then, out of this, one possesses forever that third degree of love, in which God alone is loved in the highest way. For now we do not love ourselves, except for His sake, that He may be the Reward of those who love Him and the eternal Recompense of those who love Him forever.

LOVING GOD IS OUR HIGHEST HAPPINESS

Prologue for the Letter on Love

12.34. I recall writing a letter to the saintly Carthusians some time ago, having considered these same degrees of love in it, along with some other matters. I may have made some other remarks there about love, but they would not differ from what I say here. So, I am appending the following passage to the present essay. . . .

Here begins the Letter on Love, addressed to the holy brethren of Chartreuse:

It is my opinion that authentic and sincere love comes out of a pure heart, a good conscience, and an unfeigned faith. It causes us to care as much for our neighbor's good as for our own, for he who cares for his own good only, or who cares more for his own than for that of his neighbor, demonstrates that he does not love that good purely. He demonstrates that he loves it for what he can get out of it and not for the good itself. A person like this cannot obey the prophet who says, "Praise the Lord, for he is good." He indeed praises the Lord because He is good to him but not because the Lord himself is good. . . .

LOVE FROM A PURE HEART

A first sort of recognition is the love of a slave who fears for his own skin; the second sort is that of a hireling who thinks only of himself; the third sort is that of a son who reveres his father. Therefore, he who fears and he who covets does so only for his own benefit. True love is discovered only in the Son. It does not seek its own advantage. This is why I think this virtue is implied in the text, "The law of the Lord is spotless, it converts souls," because only such acknowledgment can turn the mind away from self-love and love of the world and and fix it on loving God.

Neither fear nor self-love can change the soul. Though they change one's appearance or way of doing things from time to time, they can never change one's character. Sometimes even a slave is able to do God's work, but it is not done willingly. The slave is still igno-

TURN AWAY FROM SELF-LOVE

ble. The hireling is also able to do God's work, but not willingly. The hireling is still seen to be seduced by his own greed. Where there is self-interest, there is self-centeredness. . . .

35. Further, I have said that love is spotless. It retains nothing of its own for its own sake. Everything truly belongs to God for the per-

EVERYTHING COMMITTED TO GOD

son who holds nothing as his own, and whatever is God's must be clean. Therefore, the spotless law of the Lord is the love that seeks not what is useful to itself, but what is good for many. It is called the law of the Lord both because He lives according to it and because it is only as a gift from Him that anyone has it.

It does not strike me as absurd to say that God lives by a law, because that law is nothing other than love. What else sustains that supreme and indescribable unity in the highest and most blessed Trinity if not love? So, it is a law, the law of the Lord. It is love that somehow preserves and unites the Trinity in the bond of peace.

At the same time, I should not want you to think that I believe love to be a quality of God or a kind of accident in Him. If I did believe thus, I would be saying that there is something in God that is not in itself God. Love, I say, is the divine substance [i.e., essence]. I am only saying what St. John says, nothing new or unusual: "God is love." So, it is correctly said, love is God and love is the gift of God. Thus, love gives love; [i.e., love as the very essence of God] brings forth the quality of love. Where the term denotes the giver, it takes the name "substance"; where it denotes the gift, it is called a quality. Such is the eternal law that creates and rules the universe. . . . Even if the law does not create itself, it still rules itself.

13.36. The slave and the hireling have their own law, and it is not from the Lord. The slave does not love God, and the hireling loves something more than he loves God. I say they have a law—their own, not the Lord's—which, nonetheless, is subject to the law of the Lord. Each of these sorts can create a law for himself, but he cannot remove it from the immutable order of the eternal law. That is to say, each of these sorts wants to make his own law whenever he would rather have his own way than submit to the universal, eternal law. In **THE SLAVERY OF A** a twisted way, he tries to imitate his Creator. As **SELF-CENTERED LIFE** God is His own law for himself and depends upon himself alone, so such a person wants to rule himself and make his own will his law. This onerous and unbearable yoke lies heavily upon all the children of Adam. Alas, it makes our necks arc and bend down, so that our lives seem to approach hell. "Wretched man that I am, who will free me from this body of death?" This body, by which I am burdened and oppressed to the degree that "unless the Lord helped me, my soul would soon be living in hell!"

The soul that struggles beneath this burden says: "Why have you set me against you, and I am become a burden for myself?" Those words, "I am become a burden for myself," show that he himself is his own law and that no one but he saw to it that it was that way. Yet, that which he earlier said, speaking to God—"Why have you set me against you"—shows that he has not escaped from God's law. It is in conformity to God's eternally righteous law that the person who does not wish to accept its gentle rule will be the slave of his own will as a **SLAVE TO ONE'S** penance. He who casts off the comfortable yoke and **OWN WILL** light burden of love will have to carry unwillingly the unbearable burden of his own will.

The eternal law, by a mysterious and fair stipulation, has set the one who flees it against himself, yet it retains him captive. He can neither escape the law of righteousness, which he merits, nor stay with God in His light, repose, and glory, because he is subject to the power of the law and banished from blessedness.

O Lord, my God, "Why do you not take away my sin, and why is it that you do not remove my evil?" so that, freed from the heavy burden of self-will, I may breathe under the light burden of love; so that I may not be driven on by servile anxiety nor drawn on by the greed of **MOVED BY** the hireling? Let me be moved by Your Spirit, the Spirit of **YOUR SPIRIT** freedom, by which Your children act; the Spirit that bears witness with my spirit that I, too, am one of Your children; the Spirit that witnesses that there is only one law for both of us, that witnesses that I must also be as You are in this world. Those who follow **LIKE GOD IN** after the words of the apostle are doubtless as God is in **THIS WORLD** this world; they are neither slaves nor hirelings, but children: "Owe no one anything but to love one another."

14.37. The children are not without a law, unless one gives a different meaning to the text: "Laws are not made for those who are good." One should recognize that a law of fear, promulgated by a spirit of servitude, is different from a law of gentleness given by a spirit of freedom. Children are not bound to obey a law of fear, and they cannot exist without the law of freedom. So, do you want to know why there is no law for those who are good? It is written: "But you have not received the spirit of bondage in fear." Do you want to hear that "those who are good" are not without the law of love? "But you have received the spirit of the adoption of sons." Now hear the righteous man aver of himself that though he is not under the law, he is not lawless: "I have become as if I were bound by the law with those who are bound by the law, although I am not bound by the law; and as if I were not bound by the law with those who are not bound by the law. Although I am not without the law of God, I am bound by the law of Christ."

It is not correct to say, then, "The righteous have no law," nor to say, "The righteous are without a law." But it is correct to say, "Laws are not made for those who are good," meaning that they are not imposed on such persons against their wills, but rather that, inspired by **THE LAW OF** goodness, they are given to those who accept them **THE SPIRIT IN YOU** freely. So it is that the Savior's word is so fitting: "Take my yoke upon you." It is as if He said: "I do not impose it on the unwilling, but you who desire it, take it on; otherwise you will find toil in place of rest for your souls."

38. The law of love is good and sweet. It not only is sustained gladly and easily but also makes bearable the laws of the slave and the hireling, for it does not do away with them but fulfills them, as the Lord says, "I have not come to abolish the law but to fulfill it." It tempers the law of the slave and arranges the law of the hireling, making both lighter. Love will never be without anxiety, but it will be a chaste anxiety; it will never be without desire, but desire will take lower rank. Love submits to the law of the slave when it bestows devotion. It submits to the law of the hireling when it sets desires in order. Piety mixed with anxiety does not destroy anxiety, it chastens it. Only the punishment is taken away, the punishment without which servile fear could not exist.

On the other hand, chaste and filial fear always remains. When one reads, "Perfect love drives away fear," this must be understood in terms of the punishment that cannot be separated from servile anxiety. It is a figure of speech in which the cause is given for the effect. In turn, desire is set in proper order by the coming of love, because love moves one to reject evil altogether, and to prefer what is better even to what is good. Love moves one to desire what is good only on account of what is better. When this condition is fully attained, the body and all of the good associated with it are loved only for the sake of the soul. The soul is loved for the sake of God, and God is loved for His own sake.

15.39. Because we are fleshly and born with strong desires, our love must start with the flesh. When this is put in order, our love progresses by fixed degrees, drawn on by grace, until it is **DRAWN TO GOD BY GRACE** consummated in the spirit. Truly, "That which is spiritual does not come first, but that which is animal, then that which is spiritual." It is necessary that we first bear the likeness of an earthly being, then that of a heavenly being. So it is that the human being first loves himself for his own sake because he is fleshly and sensitive to nothing but himself. Then, when he sees that he cannot subsist by himself, he begins to seek for God by faith and to love Him as being necessary to himself.

So, in the second degree of love, man loves God for man's sake, not for God's sake. Then, when compelled by his own needs he begins to honor God and care about Him by thinking about Him, by reading about Him, by praying to Him, and by obeying Him, God gradually reveals himself in this kind of intimacy and so becomes lovable.

When man tastes the sweetness of God, he progresses to the third degree of love, the degree in which man now loves God not for man's own sake but because of God. Doubtless, one remains in this degree for a long time. I doubt that one ever attains the fourth degree in this life, that one ever loves God only for His sake. Let those who have had the experience say so; I do confess that it seems impossible to me.

Doubtless, this does occur when the good and faithful servant is inducted into the joy of the Lord and is intoxicated by the richness of God's dwelling. In some wondrous ways he forgets himself and, ceasing to be self-possessed, he passes wholly into God, and adhering to Him, he becomes one with Him in spirit. I believe the prophet sensed this when he said: "I shall enter the powers of the Lord; O Lord, I shall be mindful of your righteousness alone." He knew well that when he entered the spiritual powers of the Lord, he would then lay aside all of the weaknesses of the flesh so that he would no longer have to pay attention to the flesh, but, being entirely in the spirit, he would be mindful only of God's righteousness.

40. At last, each member of Christ can with assurance say of himself what Paul said of the Head: "If we have known Christ according to the flesh, we no longer know him thus." No one there knows himself according to the flesh because "flesh and blood will not possess the kingdom of God." This does not mean that the substance of the flesh will not be there, but that all

THE FUTURE OF THE WAY OF LOVE fleshly necessity will disappear. The love of the flesh will be absorbed by the love of the spirit, and our present, feeble, human affections will be transformed into divine affections.

Then love's net, which is now being dragged across the wide and mighty sea of time, catching all kinds of fish, will be drawn ashore; and there the bad will be tossed away, and only the good will be kept. . . .

10

WALTER HILTON
(ca. 1340-96)

Biographical Note

10

Walter Hilton (ca. 1340-96)

Biographical Note

Walter Hilton lived in spiritually vibrant but tough times as a contemporary of three of the most severe critics of the medieval church in England: Geoffrey Chaucer (ca. 1340—1400); William Langland (ca. 1332—ca. 1400), author of *Piers Plowman;* and John Wycliffe (ca. 1320-84). As a child, he experienced the awful sweep of the black death. From September 1348 to late summer 1350, the plague certainly claimed the lives of one-third, and may have claimed as many as half, of the English. As an adult, Hilton witnessed deep corruption in both church and civil government, and he saw attempts to reform both turn sour.

The Catholic Church in England suffered in Hilton's time from worldly and greedy clerics, bishops as well as priests, who as seldom as possible visited the flocks whom they were appointed to lead. They craved influence and power and leisure, and for these they needed money. So they developed a class of collection agents who knew how to extract tithes and rents and other income, however unwilling the payers might have been. But of course they could not neglect their spiritual responsibilities altogether, so they saw to the ordination of very ill educated, crude characters, and paid them pittances to baptize the babies, bury the dead, and say the masses in the parishes.

Hundreds of parish priests could not read the rituals at all. They mumbled through something that sounded like a Latin service, complete with gestures, but it was really a pious caricature. And they were not to preach. As for nurturing their people in the faith, many could not teach their people even to say the Lord's Prayer. (It too was to be said in Latin.) And all too often, the priest's moral character was as deficient as his Latin.

Of course, hundreds of priests read reasonably well and carried out their callings faithfully. They led decent and upright, even exemplary, lives. Among the bishops one could always find some who diligently looked after the spiritual welfare of their people. Thus, medieval England was not without genuinely saintly clergy.

So there were churchmen in all of the grades between careless and careful. But the careless and corrupt were everywhere; they all too often occupied even the highest posts, and they were the rule rather than the exception.

The English knew their church was a spiritual cesspool, and popular opinion lay much of the blame for its moral soiling on the papacy, their own bishops, and the bishops' bureaucracies—and not without a foundation in fact and reason.

From 1309 to 1377, the bishop of Rome and his entourage resided in Avignon, a city externally surrounded by France and internally dominated by French politics. There evidence abounded that the papal court was far more interested in controlling the politics of Europe (and therefore in obtaining the money and the power to do so) than in serving the spiritual needs of the Christian Church. In that period the popes and the bureaucrats played important roles in every major political move in Europe. And, of course, the papacy had a determinative word on who would hold any bishopric in western Europe.

In 1378 the bureaucrats' jealousies and political maneuverings brought the church to its lowest point theologically, spiritually, and morally. They managed to create two, and (shortly after Hilton's death) even three, earthly heads for the one church. They all ruled simultaneously—one from Avignon, one from Rome, and later one from Pisa. (England generally adhered to the one who was in Rome.) Each of these called himself the pope, the bishop of Rome, and each created and administered a complete, greedy, politically oriented, spiritually corrupt bureaucracy. This situation would last beyond Hilton's death until 1418, and again intermittently until 1449.

These papacies needed money to operate and to expand their power. So to gain it, they simply intensified a practice that had developed earlier and had been perfected at Avignon. They charged enormous fees for appointments to offices and for rights to the incomes from church properties. And kings and ambitious churchmen everywhere imitated them insofar as they could. Buying and selling church properties and offices to the highest bidder became a near preoccupation with ecclesiastical hierarchs. This market, and games of high-stakes politics that often involved the market, thoroughly contaminated the ecclesiastical leadership of Europe. Spiritual concerns found little entry or welcome into such a system.

But the papacy and other clergy should not bear full blame for the corruption. Civil rulers too played fiscal and political games with church properties and offices (benefices, they were called). They did this with the authority of the church itself. In England especially, the civil rulers played up nationalistic sentiments that undermined the church. By the second half of the 14th century, Parliament, reflecting those sentiments as they now affected the common people and many of the poorer clergy, enacted a series of laws considerably curtailing the power of the papacy and the English bishops. But those laws also supported the king and the high aristocracy in consistently raising taxes to support a burgeoning civil service and costly foreign adventures.

In 1381 antigovernment and antiepiscopal passions, long smoldering in the hearts and minds of the peasantry, united and gave rise to the Peasants' Revolt, also called "the Great Revolt." Riots threatened the entire governmental and social fabric. Both the civil and ecclesiastical hierarchies came under attack. The common people made their case perfectly clear when a mob savagely set upon and brutally murdered the one person who held both of the principal offices in England, Simon Sudbury, archbishop of Canterbury and chancellor.

The murder of Sudbury underlined the fact that neither church nor civil government had functioned for the good of the common people in the third quarter of the 14th century. The troubles, however, had their roots even earlier. From 1272 to 1413, only five kings ruled England, but none ruled well. In 1327 Parliament deposed Edward II, who had reigned since 1307. Rebellion finally overthrew the House of Plantagenet altogether in 1399, three years after Hilton's death, and put the House of Lancaster on the throne in the person of Henry IV. All of this was accompanied by that seemingly endless, if intermittent, string of battles and skirmishes between the English and the French that took the name of the Hundred Years War, begun in 1337.

On the other hand, the 14th century also saw the rise of some remarkable religious movements in England. Some of the greatest of England's mystics were Hilton's contemporaries or near contemporaries: Richard Rolle (ca. 1300-1349), the anonymous author of *The Cloud of Unknowing* (ca. 1350), and lady Julian of Norwich (ca. 1343—ca. 1413). Also, some devotional and pastoral writers such as Robert Manning, Dan Michel, and John Mirc gained considerable reputations across the country and across social classes.

Of course, John Wycliffe was Hilton's most remarkable contemporary. Wycliffe's early career exemplified the problems besetting the English church. He lived off the income of parishes to which he held legal title but which he did not intend to serve as priest, at least not regularly; and he took service with the government. As part of that government service, in 1377 he wrote several stinging attacks on the papacy. These landed him in jail at Oxford, a jail kept by the church. He appealed to Parliament, and Parliament, ever anxious to curtail the power of church courts, even over clergy, brought him to trial in 1378. Two courts tried him, but their decisions meant little in any practical way. He ended his days in peace as rector of Lutterworth in Leicestershire.

Most important to us at the moment is the fact that Wycliffe insisted, at least from 1378 onward, that the authority of priests and bishops rested upon their character. He declared that "Evangelical poverty" should form the character of all true Christians, including especially the clergy. Working from this principle, he rallied an army of "poor priests," who went about England preaching the gospel wherever people would gather to hear them—preaching it from a fresh English translation of the entire Bible.

In these times, Walter Hilton lived most of his life in the Augustinian community in Thurgarton, Nottinghamshire, within a few good days' walk north of Lutterworth. True to the monastic tradition to which he belonged, he took deep interest in the spirituality of ordinary people. He gave no quarter to the popular idea—one that the church itself pushed—that Christian perfection is an ideal that none can follow in this life. In fact, he wrote his *Epistle on Mixed Life* to those living in the world who yet desire Christian perfection.

Here we include a cutting from Hilton's most famous work, *The Scale (or Ladder) of Perfection*. He wrote it for a now unknown nun attached to a now unknown convent. So it has the

monastic flavor. Nonetheless, Wesleyan-Holiness people can read-
ily understand it in modern lay terms.

The Scale of Perfection

2.33. *"Reform in faith and feeling" is what I call this spiritual
opening of the interior eye to knowledge of God. I call it this because it is
at this point that the soul feels deeply something of that which it felt before only in bare believing.*

This is the beginning of contemplation, of which St. Paul speaks
in this way: "We do not look at those things which are seen but at
those things which are not seen; for those things which are seen are
temporal, but the things which are not seen are eternal" (2 Cor.
4:18). That is to say, we do not contemplate visible things, but invisible; for things visible are passing away, but things invisible are everlasting.

To this vision, every soul ought to want to come—partially here
and fully in the happiness of heaven. For the full glory of a rational
soul and its life eternal lie in that vision and in that knowledge of Jesus. "For this is eternal life: that you know the one God and Jesus
Christ whom he has sent." That is to say, Father, herein is eternal life,
that those whom You have chosen may know You and Your Son
whom You have sent, one true God.

Two Kinds of Love—Uncreated and Created

2.34. *There are two kinds of love: created and uncreated. [I write
about] what that means and how it compels us to love Jesus greatly for
creating us, more for redeeming us, and most of all for saving us through
the gift of His love.*

Now that I've said that this knowledge is the soul's glory and
end, you don't know what to make of my saying earlier that one

**DESIRE NOTHING
BUT THE LOVE OF GOD**
should desire nothing but the love of God without saying anything about this vision. Why, you
might ask, should this vision be what one
should desire?

My answer is that seeing Jesus is the soul's full glory—not simply
the vision in itself but the blessed love that arises from it. Still, since
love arises out of knowledge and not knowledge out of love, one
would say that the glory of a soul consists first of all in the knowledge
and vision of God, with love. Then, the more one knows Him, the
better He is loved.

But I earlier said that you should desire only love because it is love that causes the soul to come to this vision and to this knowledge. The soul simply cannot attain to this knowledge, or to the love that comes from this knowledge, without love to begin with. And that love is not the soul's own love for God but the love that our Lord has for a sinful soul that knows nothing at all about loving Him. It is the Lord's love that causes the soul to come to this knowledge and to come to the love that arises out of this knowledge. Let me clarify this.

What the holy writers say is true—there are two kinds of spiritual love: created and uncreated.

Uncreated love is God himself, the Third Person in the Trinity, the Holy Spirit. He is uncreated and unmade love—as St. John says it, "God is love." God is love; that is, the Holy Spirit is love.

Created love is an affection of the soul. It is produced by the Holy Spirit from the vision and the knowledge of truth—that is, from the vision and knowledge of God alone—which **PRODUCED BY THE HOLY SPIRIT** He affects and sets down. This love is called created love because it is produced by the Holy Spirit. Being created, it is not God in himself. Rather, it is the love, the feeling of the soul, that the vision of Jesus evokes and affects toward himself alone.

So now you can see that created love does not cause a soul to come to the spiritual vision of Jesus, though some think so. They want to love God so ardently out of their own strength as to merit spiritual knowledge of Him. But no, it is not like that. Rather, uncreated love, which is God himself, is the cause of all of this knowledge. Because of our sinful nature and the weakness of the body, a blind, miserable soul is so distant from clear knowledge and a blessed sense of His love that it could never attain to them were it not **GIFT OF THE FATHER** for the boundless greatness of the love of God. Because He loves us so much, He gives us His love, which is the Holy Spirit. He is both Giver and Gift, and through the Gift, He makes us know and love Him.

You should see now that this is the love of which I spoke earlier, the uncreated love, the Holy Spirit, which alone you should covet and yearn for. Anything less, any lesser gift than He, cannot suffice to bring us to the blessed vision of Jesus. So we shall wholeheartedly desire and ask of Jesus only this gift of love. We shall wholeheartedly desire and ask of Him that He would, for the sake of the greatness of His blessed love, touch our hearts with His invisible light. Thus we may know Him, and He will share with us His blessed love, so that as He loves us, we might love Him in return.

As St. John says, "We love God because he first loved us." That is to say, let us love God now, because He first loved us. He loved us greatly when He made us in His likeness. He loved us more when, in His humanity, He willingly accepted death and with His precious blood bought us from the power of the devil and from the pain of hell. He loves us most when He gives us the gift of the Holy Spirit, Love itself, through whom we know Him and love Him and are assured that we are His children, chosen for salvation. For this love, we are more bound to Him than for any other love that He ever revealed to us— either in our creation or in our redemption. For even though He created us and purchased us, to what purpose would our creation or our redemption be if He did not also save us? None whatsoever.

THE HOLY SPIRIT, GOD'S GIFT OF LOVE

So it seems to me that this is the greatest token of love shown to us: He gives himself in His divinity to our souls. He first gave himself to us in His humanity when He offered himself up to the Heavenly Father for our ransom upon the altar of the Cross. A beautiful gift this was and a great token of love. But when He gives himself spiritually, in His divinity, to our souls, for our salvation, and makes us know and love Him, then He loves us completely, for He then gives himself. He could not give us more, and less could not avail for us. This is why it is said that the justification of a sinful soul through the forgiveness of sins is attributed and allotted primarily to the activity of the Holy Spirit, for the Holy Spirit is love. In the justification of a soul, our Lord Jesus manifests His greatest love to a soul, for He disposes of all sin and unites the soul to himself. Such is the greatest thing that He is able to do for the soul, and for this reason it is allotted to the Holy Spirit to do it.

GOD GIVES HIMSELF TO US

CLEANSES FROM ALL SIN

The supreme strength and power that God demonstrates in the creation of the soul would allot that creation to the Father. The supreme understanding and wisdom that the Son showed in His humanity, overcoming the devil through wisdom, primarily, and not through might, would assign and allot redemption to Him. And Jesus' justifying work and His full salvation of a soul through the forgiveness of sins, by which He most of all demonstrates love to the human soul—a love for which we shall most of all love Him in return— would allot such salvation to the Holy Spirit, the Third Person.

All creatures, ourselves and those lacking reason, have in common the fact that He made us and them from nothing. So this work is greatest in power, but it is not greatest in love. Likewise, we and all rational souls—such as Jews, Saracens, and pseudo-Christians—have redemption in common, for He died for all alike and redeemed them if they wish to profit from it. That redeeming work was sufficient for all, though it may be that not all are redeemed. Redemption is primarily a work of wisdom, not of love. But through the gift of the Holy Spirit, our souls are justified and sanctified, and that is the work of love alone. It is not something that we **OUR SOULS ARE JUSTIFIED AND SANCTIFIED** have in common. It is a special gift to chosen souls alone. And that is truly His greatest work of love toward us, His chosen children.

This is the love of God of which I spoke earlier. This is the love of God for which you should yearn and which you should desire, for this love is God himself. It is the Holy Spirit. When this uncreated love is given to us, it produces all that is good in our souls and everything related to such goodness. God loves us before we love Him, for He first of all cleanses us from our sins and makes us love Him. Such **CLEANSES US FROM OUR SINS** love makes our will strong so that it may resist all sins. It moves us to test ourselves by means of sundry exercises, physical and spiritual, in all virtues. It also moves us to forsake the love and enjoyment of the world. It puts to death in us all of the evil stirrings of sin as well as carnal affections and worldly fears. It shields us from the malicious temptations of the devil. It routs us from worldly affairs and earthly vanity and from the camaraderie of those who love the world.

All of this is done by the uncreated love of God when He gives himself to us. We do absolutely nothing but submit and assent to Him. That is all that we do. We willingly assent to His gracious working in us. But even this willingness is not from within ourselves. It is of His making. So, as I see it, He does in us all that is well done, though we do not understand it that way. Not only does He do this in the way described, but love later does even more. He little by little, as the soul can bear it, opens the eye of the soul and in a wonderful way gives it a vision of Jesus and knowledge of Him. And through that vision, He lures all of the soul's affection to himself.

The soul then begins to know Him spiritually and to love Him fervently. Then the soul sees something of the nature of Jesus' blessed divinity. It sees how He is all, and that He works all things, and that all good deeds done and all good thoughts are from Him alone.

He is, after all, the absolute supreme Power, the absolute supreme Truth, and the absolute supreme Goodness. So every good deed done is from Him and through Him. He alone shall have the honor and thanks for all good deeds. Wretched persons steal His honor for a season, but at the finale, truth will show that Jesus did everything and that the human being, by itself, did nothing whatsoever. At that time, those who stole God's property and were not reconciled to Him in this life shall be condemned to death; and Jesus shall be rendered full honor and thanks by all blessed creatures for His gracious working.

This love is naught else but Jesus himself, who, as I have said before, accomplishes all of this in the human soul and reshapes it to His

THE FULLNESS OF HIS LOVE

likeness in the filling out of His love. And I would say, too, that this love brings into the soul the plenitude of all virtues. It makes them all pure and true, tender and good-natured; it transforms them all into love and delight.

This love lures the soul from the carnal to the spiritual, from an earthly disposition to heavenly tastes, from the vain scrutinizing of worldly things to the contemplation of spiritual beings and of the mysteries of God.

The Special Grace of the Holy Spirit

2.35. *How some souls love Jesus by way of zealous physical pieties and their own human affections stirred by grace and reason. And how some love Jesus more placidly by way of spiritual affections alone, inwardly stirred up by the special grace of the Holy Spirit.*

Now, then, I can say that anyone who has this love most of all in this life pleases God most. And because he has the greatest gift of love here on earth, he will have the clearest vision of Him in the glory of

NOT BY OUR OWN EFFORT

heaven. Some suppose that this love can be attained by one's own effort, but that cannot be. It is freely received through Jesus' giving of grace after the great labor of body and soul that preceded it. There are some lovers of God who would make themselves love Him by means of their own strength—with great vehemence they strain and pant so forcefully that they burst with physical zeal. They seem ready to pull God down from heaven, saying in their hearts and with their mouths, "Ah, Lord! I love You and I yearn to love You. For Your love, I would undergo death." In such activity they feel great zeal and much grace.

In my opinion, such behavior is good and merits reward if it be well tempered with humility and discernment. Nonetheless, these persons neither love in terms of the way in which I am speaking of loving, nor do they possess the gift of love in those terms. It is not even this sort of love for which they are asking.

One who has the gift of love of which I am talking has it through a grace-given vision of Jesus, or, at least such a person would like to have such love if he does not have it yet. Such a person is not itching to overwork himself, as if by some great physical effort he could gain, and so feel, some portion of the love of God. Rather, it seems to him that he is nothing at all; it seems to him that by himself he knows not how to do anything whatsoever. He clings to the mercy of God and is lifted up by it like some deadweight. He sees clearly that Jesus is all and does all, and therefore he asks for nothing other than the gift of His love. Because the soul sees that its own love is nothing, it yearns for His love. That is enough. For that he prays; for that he yearns—that the love of God would touch him with its blessed light so that by God's own gracious presence, he can catch a glimpse of Him, for then would he love Him. This is the way in which the gift of love, which is God himself, comes into a soul.

YEARNING FOR THE GIFT OF GOD'S LOVE

The more that the soul makes itself nothing, through grace and by grasping this truth, the nearer it comes to seeing the gift of blessed love, because then love is master. Love works in the soul, causing it to forget itself and to see and to consider only how love acts. Then the soul is more passive than active. Such is pure love.

This is what St. Paul meant when he said, "All upon whom the Spirit of God acts are children of God." That is to say, these are especially God's children who are made so humble and obedient toward Him that they do not work of themselves but allow the Holy Spirit to move them and to create feelings of love in them in a very sweet harmony with those movings, for they are most like Him.

Others do not know how to love like this. Rather, they vex themselves through their own sentiments. By thinking of God and by physical practices they stir themselves up to elicit by force, through zealous pieties and other physical signs, a feeling of love. But these persons do not love spiritually.

They do well, and they merit reward, provided they humbly acknowledge that what they do is not the true-to-life feeling of love that comes through grace. It is human action, done at the behest of the reason. Nonetheless, by God's goodness, because the soul does that which lies within it to do, these human sentiments, stirred toward God by human doing, are transformed into spiritual sentiments. They are made worthy of reward, as if they had been done in the Spirit in the first place.

This is a great blessing that our Lord shows to the humble. He transforms all of these sentiments born of natural love into the affection and into the reward of His own love as if He had brought them all about entirely on His own. So these affections, transformed in this way, may be called "affections of spiritual love by **NATURAL WORKINGS** way of purchase." They arise from the natural **OF THE HOLY SPIRIT** workings of the Holy Spirit.

Now I am not saying that one can bring about such affections on one's own, without grace. I know well St. Paul's word, that in ourselves and without grace we can neither do nor think any good. That is to say, we who love God do not suppose that we are sufficient in ourselves to love or to think that which is good. Rather, our sufficiency comes from God, for He works everything in us—both good will and good work, as St. Paul says. That is to say, it is God who works a goodwill and the fulfilling of goodwill in us.

Nonetheless, I am saying that those affections are good that are **GENERAL GRACE** made so by the general grace that He gives to all of His chosen ones. Such affections are not the effects of special grace. As I have said before, they are not the same as the affections that He works in His perfect lovers by the touching of His gracious presence. For in imperfect lovers of God, love works remotely. It works through the affections. But in perfect **PERFECT LOVERS** lovers of God, love works close in, through His own **OF GOD** spiritual affections. It slays for the time all other affections—carnal, natural, and human—in a soul. Such is properly the working of Love himself. A pure soul may have a small portion of this love through the vision of Jesus here, but in heavenly bliss it is fulfilled by the clear vision of His deity. There no affection shall be felt in the soul except that which is divine and spiritual.

Love, the Most Valuable Gift

2.36. Such love is the most valuable and profitable of all the gifts of Jesus to us. This is how He does all of the good that is done in those who love Him and does it for love alone. Such love makes the practice of all of the virtues and the doing of all good deeds light and easy.

These things being so, ask of God only this gift of love, which is

the Holy Spirit; for of all of the Lord's gifts, none is as good or profitable, as valuable or excellent, as this one. There is
THE HOLY SPIRIT,
GOD'S BEST GIFT
no gift of God except this one, this gift of love, that is both Giver and gift. Therefore, it is the best and the one most worthy of honor. The gifts of prophecy, working miracles, great knowledge, counsel, much fasting, rigorous penance, or any others like them are great gifts from the Holy Spirit, but they are not the Holy Spirit. A reprobate deserving of damnation could have these gifts as fully as a chosen soul.

So, then, all of these sorts of gifts are not to be deeply desired nor valued very highly. Rather, the gift of love is the Holy Spirit, God himself. One cannot have the Holy Spirit and be damned because that Gift alone saves one from damnation and makes one God's child and a partner in the celestial inheritance. As I have said before, such love is not the affection of love that is created within a soul. Rather, it is the Holy Spirit himself, it is Uncreated Love, who saves a soul, for He gives himself to a soul and makes the soul to love Him only for himself.

And more than that, by means of this gift, the soul, for the sake of God alone, loves itself and all of its fellow Christians as itself. This is the gift of love by means of which one may distinguish between the chosen and the reprobate. This gift produces perfect peace between God and a soul. It joins all blessed creatures fully in God. For it impels Jesus to love us, and us to love Him in return; and it makes all of us love one another in Him.

Yearn for this gift of love before all else, as I have said; for if God graciously gives it in that way, it will open and enlighten the reason of your soul to see the truth—which is God—and spiritual things. And it will stir up your affection to love all that He is with all that you are. It will work in your soul only that which He wills, and you will look reverently on Jesus with the tenderness of love and observe the way in which He acts. Through the prophet, this is what He tells us to do: "Be still, and comprehend that I am God." That is to say, you who are transformed in affection and have your inner eye open to the vision of things spiritual, leave off outward activity from time to time, and see that I am God. Simply observe how I, Jesus, God and man, act. Look on Me, for I do all things. I am love, and for the sake of love I do all that I do. You do nothing.

I shall show you that this is true, for there is no good deed done in you, there is no good thought sensed in you, except what is done through Me. That is to say, it is done through My power, wisdom, and love, powerfully, wisely, and lovingly, or it is not a good deed. So then it is true that I, Jesus, am Power, Wisdom, and blessed Love, and you are nothing, for I am God. You can clearly see that I do in you all of your good deeds, all of your good thoughts, and all of your good loves. You do nothing at all.

And yet, these good deeds are called yours. Not because you do them in the first place but because I give them to you out of the love that I have for you. Therefore, because I am Jesus and do all of this for the sake of love, stop thinking about yourself; don't give yourself another thought. Look on Me. See then that I am God, for I do all of this. . . .

So, observe and consider what love does in a chosen soul that it transforms to its likeness in affection—when the reason is given a bit of light so that it may know Jesus and sense His love. Then love **GIFTS OF THE SPIRIT** brings into the soul the perfection of virtues; they are all turned effortlessly to tenderness and to delight. The soul does not struggle vehemently to gain them as it did earlier, but it possesses them without difficulty and senses them placidly and solely through the gift of love, which is the Holy Spirit.

Now, this is a very great release, a joy unspeakable. The soul suddenly senses—never knowing how—that the virtues **THE JOY OF FULL SALVATION** of humility and patience, sobriety and constancy, chastity and purity, kindness toward the fellow Christian, and all of the other virtues, which had been onerous and painful and difficult to maintain, are now turned to tenderness and delight and a wonderful cheerfulness of heart. This, to such an extent that one does not find it difficult or a burden to maintain any virtue, but quite delightful. And all of this is the work of love.

There are other persons who are on the usual road of love but are not so far along in grace, who work under subjection to reason. In order to acquire virtues, they constantly wrestle and battle against sins, and, like wrestlers, they are sometimes on top and sometimes underneath. These persons do quite well. It is in the reason and in the will that they possess virtues; they do not have them in appetite or in love. They fight for them, as if gaining them depended on their own **WHOLLY IN THE HAND OF GOD** strength, and therefore they are not able to come to perfect rest or fully to conquer. They shall have great reward, but they are not yet sufficiently humble. They have not placed themselves wholly in the hand of God because they do not yet see Him.

A soul that possesses a spiritual vision of Jesus gives little heed to the struggle for virtues. It is not particularly interested in them. Rather, such a person puts all of his labors into maintaining that vision and that contemplation of Jesus that he has. He invests all of his efforts in focusing his mind firmly upon it and in binding his love to that alone, so that it does not fade away. Insofar as it is possible, he forgets everything else.

When one does this, Jesus truly has the mastery of all sins in the soul. He shields it with His blessed presence and obtains all of the virtues for it. And the soul is so comforted and so lifted up with the tender sense of love that comes from the vision of Jesus that it feels no great external distress. In this way, love puts to death all sins as a whole in the soul and reforms it with a new feeling for the virtues.

How Love Puts Sins to Death

2.37. *How love puts to death all stirrings of pride and makes the soul perfectly humble through the graciously given vision of Jesus. His love makes the soul lose its taste for any earthly honor.*

I will say still more precisely how love puts sins to death and reforms the virtues in a soul. First, I would speak about pride and its opposite, humility.

You should understand that there are two kinds of humility. One is possessed—through the working of reason; the other is **TWO KINDS OF HUMILITY** sensed—through the special gift of love. Both are from love, but love operates the former through the reason of the soul; the other it effects through itself. The former is imperfect; the latter is perfect.

One senses the former humility by pondering his own sins and his own misery. Through such pondering one thinks himself unworthy of any gift of grace or reward from God. It seems to **HUMILITY THROUGH SELF-DISCIPLINE** him sufficient that God, in His great mercy, would grant him forgiveness of his sins. And it also seems to him that because of his own sins he is worse than the greatest sinner who has ever lived—that everyone does better than he. With such ponderings he mentally throws himself lower than all others. He diligently tries to resist, as much as he can, the stirrings of pride in body and soul. He hates himself, and so he does not assent to prideful feelings. And if his heart is ever captured by it and defiled by the vain joy of honor, knowledge, praise, or anything else, he is unhappy with himself and mourns over it in his heart as soon as he is able to perceive it. He begs God's forgiveness for it, reveals it to his confessor, meekly accuses himself, and accepts his penance. This is good humility, but it is not yet perfect because it is the humility that pertains to souls that are starting out and gaining in grace, the humility caused by pondering one's sins. Love brings this humility about by way of the reason of the soul.

The soul senses perfect humility from the vision and spiritual knowledge of Jesus. For when the Holy Spirit enlightens the reason to

HUMILITY THROUGH THE HOLY SPIRIT

see the truth that Jesus is all and that He does all, the soul finds great love. There is joy in that spiritual vision—because it is so real. The soul forgets itself and leans entirely upon Jesus with all of the love that it possesses in order to gaze upon Him. It pays no attention to its own unworthiness or of sins already committed; it accounts itself as nothing, along with all of the good that it ever did, as if nothing existed but Jesus. Such was the humility of David when he said, "Surely my being is as nothing before you" (Ps. 38:6, Vulgate [cf. 39:5, most versions]). That is to say, Lord Jesus, the sight of Your blessed uncreated substance and Your limitless being shows me clearly that my substance, the very being of my soul, is as nothing before You.

Such a person pays no heed to his fellow Christians, not judging them to be either better or worse than he. He accounts himself and

LOVES OTHERS AS HIMSELF

all others as equal—as nothing in themselves, compared to God. And that is correct, for all of the goodness done in him and that done in them is from God alone, whom he sees as all. So he accounts all other creatures to be nothing, as he accounts himself. Such was the humility of the prophet when he said, "All are as nothing before our Lord; they are accounted to him as vain and without being" (Isa. 40:17, Vulgate). That is to say, humankind is nothing compared with the eternal being and unchangeable nature of God, for man is made from nothing and to nothing he shall return unless He who made man from nothing maintains man's being.

This is truth, and it should make a soul humble—if it sees this truth through grace. Therefore, when love opens the inner eye of the soul to see this truth, given its context, the soul begins to be truly humble, for then, through the vision of God, it feels and sees itself as it is. Then the soul ceases to look and to incline itself toward itself. It turns completely to beholding Him. And as it does so, it thinks nothing at all of the joy and honor of the world, because the joy of worldly honor is so small and so valueless in comparison with the joy and love that it feels in the spiritual vision of Jesus. In the knowledge of that truth, it wants nothing of worldly honor, even if it could be had without sin.

And though some would want to honor such a person, praise him, hold him in high esteem, and give him great eminence, it is no pleasure to him. Even to have knowledge of all seven of the liberal arts, indeed of all of the arts under the sun, with power to do miracles of all sorts—all of this gives him no more delight or enjoyment than gnawing on a dry twig. He would much prefer to forget all of these and to be alone, out of sight of the world, than to ponder them and to be honored by everyone.

The heart of a true lover of Jesus comes to be of such great value and so sublime through even a slight glimpse of Him and a slight sense of His spiritual love that all of the pleasure and all of the joy of the entire earth is insufficient to fill even a corner of it. At this point, then, it seems right to say of those miserable souls who **LOVE NOT THE WORLD** love the world, who are, as it were, enraptured with the love of their own honor and chase after it with all of the strength and cunning that they have, that they find this humility tasteless. And they are a long way from it. But the soul that loves Jesus always has this humility, not through peevishness or striving but with delight and mirth. And it has this mirth, not because it forsakes the world's honor (for such would be the prideful humility of the hypocrite), but because, through the gift of the **THROUGH THE GIFT OF THE HOLY SPIRIT** Holy Spirit, it has a vision and a spiritual knowledge of the truth and worthiness of Jesus.

That sacred vision and loving contemplation of Jesus comforts the soul so marvelously and buoys it up so powerfully and tenderly that it cannot take pleasure or fully rest in any earthly joy. Neither does it wish to. As for such a person himself, he cares not whether people abuse or laud him, honor or hate him. He does not take the matter seriously— whether to be pleased if he be hated, so seeming to have more humility, or to be displeased with honor or praise. He would rather forget those alternatives and ponder Jesus alone—and gain humility in that way. If anyone could attain humility, this latter is much the more secure course to it, as David knew: "My eyes are always on the Lord, for he will pluck my feet from the snare" (Ps. 24:15, Vulgate [25:15, usu.]). That is to say, my eyes are always open to Jesus our Lord because He shall keep my feet from the snares of sins.

When one does keep one's eyes open in this way, he utterly forsakes himself and submits wholly to Jesus. Then he is securely guarded, for the shield of truth that he holds keeps him safe. As long as he stays behind that shield, he will not be injured by any stirring up of pride. This is as the prophet says: "Truth will surround you with a shield; you shall not fear for the terror by night" (Ps. 90:5, Vulgate [91:4-5, usu.]). That is to say, truth will surround you with a shield—if you look to Him alone, forsaking all other things. And then you will not fear the terror by night, which is to say you will not fear the spirit of pride, whether it comes by night or by day—as the next passage says: "or the arrow that flies in the day" (Ps. 90:5, Vulgate [91:5, usu.]).

SAVED FROM PRIDE

Pride comes at night to assail a soul when it is hated and condemned by others. It comes to make that soul fall into despair and sorrow. It comes also as an arrow flying by day, when one is honored and lauded by all for worldly or spiritual deeds. It comes to give him the staff of vain joy to lean upon, in himself or in some passing thing. This arrow is a sharp one, a dangerous one. It flies swiftly, it strikes softly, and it wounds mortally. But the one who loves Jesus, the one who steadfastly sees Him by way of pious prayers and assiduous attention to Him, is so enwrapped by the safe shield of truth that he is not afraid. For this arrow cannot enter the soul. Even when it comes, it does no harm but glances away and passes on.

Thus, as I understand it, the soul is made humble by the working of the Holy Spirit—that is, the gift of love. For He opens the eye of the soul to see and to love Jesus. And He keeps the soul calmly and safely in that vision, putting to death secretly and quietly all of the agitations of pride. He also brings in the virtue of humility in the same way, in truth and in love. All of this is done by love, but not to the same degree in all of its lovers. Some have this grace only fleetingly and in a small dose, as if they were at the beginning, making little attempt to attain to it because their conscience is not yet wholly cleansed by grace.

SOME ARE NOT YET FULLY CLEANSED BY GRACE

Others have it more fully, because they have a clearer vision of Jesus, and they feel more of His love. And some have it quite fully, for they have the full gift of contemplation. Nonetheless, one who has it in the slightest degree that I have described truly has the gift of perfect humility, for he has the gift of perfect love.

THE GIFT OF PERFECT LOVE

11

HOLINESS IN THE REFORMATION: THE ANABAPTISTS

P ETER R IEDEMANN (1506-56)

Biographical Note

Account of Our Religion, Doctrine, and Faith

We Also Believe in Jesus Christ,
His Only Son, Our Lord

We Believe in the Holy Spirit

Through Whom Is Gathered Together One Holy,
Christian Church

What the Church Is

How One Is Led [to the Church of Christ]

Community of Saints

11

Holiness in the Reformation: the Anabaptists

Two traditions are underrepresented in this volume: Orthodoxy and Anabaptism. John Wesley, whose sources we are trying, though not slavishly, to reflect here, seems to have paid but slight attention to either one. He understood himself to be a child of the patristic, Western, and (as we call it) magisterial or state-church Protestant traditions. Orthodoxy and Anabaptism simply were not on his cognitive map.

The early Anabaptists fit with those whom Wesley called "enthusiasts." They seemed far more interested in "signs and wonders" indicating the presence of the Holy Spirit than in doctrinal carefulness, orderly and traditional worship, and civic allegiance. When they arose in the mid-1520s around Zurich, they at first appeared to be simply a group of Protestant literalists, mostly laity. But as Zwingli, the Protestant Reformer in Zurich, was to discover, these were highly sophisticated interpreters of Scripture whose studies had led them to a radical conclusion.

Luther, Zwingli, and the other great Reformers had certainly helped to free Christians from the bondage of works righteousness with their principle of salvation by grace alone through faith. They had also freed Christians from bondage to tradition and ecclesiastical autocracy by insisting that Scripture alone is the Rule for faith and practice.

But Luther and Zwingli had not come far enough, said the Anabaptists—the Church must return to its apostolic roots and faith. Especially must the Church sever its close relationship with the state, because the present relationship was the source of corruption. It forced the Church to proclaim one Master and in reality to serve another.

In the light of their Bible study, Anabaptists soon were making another critique of Luther in particular. He was carrying his doctrine of justification by grace too far, they said, insisting that the human will is absolutely bound morally and that the believer cannot truly keep the law of God. They insisted instead that God's grace transforms the believer and makes one truly righteous. For them, there was no "mere" imputation of Christ's righteousness to the Christian's account.

Luther's reading of the Bible and human nature had led him to teach that the Scripture's invitations to holiness and its promises of entire sanctification had to do with ideals and goals for the life to come. The Anabaptists' reading of the Bible led many of them—probably the majority—to declare that holiness, even perfection in holiness, is possible in this life, though they differed regarding its precise dimensions.

Scholars, including Anabaptists themselves, have argued over which of several dimensions of the Anabaptist perspective was most basic:

Was it their understanding of Scripture, which for them finds its summation in the Sermon on the Mount?

Was it their understanding of the Christian life, which for them is essentially summed up in obedience to Christ, in discipleship that finds its center in vicarious suffering?

Was it their understanding of Christian community, an understanding of the Church as a community in radical obedience to Christ as it faces the disobedience of pseudochurches and the kingdoms of this world?

Was it their understanding that Christ is coming again—soon?

There is no dispute over the fact that Anabaptists emphasized holiness of heart and life, often in the face of great opposition from the other major voices of the 16th-century Reformation. Those voices had great difficulty understanding that the Anabaptists truly believed, as firmly as they themselves, that salvation is by grace alone, through faith. The Reformers thought they heard the popular Roman Catholic understanding reasserting itself: that one works at being holy until one is sanctified sufficiently that God can justify that person. And certainly the seriousness with which Anabaptists went about being holy seemed to support the truth of that impression. But the Anabaptists insisted that we are not only saved by grace through faith but also sanctified by grace through faith. They insisted that their discipline was not intended to make them holy, but rather to give witness to the holiness that God in Christ had given them.

That is what the Anabaptists said when they were theologically careful. Unfortunately, like later Holiness movements, they were not always careful, and they sometimes talked about their discipline as if it were a *means* of salvation or sanctification rather than its *consequence*.

Then, too, the Anabaptists sought to contradict Luther's insistence that our wills are so fallen as to make them utterly useless at the point of our salvation. They talked about the absurdity of salvation by a God who arbitrarily elects to salvation and damnation. In the course of that argument they often defended a freedom of the will that made the grace of God absolutely amenable to it. Some saw free will as part of our natural human equipment (rather than as a divine gift of grace). They argued as if our salvation was really up to us, essentially a consequence of our choosing.

These rather grassroots ways of putting things often left the Anabaptists exposed to pouncing and pummeling by the magisterial Reformers. But in fact, Anabaptist documents show a much more grace-oriented understanding of sanctification and holiness than the magisterial Reformers seem to have been willing to recognize. What the documents also show is the reliance of Anabaptist writers on Scripture, almost exclusively—this in clear contrast to the tendencies of Luther, Calvin, and others to utilize Christian theological traditions to guide the interpretation of Scripture.

So it is that the Anabaptists are indeed "radical" reformers. They insist that justification and sanctification both are by grace. Therefore, God gives not simply imputation and hope. He imparts himself and transforms the life of the Christian. The life He gives is the pure and gracious "new Adam," not the life of corrupt and selfish "old Adam." This is the measure for the possibilities of grace in human life. The Anabaptists insisted that *sola scriptura* means just that—the Bible is to be the absolute Authority for all, at all times, on all issues.

As we have noted, the term "Anabaptist" is a general one denoting a number of groups, several of which still exist. The largest of these is the Mennonites, who are themselves divided into several denominations. Also significant as an existing Anabaptist group with its roots in the 16th century is the Church of the Brothers, known as Hutterians or Hutterite Brethren. The document that follows comes from this latter group. It is the work of one person but has been accepted by the Hutterites across the centuries as one of their basic statements.

PETER RIEDEMANN (1506-56)

Biographical Note

Peter Ridemann, or Riedemann (pronounced REED-eh-mahn), was born in 1506 in Silesia, which is along both sides of the Oder River in what is now Germany, Poland, and Czechia. At age 23 he was elected a "servant of the Word" by an Anabaptist group and was almost immediately jailed in Gmunden for three years. There he wrote his first "Account and Confession of Our Faith"—and then escaped.

He fled to Moravia and there joined the Hutterites and married. The fellowship in Moravia sent him as a missionary to Franconia, where he was again thrown into prison. There he stayed for four years while a procession of Protestant clergy and jurists came by to convince him of the error of his ways.

While he was in prison, the Hutterites suffered a division, which, upon his release, Riedemann was able to mend to the point that he is often referred to as the second founder of the Hutterites. Two years after his release, the community sent him to Hesse to end some serious confusion among the Brethren, and from thence he returned the same year to Stainabrunn, Austria, which was becoming an Anabaptist gathering place. In Stainabrunn he witnessed the imprisonment of about 150 of his spiritual brothers, and it moved him to write them letters of consolation and counsel on the necessity of Christians suffering.

Not long after coming back to Austria, Riedemann again found himself sent to Hesse with the task of strengthening ties between the brethren in Moravia and those in Hesse. And again he found himself jailed. The year was 1540, and toward the beginning of his two years in jail there he wrote his *Account of Our Religion, Doctrine, and Faith*, or, as it is commonly called, his *Confession of Faith*.

While we have many of his writings, including hymns and letters, we know almost nothing of Riedemann after his release from the Hessian prison in 1542 except that he died in 1556, apparently of natural causes.

The cutting that follows is from the 1540 *Confession of Faith*, in which, in the First Part, he is expounding the Apostles' Creed.

Account of Our Religion, Doctrine, and Faith

We Also Believe in Jesus Christ, His Only Son, Our Lord

We believe in Jesus Christ. We believe that our entire salvation and redemption is in Him. We believe that He has quieted the ire of the Father. We believe that through Him God is reconciled to the world, as Paul says: "God was in Christ reconciling the world to himself, not counting their trespasses against them." So we are reconciled to God through Him. And there is no other name whereby we may be saved than that of Jesus Christ of Nazareth.

Now, to begin with, we believe that we have redemption in Christ, that Christ has redeemed us from the power and snare by which the devil held us captive. For Christ has robbed the devil of his power. He has overwhelmed him. He has overcome him. The

CHRIST DWELLS IN US
BY FAITH

snares by means of which the devil held us captive are the sins in which we lay bound. And we served the devil by lying bound until Christ came to dwell in us by faith. Then, by His might working in us, He debilitated, quenched, killed, and took away sin, in order that we might be without sins and might live unto righteousness. Even so, He himself works and produces this righteousness in us, for without Him we can do nothing.

Now, He is truly our Redeemer, since He, the Lord himself, works in us and takes away the sins from which we could in no other way become free. [We are] now freed, through Him, to the degree that the sins to which we were long enslaved no longer can rule over us, though they do stir within us. The person who says that Christ has redeemed him but continues in sins, lying therein as one held captive, is like a prisoner lying bound hand and foot saying he is free. Surely anyone would consider this foolish. For he who says he is free but is bound has little desire to become free. Likewise, the person who says that Christ has redeemed him from sin and yet continues to live in it

FREED
FROM SIN

demonstrates that he does not wish to be free. But, as we have said, by Christ's coming to us, He has freed us from sin in order that we might be servants of righteousness.

Still, many—especially the Lutherans—say that Christ is their Righteousness and Goodness, while they still live in utter abomination and lewdness. This is nothing else than drawing near to God with the mouth while the heart is far from Him. Therefore, this is a seduction away from Christ rather than a confessing of Christ. And why is this the case? Because it hinders persons from seeking the true righteousness that is in Christ Jesus; it draws them away so that Christ might not be their Righteousness; and so, they continue in their sins.

But we confess Christ to be our Righteousness and Goodness because He himself works in us the righteousness and goodness by means of which we become God's beloved, pleasing to Him. For we have no goodness apart from that which He alone works in us, although many say of us that we seek to be good through our own works. To this we say, "Not so!" For we know that all our work, to the degree that it is our very own work, is nothing but sin and unrighteousness. But to the degree that it is of Christ, done by Christ in us, it is truth. It is just and good, loved by God, and well pleasing to Him. And this we are not ashamed to proclaim and aver, for the angel says to Tobias, "It is good to keep to yourself the secret of a king, but it is honorable to reveal and declare the works of God" (Tobit 12:6-7).[1]

This is so because it is through His actual strength and working that He directs us into His own nature, essence, and character. So it is a goodness that makes us blessed and leads us to God. And so it is that Christ is our Righteousness and Goodness, as well as our Life, for we ourselves do not live, but Christ lives in us. And so it is that He is also our Resurrection and Salvation and our All in All. We likewise believe that the incarnation of Christ signifies our transfiguration, and His suffering and death signify our salvation and life. This means that in Him we have all things.

We Believe in the Holy Spirit

Because the strength, the power, the nature, the character, and the essence of the Godhead are illustrated for us in the creation . . . we say it this way: the Holy Spirit comes from the Father and the Son, or from the Truth and the Word. . . . And, as the Son or the Word proceeds from the Father yet still remains in Him, so the Holy Spirit proceeds from them both and remains in them both for ever and ever.

So we acknowledge [the Holy Spirit] to be God, with the Father and the Son. There are three names, but there is only one God. And He is more than generous to any who call to Him, especially to those

---

1. At the time Peter Riedemann wrote (1545), most Chistians still considered the Old Testament Apocrypha to carry canonical authority. Tobit is one of those apocryphal work.

who call to Him trustingly. For just as fire, heat, and light are three names and yet one in substance, or nature, or essence, even so God the Father, Son, and Holy Spirit are three names but still one being. And even as fire, heat, and light do not separate . . . one from another—all three being present where one is and none being present where even a single one is lacking—so it is with the Father, Son, and Holy Spirit. Where one of them is, there are all three; but where one of them is lacking, all three are lacking. Just as unlikely as it is that someone could take heat and light from fire and still leave fire behind, even so, and still less, can one take the Son and the Holy Spirit from the Father.

Just as the breath determines the word and gives it shape and sound, so the breath, wind, and Spirit of God make the Word alive and active within us, leading us into all truth. This—yes, this!—is the power of God, which does all things, coordinates and perfects all things, confirms all things, unites, comforts, teaches, and instructs. And by means of His working in us, we are assured that we are children of God.

We believe that it is in the Holy Spirit that we have all comfort, delight, and fruitfulness; and we believe that He confirms, brings to pass, carries out, and perfects everything. We believe that He also teaches, directs, and instructs us, assuring us **THE HOLY SPIRIT MAKES US ONE WITH GOD** that we are God's children. And He makes us one with God, so that through His working we are incorporated into the divine nature and character and are partakers of them. And we experience this work of His—praise God!—in our very selves: in truth and power in the renewal of our heart.

Being in God, we are utterly certain that He has drawn our heart to himself and made it His abode; He has removed and excised evil, sin, and the propensity to sin from our heart. So it is that He has made our heart to depend upon His Word—to seek, to love, and to hear it diligently, and not only to hear but to keep and to follow it diligently. And we believe that the one Holy Spirit does and works all of this in us.

Through Whom Is Gathered Together One Holy, Christian Church

We also confess that through Christ God has chosen, accepted, and sought a people for himself, a people not having spot, blemish, wrinkle, or any such thing. They are a people pure and holy as He

HOLY AS HE
HIMSELF IS HOLY
himself is holy. Therefore, such a people, or community, or Church are drawn together and led together by the Holy Spirit. And the Holy Spirit, who from that point rules, controls, and orders everything in her, leads all her members to be of one mind and intention. Thus they want only to be like Christ, to partake of His nature, and to do His will diligently. The Church cleaves to Him as a bride, as a spouse to her bridegroom, as one body with Him, one plant, one tree, bearing and giving one kind of fruit. As Paul says: "As many as are led by the Spirit of God, they are the children of God"; and again, "The same Spirit assures us that we are children of God."

The Church is an assembly of the children of God, as it is written, "You are the temple of the living God"; and "I will dwell in them and walk with them; and I will be their God, and they shall be my people." Since, then, the Church is an assembly of the children of God, "Come out from among them [the sinners], and be separate, says the Lord, and touch no unclean thing; and I will receive you, and I will be your Father, and you shall be my sons and daughters." The children of God become such through the work of the unifying Spirit. So it is evident that the Church is brought together by the Holy Spirit, that she has her being and is kept by Him, and that there is no other Church than that which the Holy Spirit builds and gathers.

Therefore, vain is the assembly of the unjust and sinners, prostitutes, adulterers, brawlers, drunkards, the covetous, and the selfish. And all those who lie in word and in deed are no church of God. They do not belong to Him. As Paul says: "If any man does not have the Spirit of Christ, he does not belong to him." So not only is their assembly not a church of Christ, but also none of them can be a church of Christ nor continue in the Church of Christ unless they repent of their sins. As David says: "The sinner shall not stand in the congregation of the righteous." And after [David], John says: "In no way shall anything enter it that defiles or works abomination or lies; rather, they shall enter whose names are written in the living book of the Lamb." And "outside are dogs, sorcerers, and whoremongers, idolaters, murderers, and whoever loves lies and makes them up."

What the Church Is

The Church of Christ is the foundation and ground of truth, a lamp of righteousness, in which the light of grace is carried about and held up in front of the whole world. In this way the world's darkness and unbelief and blindness are seen and made light; and in this way people may also learn to see and know the way of life. For this reason, the Church of Christ is, in the first place, completely filled with the light of Christ, as a lamp is lit and made bright by the light. In this way, His light can shine through her to others.

And as the lantern of Christ has been lit and made bright and clear, enlightened by the light of the knowledge of God, its brilliance and light shine forth to give light to others still walking in darkness. This is as Christ commanded: "Let your light shine before men that they may see your good works and glorify God, the Father, in heaven." However, this cannot happen apart from the strength and working of the Spirit of Christ within us. Moreover, as the physical light sheds a ray and a beam to give light to men, according to its own character, so the divine light, wherever it has been lit in a person, emits its divine ray and beam. And the nature of this light is true, divine righteousness, brilliance and truth, which is shed abroad more brightly and clearly than the sun to give light to all by the lamp, which is the Church of Christ.

THE SPIRIT OF CHRIST ENLIGHTENS US

Thus the Church of Christ is and continues to be a pillar and ground of truth, for the truth itself shows itself and expresses itself in her. And that truth is confirmed, ratified, and accomplished in her by the Holy Spirit. So whoever endures and allows the working of the Spirit of Christ is a member of the Church. But whoever does not allow this work, but allows sin to have rule over him, does not belong to the Church of Christ.

How One Is Led [to the Church of Christ]

The Church of Christ is the foundation and ground of truth, and the truth is either built upon her or entrusted to her. Therefore, no one can or may come to her (much less continue to live in her) except by living and walking in the truth—that is, in God. One continues to be a part of the Church by having the truth within himself, and by allowing only the truth to rule over, carry on, and direct its work within him. This, so that the truth may shine forth and stream out like a light from him.

However, as we have said, God gathers His Church through His Spirit. She cannot be gathered in any other way. And therefore those who are to gather persons to her must have the same Spirit. So it is that when Christ wanted to send His disciples out to gather His

ENDUED WITH POWER FROM ON HIGH Church, He ordered them not to leave Jerusalem until they were endued with power from on high, which is the means by which they were to do this work. He gave them an order and a method by means of which they should gather the Church; namely, by word and sign.

The covenant of God's grace is a covenant of the knowledge of God (as the Word says, "They shall all know me, from the least to the greatest"). It is, therefore, the will of God to call persons to the covenant by His Word. And He will reveal himself and make himself known to them through the covenant. For as soon as one believes His Word with a whole heart, God wills to seal the covenant in us with [the gift of] His Spirit. And that Spirit will lead us into all truth and will reveal all things to us.

However, since Christ would not send out His disciples until they had received the grace of the Holy Spirit, it is quite clear that He will not have this order—that is, His Word and signs—treated cavalierly or carelessly. Rather, they should be seen as the Spirit of Christ inspires us to see them, not as the human spirit would think. However, when the Word is spoken in the Spirit of Christ and **THE WITNESS OF THE SPIRIT** one is moved by it and believes, he should be given the sign in that same Spirit and not without the Spirit. After all, it is the Spirit of Christ that leads the Church, not human beings. What the Spirit is building now has continuance through Him; but what a man does, as man, does not last. Therefore, his work is in vain, as David says: "Except the Lord build the house, they labor in vain that build it."

Community of Saints

Every good and perfect gift comes down from above, from the Father of lights, with whom is no variableness nor change to darkness. He gives and shares all things with us who believe in Him, as Paul says: "If God be for us, who can be against us?" He that spared not His only begotten Son, but gave Him up unto death for us all, how shall He not, with Him, also give us all things? So the Father wants to pour out all good things upon those who believe His Word and walk justly and faithfully before Him. His promise demonstrates this when He says to Abraham, "I am God Shaddai"—one with authority and power, with fullness to overflowing, and with a sufficiency of all good things. "Walk before me and be steadfast, devout and faithful to me, and I will make my covenant betwixt me and you. And I will multiply you greatly. And it shall be a perpetual covenant, in order that I may be your God and the God of your progeny forever."

It is as though He says, "If you cling to Me and do and keep My will, you shall have everything good in Me; in fact, I will give you all that is useful and lovely." Just as the Father is the fullness of all good things, He has given authority to the Son to be like himself, as it is written: "For it pleased the Father that in him should all fullness dwell"; and "The Word became flesh and dwelt among us, and we beheld his glory, the glory as of the only begotten of the Father, full of grace and truth." And yet again, "In him dwells all of the fullness of the Godhead, in essence, and you are full of that selfsame thing."

However, we become partakers of this grace of Christ through faith in the truth, as Paul says: "And Christ dwells in your hearts

PARTAKERS OF GRACE THROUGH FAITH

through faith." Faith like this comes from the hearing of the preaching of the gospel. So through attentive hearing and the observation of the gospel we become partakers of the community of Christ. This may be recognized from the words of John, when he says: "That which we have seen and heard we declare to you, in order that you may also have fellowship with us. Our fellowship is with God the Father and with His Son, Jesus Christ our Lord," who has given us everything that He has heard and received from His Father.

Community is nothing else, however, than those having fellowship having all things in common; no one having anything for himself, but each having all with the others, even as the Father has nothing for himself—all that He has, He has with the Son. And the Son has nothing for himself; but all that He has, He has with the Father and with all who have fellowship with Him.

So, likewise, all those who have fellowship with Him have nothing for themselves. They have all things with their Master and with all of those who have fellowship with them, in order that they might be one in the Son as the Son is in the Father.

It is called the communion of saints because they have fellowship in holy things—especially in those things by means of which they are sanc-

SANCTIFIED IN THE FATHER AND IN THE SON

tified, that is, in the Father and the Son. Sanctified in the Father and in the Son, who sanctifies them himself, and sanctifies all that He has given the community. So everything serves to the betterment and building up of one's neighbor and to the praise and glory of God the Father.

12

LUTHERAN PIETISM

Introduction

JOHANN ARNDT (1555—1621)
Biographical Note
True Christianity
Book 1
Foreword
Chapter 40: Some Fine Rules for a Christian Life
Chapter 41: Reestablishment of the Image of God
Chapter 7: A Christian Ought to Die to Himself
Chapter 12: Of the Love of God and Our Neighbor
Book 2
Part 1, Chapter 1: An Introduction into
the Holy Life of Christ

AUGUST HERMANN FRANCKE (1663—1727)
Biographical Note
On Christian Perfection (1690)

12

Lutheran Pietism

For most adherents of the Holiness Movement, it may seem novel to see the work of Lutherans listed among *Great Holiness Classics*. Most Wesleyans who have given attention to the matter have accepted as true the usual judgment that Luther, and therefore his followers, did not develop a doctrine of sanctification. Rather, says the conventional wisdom, Luther and his disciples simply transformed the medieval doctrine of sanctification from a doctrine of doing good works in order to become justifiable to a doctrine of doing good works in response to the fact that one is already justified.

Already in Luther's lifetime, his "response ethic" came under severe criticism, not just from Roman Catholics, but from his own followers and Calvinists and such "radicals" as the Anabaptists. "If good works and a pure life do not contribute to our salvation in any way," said his questioners, "why is the Bible so full of commands to love and purity?" His answer followed two lines: First, we are so ensnared by sin that even if we loved God with all of the heart and soul, mind and strength, and neighbor as self, we would not know how to express that love. In fact, we would most likely attempt it in ways that would have just the opposite of their intended effect. Therefore, God has revealed in the Bible the directions our response to divine grace are to take. Second, the commands to love and purity are in Scripture as ideals whose very unreachability, coupled with the fact that they are indeed commands, drive us back to trust in Christ and Christ alone for our salvation.

Theoretically, Luther's position seems to lead to antinomianism, that is, to the belief that morality is not really necessary to salvation. Practically, it did not. Self-consciously, Lutherans did not generally develop the activist moral and ethical sensitivity that was found in the Reformed, Anabaptist, and Anglican traditions. Lutherans seldom engaged in attempts to open existing society to radical change. Nevertheless, they insisted on the authority of the Bible as God's written Word. They also insisted on their understanding that the believer will indeed respond with a grateful heart to the Living Word according to the foundation established by the preaching of the written Word. Thus, serious Lutherans attached ethical meaning to the word "Christian"—and came up with a set of theological faults different from but not worse than other traditions.

To speak of sanctification in the context of this understanding of salvation is to speak of a process; and to speak of *entire* sanctification is to speak of the end of that process. Medieval Roman Catholics believed one to be entirely sanctified when, through rigorous discipline and long practice, aided by the means of grace provided by the church, one finally had developed an entirely loving disposition—loving God with all of the heart and soul, mind and strength, and neighbor as self. When one reached this point, when such loving was the unswerving disposition of the believer's heart, then God could justify; then the believer was really saved.

So to apply Wesleyan language to the medieval Roman Catholic idea, one must first be entirely sanctified before he or she can be saved. Further, it was believed that very few reach this fixed disposition to love (are entirely sanctified) in this life. Therefore, few go straight to heaven from earth. Instead, most believers, said Roman Catholicism, must go to purgatory, where that loving disposition is instilled through further rigors and disciplines until one is holy enough to be saved, that is, until he or she is entirely sanctified.

The Lutheran tradition rejected the notion of salvation by works that is implied here. So sanctification could not be the road to justification. Further, Lutherans rejected the notion of purgatory as well. Luther's followers could come to no agreement as to what kind of state we are in between this life and our everlasting presence with the Lord. They were certain, however, that it would not involve doing good works in order to be prepared for heaven.

But in leaving the doctrine of purgatory behind, Lutherans had to answer several earnest questions: "How is it possible, then, that persons not yet perfected in love (that is, all of us) get to heaven? If we enter heaven unperfected, would that not make heaven less than perfect—something that it cannot really be? And if the imperfect, the truly sinful, can get into heaven as they are, does that not destroy the whole fabric of Christian discipline and set at naught the teachings of Christ and the authority of the Bible?"

In the generation after Luther himself, Lutherans hotly debated the matter of sanctification. The debate ran along two lines. First, is sanctification really simply that which happens to us as we develop a disposition of pure love of God and neighbor, in response to God's having justified us by grace through faith? Or is sanctification somehow itself a gift of grace? Second, is entire sanctification possible in this life?

The consensus, finally reached in 1577, was put in literary form in the *Book of Concord* in 1582. It declared that sanctification is a gift of grace. That which was declared to be true legally in the earlier gift of justification becomes true in fact in sanctification. In justification, one is accounted as righteous by God; this righteousness is imputed to him or her. In sanctification one actually becomes righteous; righteousness is imparted to him or her. Thus, in sanctification, the believer becomes in experience what he already is in Christ. The Christian life, then, begins with God's simple imputation of Christ's righteousness to us and develops to the point that the believer, through divine grace, actually comes into the genuine possession of Christ's holiness.

This holiness, which was at first simply put to the believer's account, now becomes a genuine possession of the Christian. It is as if it were the believer's own. The Church makes this possible, because from the Church's means of grace the Christian gains the strength to live according to the teachings of the gospel.

The Lutheran consensus went on to declare that all holiness, all sanctification, is totally dependent upon our being "in Christ." This state of being "in Christ" has two sides to it, as it were. First, it means that when the Heavenly Father looks upon us, He sees us through Christ—He sees us dressed in Christ's righteousness; He sees us clothed in the absolute holiness of His Son. So we are indeed entirely sanctified in this life by imputation when we are justified, because that is when we are "hidden in Christ." There is no such thing as a Christian who is not always entirely sanctified. Second, being "in Christ" also means that Christ's character is actually imparted to us. We really become "new creature[s] . . . in Christ Jesus" (Gal. 6:15, KJV). So we are sanctified by impartation.

But while the imputation is complete, it cannot be completed in this life, which means that believers cannot be entirely sanctified in this life. It is not that the body and the material world are in themselves bad. In fact, they are good, for they are God's creations. But they are weak and deprived and are therefore all too open to the manipulation of our depraved wills. They are not sinful, but they easily become the instruments of sin. So it is only when we leave behind the fallen world and our fallen bodies and wills and are resurrected from the dead that we can be entirely sanctified. We leave this life not yet entirely sanctified, but we enter heaven itself perfected in love.

In Lutheran theology, death itself is not the sanctifier, but it does loose justified persons from the effects of the Fall. It makes it possible for us to be entirely sanctified. Or, to put it in good, traditional Lutheran language, sanctification is the process of becoming what we already are in Christ; and since Christ is risen from the dead, it means that the process cannot be completed until we too are risen to life everlasting, free of this fallen world and our own fallen natures.

Technically, in Lutheran thought there is this difference between sanctification and perfection: sanctification is the process of really becoming what we are declared to be at the moment of our justification. Sanctification is a this-earthly-life process, except that it is not completed here. Perfection is not a process at all but is rather Christ's righteousness applied to us in this life and our absolute likeness to Him in the life to come. It is in these terms that the Lutherans whose works we shall present here can speak of our perfection and at the same time maintain the truth of the Lutheran conviction that every Christian is "at the same time justified and a sinner." We are always perfect, but we are entirely sanctified only "when this corruptible shall have put on incorruption, and this mortal shall have put on immortality" (1 Cor. 15:54, KJV).

Lutherans hammered out this consensus in a period of great political and theological stress, during the three and a half decades between Luther's death (1546) and the publication of the *Book of Concord* (1582). Then, for the next century, they sought to refine it, theologically, as they faced another fundamental change. Between 1555 and 1648, Lutheranism (they themselves more often called it Evangelicalism) was transformed from an illegal, German-speaking sect in Saxony and surrounding territories to the state church in the northern and central duchies of the Holy Roman Empire. And beyond that, Lutheranism had won over all of Scandinavia and Finland, also Prussia, and what we now call the Baltic States.

During that era, almost everyone believed that church and state were two sides of a single coin. State and church together were society—"state" was one way of looking at society, and "church" was the other way of looking at society. Both sides of that coin, they believed, needed carefully constructed rationales, explanations, and "operating instructions." So, as Evangelicalism became the official religion of political states, many of its leaders sought to develop a theological base as clearly defined and as thorough as the civil laws that governed the state. What is more, until well into the 17th century, serious believers could not conceive of a state without an official religion; just being Christian would not do—not since about 1520.

Christian people came little by little to see that they might tolerate other than official expressions of Christianity (and even more or less tolerate Jews). They could even grant others considerable rights, but the state had to be officially Lutheran or Reformed or Anglican or Roman Catholic. This meant that each state defined citizenship in terms of its branch of the Christian faith—to be a good citizen was to practice the given state's official faith acceptably and to be at least minimally schooled in it. So the church undertook catechism for the sake of the state as well as for its own sake. It was also believed that the religion of the given state has to be defined over against other religions, even if others were tolerated and accepted as more or less Christian. This polemic process often became very bitter, fastidious, censorious, and unfair.

Of course, each of the forms of Christianity that came to be officially established already had some foundational statements in place. The creeds of the first five Christian centuries served as the norms for almost all Christians in whatever state. Then these were augmented by the creeds and confessions of the Reformation era. Among Lutherans, these were the Augsburg Confession and its official interpretation, the Apology, both of them the work of Philipp Melanchthon.

These documents were attempts to explain and defend the Christian orthodoxy of Evangelicalism to Roman Catholic rulers, secular and ecclesiastical. The Schmalkald Articles were written by Luther as a brief statement of Evangelical faith to be presented to a church council, which never met. Melanchthon also wrote a treatise against the pope and Roman Catholic claims to be the one true Church. Then came the two catechisms written by Luther—the Small Catechism, which is for use among the grass roots, and the Large Catechism, which is especially for ministers of the gospel. But even all of these were not enough, because the faith was alive among the people, and that meant that every new day brought new questions.

Think, for instance, how different it would have been to reflect on the phrase "I believe in God the Father Almighty, Maker of heaven and earth" in 1540, in 1590, and again in 1640. In 1540 Earth was thought to be the center of the universe, and heaven was the space in which were found many bodies that revolved around that center. In 1590 both heaven and Earth had expanded enormously, and Earth, at least, was found to be peopled with all sorts of heretofore unknown folk, and even mighty civilizations, which had never heard of Christ and Church but who could be converted to Christianity.

By 1640 Francis Bacon and René Descartes, reflecting on the entirely different view we now had of the "stuff" of both heaven and Earth, and of how they relate, convinced thinking people that we needed entirely new ways of thinking about them and about ourselves.

All of this guaranteed that no doctrinal stone went unturned, and, almost in spite of themselves, Christian thinkers came to believe that doctrine arrived at by logical analysis of the Scriptures was as much a part of the faith as the Bible itself. Should a person confess an inability to understand much of the mysterious lore that was going under the name of theology, the Evangelical Church gave much the same answer that the Roman Catholics had long since given: "Trust the Church."

In this circumstance, the clergy were encouraged to look upon the church as the Department of Morality for the state. Even ecclesiastical appointments were made from this perspective. Preaching, celebrating the sacraments, and the round of pastoral duties all became instruments of this mentality. The good preacher was one who could get people to be very self-conscious in the keeping of civic virtues, such as obedience to authority and patriotism. The celebration of the sacraments was a celebration of citizenship in the heavenly kingdom of which one's earthly society was a true expression.

So, if one was baptized in Saxony, the same rules made one both a good Saxon and a good Christian: one was loyal to the duke of Saxony and to the duke's church. Under ordinary circumstances, loyalty to one was accounted loyalty to the other. Celebration of the Lord's Supper was celebration of one's heavenly citizenship, of which citizenship in Saxony was to be a foretaste. Clergy could not generally separate their roles as ministers of the gospel from their roles as agents of the state.

In all of this concern to serve the state well as its Department of Morality, especially through careful theologizing, the Evangelical Church little by little came to satisfy itself with confessions of orthodoxy. Earlier, it had proclaimed that the true and living God meant to redeem folks, and it had encouraged people to open themselves to Him. But now, at the heart of Evangelical faith, right doctrine replaced evangelical experience. To be a Christian was to be baptized, to give the church due regard, to agree with the church as to right doctrine, to live a life of simple moral decency and patriotism, and to exercise good workmanship whatever one's calling.

The religious movement called Lutheran Pietism arose in reaction to this later vision of the nature and role of the Christian Church and of the heart of the Christian faith. But it took great care to keep free of novelties, and its adherents took pains to remain within the established church. On into the 18th century, some Pietists were ejected from the state church, but most of their opponents conceded that they should not be excluded from it, and the Pietists themselves generally did not think of themselves as separatists. They thought of themselves as Lutherans who sought to reform the church from within. So they grounded themselves very firmly in the theology of Luther himself and mastered the great creed to which Lutheranism gave allegiance. But their primary concern was not doctrine. It was Christian experience and the development of a Christian lifestyle. To speak from a Lutheran point of view, it was sanctification, and it came to involve perfection.

JOHANN ARNDT
(1555—1621)

Johann Arndt

Biographical Note

Tradition has given two persons the title Father of (German) Pietism: Johann Arndt and Philipp Jakob Spener (1635—1705). The title commends them to many and condemns them for yet others. Neither had designs on siring a new religious movement, but each took keen interest in reviving the Lutheranism he saw about him as a pastor—and Arndt as superintendent-minister.

Arndt had originally planned to practice medicine, but during an extended bout with illness he began to read theology, including the medieval mystics, and became convinced that ministry, not medicine, was his calling. And he had rather clear aims for that ministry.

By the early 1580s, Lutheranism had undergone long, bitter struggles with Roman Catholicism, with the "enthusiasts," and with the Calvinists. Along with these, wrangles among disputatious Lutherans themselves had created a situation in his beloved Lutheranism that Arndt saw as spiritually dangerous. On the one hand, Christian morality had suffered. On the other hand, ethical and moral carelessness often coexisted with doctrinal punctiliousness.

Luther had led in a deep and lasting reform of the church and of doctrine, but many used the very watchword of that Reformation—salvation by grace alone, through faith—to avoid serious ethical and moral reflection. The need to educate a Lutheran ministry and the endless bickering over doctrine on so many fronts had originally given birth to deep sensitivity to what was orthodoxy and what was not. But now sheer pickiness and the state's concern that clergy guard the social order often replaced sensitivity in theological matters.

Arndt responded by advocating a Christianity that would be both doctrinally correct and morally appropriate. He sought to inculcate a faith that is theologically down-to-earth. This was no easy task because it seemed to require a concern for religious experience. This position was a "stone of offense" for most Protestants and Roman Catholics alike in those days. It was also a "stone of offense" because of its tendency to give the individual sovereignty in all things. It threatened the Protestant insistence that the Bible alone is the sole Authority for faith and practice; and it threatened the Roman Catholic insistence that the Bible and the tradition held coordinate authority. It also undercut the authority of those directing the church.

Arndt knew all of this but seems to have believed that it should not be allowed to prohibit nor inhibit a proper internalization of the faith and its reexternalization in holy living. He put three safeguards in place, not because they are strategic, but because he believed they are biblical.

First, he grounded religious experience in repentance. True repentance makes sheer subjectivism impossible because the truly repentant person will, in gratitude and trust and obedience, fix his or her gaze on Him who gives that repentance and who has forgiven his or her sin. In modern terms, this is to say that repentance is not primarily a feeling and is not strictly personal—it is the fundamental dimension of a personal relationship. Second, this relationship is absolutely dependent upon life in community. It is ordinarily initiated by the Church, in baptism in the name of the Triune God. This relationship is also maintained by life in the Church, understood as the Body of Christ and the communion of saints. Here the means of grace are proffered—the Word is heard and preached, and the sacraments are rightly administered.

In addition to the two safeguards that Arndt stated in so many words, he constructed also a third, which shows up in the way in which he writes. For him, valid religious experience absolutely depends upon an "appropriate form of words," in this case, the language afforded by the Bible. Arndt was no fundamentalist, but he was very seldom more than a logical step away from the biblical text when he described "true Christianity." Often his language is that of the biblical text itself.

In this regard, he sounds very much like Luther. While one rejoices in one's salvation, one constantly remembers one's sinfulness. While one rejoices in having drawn closer to Christ in character, one constantly deepens one's understanding of how much farther one has to go. While one delights in the victory won, one deeply rues the skirmishes lost. While one marvels in the spiritual strength given, one confesses great spiritual weakness.

Luther said over and again that the believer is "at one and the same time justified and a sinner." Arndt accepted that dictum as a presupposition. But Arndt understood that the grace of Christ may so work in the believer that his or her being a sinner has little or nothing to do with his or her fundamental spiritual disposition. That is to say, that person who is at one and the same time justified and a sinner may also, by the workings of divine grace, love God with all of the heart and soul, mind and strength, and neighbor as self.

But Arndt was concerned for holy living. And he almost invariably put that concern in biblical language, with all of its complexity. So he could not say, "There will be imperfections in practice; only intention counts." Practice counts too. Sanctification is a matter of both heart and hand, intention and practice. But here Arndt distanced himself from standard Lutheran thought. Luther claimed fairly consistently that we are sanctified by imputation and that we then spend our lives working out the implications of that imputation. We actually sanctify ourselves in response to God's having sanctified us by imputing Christ's holiness to us. Arndt believed that God, for Christ's sake, actually imparts holiness to us, and, since that holiness is a divine gift, it is a perfect gift. It is the gift of a perfect relationship, a divine presence, which transforms us into its own likeness.

Still, Arndt spoke biblical language in Luther's dialect. And Luther's dialect was a direct descendant of Augustine's, as Augustine fought Pelagianism. For instance (a critical instance, for our purposes), Arndt used the broadest possible definition of sin as his principal operating definition, namely, "Whatsoever is not of faith is sin" (Rom. 14:23, KJV). So much to a Wesleyan's consternation, the language of purity and perfection, of sanctity and holiness, is mixed with the language of continuing sinfulness. Mixed with it and equivocated by it. So, for instance, Arndt spoke of perfection as both a gift and an attainment. And in speaking of it as attainment, he almost denied its possibility in this life:

> Perfection is not the high, great, spiritual, celestial joy and contemplation that some think it to be. Rather, it is a negation of one's own will, love, and honor; a comprehension of one's nothingness; a continual fulfilling of God's will; an ar-

dent love for neighbor; and fervent compassion. In a word, it is a love that wants, thinks, and seeks nothing other than God alone, insofar as this is possible in our earthly weakness.[1]

Here, then, is a source of Arndt's thought that Wesley recognized and commended to others, though he recognized, too, the problems in terminology. Wesley was concerned that holiness be lived, not simply admired as an ideal, and he was concerned for the Christian's assurance regarding his or her spiritual standing. These concerns made Arndt's work almost a natural for the very first volume of the *Christian Library*. In the preface to the *Library*, Wesley wrote, "John Arndt's nervous [we would say "vigorously expressed"] account of true Christianity [is] worthy of the earliest ages." Wesley printed Arndt in particular, and the *Christian Library* in general, to help the ordinary reader who needed guidance through the increasingly dense forest of Christian materials written or translated into English. For his version of Arndt's work, he chose the translation by Anthony William Boehm, done in 1712, and dedicated to Queen Anne.

Choosing a translation was a difficult task then, for many German editions of Arndt carried the insertions and deletions of their editors. Comparison of the Boehm/Wesley translation/edition with the widely circulated and most nearly standard edition, the Braunschweig (Brunswick) edition, published between 1605 and 1609, seems to confirm the general accuracy and faithfulness to the original of the Boehm/Wesley text. So we really do have Arndt in the *Christian Library*, often with a surprising degree of his originally equivocated language.

Wesley and Arndt had much in common, for Arndt too saw through the centuries of theological give-and-take, differences in expression, and genuine commonalities. Arndt quoted and paraphrased at length in his spirited encouragements to holiness of heart and life. Unlike Wesley, however, Arndt lived in an age when such an ecumenical spirit was dangerous; at least it was dangerous in Brunswick, where he was (unsuccessfully) tried for heresy. Wesley lived in an age when many had knee-jerk reactions to Roman Catholicism and to "enthusiasm," but nothing else in doctrine or piety seemed to faze them. Arndt's task was to reroute religious interest; Wesley's was to revive it.

---

1. "Liber Conscientiae," in *True Christianity*, Braunschweig ed., Proem. 7.

We have included some sections from the *Christian Library* translation/edition here to give a taste of the tradition that John Wesley thought important to his own work.

The excerpts from chapters 7, 12, and Book 2, Part 1, have been taken from Wesley's *Christian Library*. They were translated by Boehm and Wesley from a now unidentifiable edition of Arndt's *True Christianity*. The editor of this volume has modernized Wesley's English somewhat.

True Christianity, Book 1

Foreword

Dear Christian Reader:

The unrepentant life of [formal Christians], which is one of praising Christ and His Word with the mouth yet walking as dwellers in heathendom rather than as inhabitants of the Christian world, only proves the subjection of the holy gospel to gross and degrading abuse these days. Such behavior gives me reason to write this book— to show ordinary readers the ingredients of true Christianity, namely, manifestation of a true, living faith, operative in genuine godliness, productive of the fruits of righteousness.

I also want to show that we carry the name of Christ not simply

CHRIST MUST LIVE IN US because it is incumbent upon us to believe in Christ but because we are to live in Christ and He in us. And I want to show how genuine repentance must come from the deepest fountain of the heart, how heart and mind and affections must be changed in order that we might be conformed to Christ and His holy gospel—how we must be renewed by the Word of God, becoming new creatures. Just as every seed produces fruit after its kind, so the Word of God must produce new spiritual fruit in us every day. If we are to become new creatures by faith, we should live consistent with the new birth. In short: Adam must die and Christ must live in us. Knowing God's Word is not enough; it must be practiced with vitality.

Many think theology to be merely a field of formal knowledge or rhetoric, when it is really vital experience and practice. These days, everyone strives to be prominent and distinguished, but no one wants to learn to be pious. Everyone looks for men of great learning from whom one may learn the arts, the languages, and wisdom. But no one wants to learn meekness and unfeigned humility from our only teacher, Jesus Christ. It is His holy, living example that is the proper rule and model for our lives. In fact, He is the highest Wisdom and Knowledge, so we can unequivocally say, "The life of Christ can teach us everything." Everyone wants very much to be a servant of Christ, but no one wants to be His follower. Yet, He says in John 12:26: "If one would serve me, he must follow me." So, a true servant and lover of Christ must be Christ's follower.

And he who loves Christ will also love the example of His holy life, His humility, His meekness, His patience, suffering, shame, and contempt, even when the flesh suffers pain. And though in our current feebleness, we cannot perfectly imitate Christ's holy and virtuous life (and this book has no intention of saying that we can), nonetheless, we ought to love that life and ache to imitate it. We do live in Christ, and Christ lives in us. As it says in 1 John 2:6: "He who says he abides in him ought to walk as he walked."

These days, the world wants to know everything, but no one wants to know that which is better than all knowledge, namely, "to know the love of Christ" (Eph. 3:19). No one can love Christ who does not follow the example of His holy life. And in fact, many in this world are ashamed of Christ's holy example, specifically of His humility and lowliness. That is to say, they are ashamed of the Lord Jesus Christ. And of them, the Lord says in Mark 8:38: "Whoever is ashamed of me and of my words in this adulterous generation, of him, too, shall the Son of Man be ashamed when he comes." These days, Christians yearn for an imposing, magnificent, rich Christ, a Christ conformed to this world; no one wants to receive or to confess and to follow the poor, meek, humble, and despised Christ. Therefore, He will say: "I never knew you; you were not willing to know me in my humility, and therefore I do not know you in your pride" (Matt. 7:23).

KNOW THE LOVE OF CHRIST

Moreover, the ungodly mode of life not only is in complete opposition to Christ and to true Christianity but also daily piles up the wrath and punishment of God, so that God capacitates all creatures to be avengers against us. And heaven and earth, fire and water must strive against us. In truth, this distresses all of nature and nearly overmasters it. And so there must be a period of difficulty, war, famine, and pestilence. Indeed, the final plagues are bearing down so violently and so powerfully that one cannot be sure about any creature. Just as the horrible plagues overtook the Egyptians before the redemption and exit of the children of Israel from Egypt, so dire and

UNGODLY LIFE OPPOSES TRUE CHRISTIANITY

unheard-of plagues will overtake the ungodly and impenitent before the ultimate redemption of the children of God.

Therefore, now is a fitting time to repent, to start on another life path, to turn from the world to Christ, truly to believe in Him, and to live in Him as a Christian, so that we may securely "dwell in the shelter of the most High, [and] abide in the shelter of the Almighty" (Ps. 91:1). So the Lord admonishes us in Luke 21:36: "Watch therefore always, and pray that you may be worthy to escape all of these things." Ps. 112:7 attests the same admonition.

So, dear children, this book will serve as a guide to this end. It will tell you not only how you may obtain the forgiveness of your sins

GRACE TO LEAD A HOLY LIFE

through faith in Christ but also how you may appropriate the grace of God in order to lead a holy life and how you may manifest and furbish your faith by a Christian way of life. Rather than being a matter of words and external display, authentic Christianity consists in living faith from which spring the fruits of righteousness and all kinds of Christian virtues—as from Christ himself. Since faith is hidden from human eyes and is invisible, it must be shown by its fruits; and faith does create, from the presence of Christ, all that is good and righteous and holy.

Now, hope arises from faith, since faith awaits the promised blessings. Other than a faithful and steadfast expectation of promised

FAITH BRINGS HOPE

blessings, what might hope be? Now, if faith shares with a neighbor the blessings that it has itself received, love emerges out of that faith; and that love bestows upon the neighbor that which it has itself received from God. If faith withstands the test of the cross and submits itself to the will of God, patience sprouts forth. When faith sighs beneath the cross, or gives thanks to God for mercies received, prayer is born. When faith compares the splendor of God with the misery of the human being, and submits and bows to God, humility is born. When faith is mindful not to lose the grace of God, or, in the words of St. Paul, "works out its salvation with fear and trembling" (Phil. 2:12), fear of God is born.

So you see how all of the Christian virtues, if they are indeed genuine . . . take their rise from God, from Christ, and from the Holy Spirit. They are the offspring of faith. They arise and grow from faith; they cannot be separated from faith as their source. Hence, no work can be pleasing to God apart from faith in Christ. How can authentic hope, love rightly defined, constant patience, earnest prayer, Christian humility, and a childlike fear of God exist without faith?

RIGHTEOUSNESS THROUGH FAITH Both righteousness and the fruits of righteousness must be drawn from Christ, the Wellspring, through faith. You must be careful not to relate your works and the virtues that you have initiated, or the gifts of the new life, with your justification before God. None of our works, our merit, our gifts, our virtue, however, rests here, but rather on the exalted, perfect merit of Jesus Christ, received by faith. . . .

So be careful not to confuse the righteousness of faith with the righteousness of a Christian life. Rather, make a clear distinction because the entire foundation of our Christian religion depends on this point. On the other hand, your repentance must be made with no less righteous zeal, for otherwise you do not have that righteous faith that purifies, changes, and amends the heart daily. Understand, too, that the consolations of the gospel cannot be applied until there has been genuine and righteous sorrow, a sorrow by which the heart is broken and made contrite—as we read: "To the poor has the good news been preached" (Luke 7:22). How can faith enliven a heart not yet mortified by sincere regret and sorrow and a thorough knowledge of sin?

So do not think that repentance is an insignificant, easy business.

SALVATION BEGINS IN REPENTANCE Remember the solemn and sharp words of the apostle Paul, commanding us to mortify and to crucify the flesh with its lusts and desires, and to offer our body as a sacrifice, to die to sin, to be crucified to the world (Col. 3:5; Rom. 6:6; 12:1; 1 Pet. 2:24; Gal. 5:24; 6:14). Truth to tell, none of these is a result of gratifying the flesh; nor do the holy prophets describe repentance in pleasant terms when they urge and demand a contrite and a broken spirit and say: "Rend your heart; weep and lament" (Joel 2:13, 17; Jer. 4:8).

Where is such repentance found these days? The Lord Jesus Christ describes it: one should hate himself, deny himself, and renounce all that he has if one wishes to be His disciple (Luke 9:23; Matt. 16:24). Indeed, none of this can ever arise out of idle chatter. There is a living example and portrait of all of it in the seven Penitential Psalms (6; 32; 38; 51; 102; 130; 143). The Scriptures are full of the jealousy of God demanding both repentance and the fruits of repentance, without which eternal salvation is lost. From that point, the consolation of the gospel is able to show its true natural power;

but, by way of the Word, the Spirit of God has to work both repentance and the fruits of repentance in us.

This book . . . is about such sincere and genuine, inner, profound repentance; the demonstration and practice of authentic faith; and the love that a Christian should have in all that he does, for what proceeds from Christian love proceeds from faith. . . . So I would kindly remind the Christian reader continually to take into account the larger aim and purpose for which I wrote the book. He will find its principal purpose is to teach the reader how to understand the hidden, inherited abomination of original sin; how **THE ABOMINATION OF ORIGINAL SIN** to learn to see our misery and helplessness; how to refuse to place any confidence in ourselves; how to remove all moral self-accrediting and to ascribe all to Christ. Thus He alone may abide within us, work all things in us, alone live in us, and do all things in us, for He is the Beginning, the Middle, and the End of our conversion and our salvation. . . .

May God enlighten us all by His Holy Spirit, so that we may be pure and without offense in faith and life, until the **ENLIGHTENED BY THE HOLY SPIRIT** day of our Lord Jesus Christ—which is near at hand—be filled with the fruits of righteousness, to the honor and praise of God. Amen.

Chapter 40
Some Fine Rules for a Christian Life

Train yourself in godliness, for while bodily training is of some value, godliness is a value in every way, as it holds promise for the present life and also for the life to come (1 Tim. 4:7-8).

This verse describes the Christian life and teaches us the best possible way for the Christian to carry out that life, namely, with a godliness that carries all of the Christian virtues in itself. The apostle notes two important motives. First is the pervasive usefulness of that godliness. If one's godliness inhabits one's entire walk, all works and deeds, it renders everything good and chaste. It blesses everything. Second, such godliness has its reward in this life, as may be seen in the lives of Joseph, Daniel, and others. In eternal life, we will reap without ceasing.

I

If you are unable to live a perfect life, as is commanded in the Word of God and as you would very much like to do, you are

YEARN FOR A PERFECT LIFE nonetheless to yearn to live it. Such holy desires truly please God, and He accepts them as if they were deeds, for He looks on the heart, not on works. Nonetheless, you are always to mortify your flesh and forbid it to rule.

II

In all that you think or do, be sure that you guard the purity of **PURITY OF HEART** your heart. Do not become impure through prideful thoughts, words, or deeds, with ire and similar carnal and devilish works, for by way of such things your heart will be left ajar to Satan and closed to God.

III

Strive to keep your soul free in such a way that you do not, through some inordinate yen for temporal goods, make it a slave to earthly things. Your soul is more precious than the whole world. Why then should you sell it and make it subservient to worthless, passing baubles that are nothing in themselves? Are you going to let your heart cling to these things that have no eternal value?

IV

Shun worldly grief, for it brings about death—death that arises from covetousness, envy, from mourning for food, from unbelief and impatience. Godly sorrow, which arises from the knowledge of sins and from reflection on the eternal pains of hell, sanctifies and produces blessedness for remorse that no one regrets. It gives birth to joy and to peace in God (2 Cor. 7:10). No one ought to be sorrowful for temporal things, but for his sins.

V

If you cannot take up your cross with joy—as is intended for you—do take it up with patience and humility, at least; and always let divine providence and the divine will be your consolation. God's will is **GOD'S WILL IS ALWAYS BEST FOR ME** always good; it seeks our best interest and our blessedness in everything. Should God wish you to be sad or happy, rich or poor in spirit, low or high in station, honored or unhonored, understand that it is for your good. And because it is for your good, it is for His pleasure. God's pleasure is to be your pleasure. In fact, it is to be your consolation that God seeks your blessedness precisely by the way in which He treats you (Ecclesiasticus 39:21; Ps. 145:17). It is always better to allow God to work and to perfect His will in you and through you than for you to perfect your will in yourself, for His will is always aimed at good, yours at evil.

VI

If God grants you heavenly consolation and joy, accept it with humble thanks. However, if God removes His consolation, understand that this is a mortification of the flesh; it is better than joy of spirit. Pain and suffering make a sinner healthier than joy and happiness do. Spiritual joy that is too great leads many of you into spiritual pride. God knows equally well those whom He leads into eternal life by way of the path of full, heavenly consolation and light and those

NOT MY WILL BUT THY WILL whom He leads along an unattractive, gloomy, stony, and bleak path. It is much better for you to go into eternal life by the way ordained for you by divine wisdom than by the way your own will and pleasure demand (Eccles. 7:4).

VII

If you cannot bring to the God you love many and large offerings—such as meditation, prayer, and thanksgiving—bring what you

GIVE TO GOD WHAT YOU HAVE have and can. Bring with these offerings a goodwill and holy desires, and hope that you might please Him in your worship. Having such a holy desire, or even wishing to have one, is no small gift or sacrifice. That too pleases God. Our meditation, holy yearnings, prayer, and thanksgiving are as great in the eyes of God as we wish them to be. God demands no more from you than His grace works in you, and you cannot give Him more than He has given you. Pray to your Lord Jesus Christ that He may make your sacrifice and gifts perfect through His perfect sacrifice, for our perfection is in Him, [though] it is in part in us.

Here is what to say: Dear God and Father, take my meditation, faith, prayer, and thanksgiving through Your dear Son, and do not look on it as it is in itself but as it is in Christ. In this way, it will please You as a perfect work; my Lord Jesus will make perfect that which is lacking in me.

So it is that our meditation, prayer, and thanksgiving succeeds; and even if it is in itself feeble and dim, and even if it has shortcomings, it is a great work of perfection, a great light and glory from the merit of Christ. It is uncomely in the same way that a naked, miserable child is unattractive when it is bare and dirty. If a person adorns it and cleanses it, however, it brings pleasure. In themselves, your own acts are nothing, but all of your works truly please God if they be adorned with Christ's perfection. . . .

VIII

Your sins and many trespasses should truly make you sorrowful— but not dejected. Even if they be many, understand that much more grace, nay much more mercy, is there with God (Ps. 130:7). If they are **FORGIVENESS OF SINS** great, remember that Christ's merit is greater **FOLLOWS REPENTANCE** (51:2). If you are sorry for your sins, God also rues His punishment (Ezek. 18:23; 33:11). The forgiveness of sins follows repentance, and it occurs as often as the sinner is sorrowful. As soon as the leper said to the Lord, "Lord, you can truly cleanse me," the Lord said to him, "I will do so; be cleansed" (Matt. 8:2-3) God also quickly purifies you within, saying: "Take heart, my son; your sins are forgiven" (9:2). This is an image and mirror of internal purification and the forgiveness of sins. The great mercy of God toward humankind should not cause humankind to sin more, but to love God more and more profoundly (Ps. 103:1).

IX

You must not only accept insult, rejection, and injury without anger, a wrathful spirit, or yearning for revenge; you must also look upon such treatment as a test of your heart. . . . God wants to reveal what is hidden within you, whether it be meekness and humility or pride and a wrathful spirit. As the saying goes: One's response to libel shows what is within. If there be meekness and humility in you, you will overcome all libel with meekness. (1) In fact, you will consider it to be the Almighty's chastisement of you. . . . (2) In large part, Christ's suffering was the suffering of insult, and this must be the case with true members of Christ as well. Heb. 13:13 says: "Let us go forth to him outside the camp, bearing abuse for him." Notice the meekness of heart with which Christ bore abuse. For the sake of that patient heart of His we, too, are **ACCEPT ABUSE** to bear our abuse with meekness. Do not say: "Must I **LIKE CHRIST** take this off such a scoundrel?" For the sake of the meek and patient heart of Christ, you are to "take it."

(3) God is so good and faithful that He will give much greater honor and glory for unmerited injury. King David believed it a sure sign that God would again honor him when he suffered injury. And, in fact, this is how it came out, for he said: "It may be that the Lord

will look upon my affliction and that the Lord will repay me with good for today's cursing of me" (2 Sam. 16:12). So, as the apostle says in 1 Pet. 4:14, you do not have to worry about what people say against you, but you should be happy that the Spirit of God rests upon you.

X

You are to learn to overcome with good deeds and a good spirit all of your enemies and evildoers, and to forgive. Looking for revenge, a wrathful spirit, and striking back do not make one victorious over an enemy. As the saying goes: "Victory lies in virtue, not in vice." Wrath, the yen for revenge, and hitting back are sins and vices; therefore, one cannot conquer through them. Only through virtue may one conquer. No devil drives away another devil; no vice will drive away another vice; and no quest for revenge, nor any blow, will subdue your antagonist. It will only make him worse.

CLEANSED FROM REVENGE

If one saw a person full of maledictions and invective and wanted to pummel him, would pummeling solve the problem? Of course not. An evil, venomous person is full of maledictions, so one must heal him with tenderness. Look what the Lord God himself did to subdue us. Did He not overcome our evil with good, our wrath with love? Did not His goodness draw us to repentance? St. Paul described this method in Rom. 12:21: "Do not be overcome by evil, but overcome evil with good." This is the victory.

XI

When you see that someone has received a gift from God that you do not have, do not envy it nor begrudge it. Rejoice in it; thank God for it. The elect and faithful are one body, and a gift, an embellishment of one faithful member, is meant for, and honors, the whole body. On the other hand, when you see someone in misery, you are to take it to yourself as your own misery and grieve over it, for it is a common human sorrow under which all flesh passes. One who has no compassion and no mercy is not a member of the Body of Christ. Did not Christ consider our misery to be His own, and in that way redeem us from our misery? So it was that St. Paul said: "Bear one another's burden, and so fulfill the law of Christ" (Gal. 6:2).

CLEANSED FROM ENVY

XII

One should distinguish between loving and hating one's neighbor. To be sure, you are to hate a man's sins and vices as the work of

the devil. But you are not to hate the sinner himself. You are to have
mercy on him because such vices dwell in him; and
CULTIVATE CHRISTLIKE LOVE you are to pray to God for him as the Lord Jesus
Christ on the Cross prayed for those who did evil to
Him (Luke 23:34). You must also understand that no one who inwardly hates his neighbor can please God. God is pleased to help all
(1 Tim. 2:4). If you seek to destroy someone, you are working against
God and contrary to His pleasure. Therefore, no one who seeks another's destruction can please God. The Son of Man came not to destroy lives but to save them (Luke 9:56).

XIII

Because you know very well that all are sinners and full of error,
you are to think of yourself as the weakest and most erring of them
all, and as the greatest sinner. As the old saying goes: "All are frail;
moreover, consider no one more frail than yourself."

(1) All stand under the same damnation before God; and before
Him there is no distinction. "We have all sinned and fall short of the
glory of God"—glory that we are to have before God (Rom. 3:23).

(2) If your neighbor is a greater and more baleful sinner than
you, do not think that this makes you better in God's eyes. "He who
thinks that he stands, take heed lest he fall" (1 Cor. 10:12). If you
humble yourself and lower yourself before all, God will raise you up
by His grace.

(3) Truth to tell, as the greatest of sinners, you need His grace and
mercy. And where humility abounds, grace abounds. That is why St.
ALL OF US NEED MERCY Paul thought of himself as the greatest and chief of sinners: "The saying is sure and worthy of full acceptance,
that Christ Jesus came into the world to save sinners.
And I am the foremost of sinners; but I received mercy for this reason,
that in me, as the foremost, Jesus Christ might display his perfect patience for an example to those who were to believe in him for eternal
life" (1 Tim. 1:15-16); and "I will all the more gladly boast of my
weaknesses, that the power of Christ may rest upon me" (2 Cor. 12:9).

XIV

Authentic enlightenment brings with it the world's libel. The
children of this world have their inheritance here—in temporal honor, passing wealth, earthly glory (which they believe to be the greatest
treasure). The children of God have their treasure in earthly poverty,

calumny, persecution, injury, suffering, death, martyrdom, and pain. Like Moses, they consider injury suffered for Christ's sake to be worth more than the treasures of Egypt (Heb. 11:26). This is authentic enlightenment.

XV

The Christian's true name is written in heaven (Luke 10:20). It is there because of genuine knowledge of Jesus Christ through faith. By means of this, we are planted in Christ; indeed, we have our names inscribed in Christ as they are inscribed in the Book of Life. From this condition spring living virtues that God will laud on the final day (Matt. 25:34-40). On that day, all of the treasures brought together in heaven will be brought out (1 Tim. 6:19), and all of the works wrought in God will be brought to light (John 3:21). One will find no saint unhonored by such virtue, and such virtue will never again be forgotten (Ps. 112:6). This is the name written in the Book of Life (Rev. 2:17; 3:12). The virtues of faith, love, mercy, patience, and similar things . . . point to true saints and eternal names in heaven.

Chapter 41
Christianity in its entirety consists in the reestablishment of the image of God in man and the extirpation of the image of Satan in him.

And we all, with unveiled face, beholding the glory of the Lord, are being changed into his likeness from one degree of glory to another, for this comes from the Lord who is the Spirit (2 Cor. 3:18).

Eternal life consists in authentic knowledge of Christ—of His person; His calling; His blessings; His heavenly, eternal possession (John 17:3). All of this is ignited in our hearts by the Holy Spirit, ignited as a new light that shines ever brighter and clearer, like a polished brass or a mirror. Or we might say it is as a small child that grows and matures in body every day.

Chapter 7
A Christian ought to die to himself, and to the world, and to live for Christ.

1. We ought to live not to *ourselves,* but to Him who died for us. But to live to Him, before we be dead to ourselves, and to the world, is utterly impossible. If therefore you have a mind to live in Christ, you must be dead to all the desires of the world; and if you

DEAD TO THE WORLD have resolved to live not to yourself, but to Christ, then you must be ready to renounce your own natural life, with all that belongs to it. But if you are inclined to live to yourself and to the world, then you must be ready to renounce all fellowship with Christ. For "what communion has light with darkness," or Christ with the world? And what agreement can the Spirit have with the flesh?

2. There are *three* kinds of death; the one is *spiritual,* the second *natural,* and the third *eternal.* The first is when a man dies daily to himself; that is, by a death to avarice, pride, voluptuousness, wrath, and all other sins and passions of the corrupt nature. This death is the beginning of life.

3. Of the *second* the apostle speaks to his Philippians: "To me to live, is Christ; and to die is gain." As if he should have said, even when a Christian shall pass through *natural* death, Christ still remains his life; and thus death is gain to him. For in that he exchanges a short and miserable life, for an eternal blessed one; this cannot but be a most gainful exchange. And because Christ has here been his life, when he comes to be translated into the arms of his Beloved, whether it be gain for such an one to die, to leave this world of sin and misery to go to Him, none can doubt.

4. Yes, thrice happy is that soul, to whom to *live is Christ:* the soul wherein Christ lives; or that has in her the life of Christ, by a most lively copying after the original graces which shine so bright in Him. Blessed is the man who thus lives in Christ! But alas! the far greatest part of men have clothed themselves with the devil, have put on his life instead of Christ's, and *to them to live is the devil,* seeing that their life is the devil all over. It is pride, wrath, lying, idolatry, covetousness, concupiscence; and all this is the *life of the devil.*

5. But you, O man! Consider who it is that lives in you. Blessed are you, if you can say, *to me to live is Christ;* not only in the world to come, but even in this present world. Here, even here, let Christ be **IN THIS PRESENT WORLD** your life; that He may be so forever. And here die to the world and to sin, and account that loss all gain. For is there anything more gainful than the thorough mortifying of all the sinful lusts and affections in order that Christ may live in you, and you in Him? For the more anyone dies to the world, and to himself, the more Christ lives in that person. On then courageously, and faint not; but let Christ now live in you in time, so that you may also live with Him in eternity.

6. It is written of Him, "The Son of Man came not to be served, but to serve others, and to give His life a ransom." And again, "I am among you as he that serves." And shall we [hesitate to follow Christ in this?] God forbid. How can we ever refuse such love as this? He took the form of a servant for us. And for us, He makes war all our lives against His and our deadly enemy, the world. How is it that the love of Christ does not even *constrain* us henceforth to die to ourselves, that we may live to Him who died for us? Because we must judge, "That if one died for all, then were all of us dead!" Oh! can there be the least hesitation in returning Him life for life, body for body, and soul for soul! Shall we after this, refuse to fight under His banner, to resist for His sake, even unto blood? No! Let us in His name, defy the world to do its worst, which we have solemnly renounced: and never be so base as to entertain the least thought of ever *deserting to it.*

7. For the sake of Christ, you must die to yourself; for the love of Him be willing to die to all your sins, and to the whole world. All good works must be done and an holy and innocent **DIE TO YOURSELF AND TO ALL SIN** life must be lived; but this, not to *merit* anything thereby: but only out of *pure love* towards Him. You can merit nothing for yourself; Christ has done that for you, when He made himself *poor,* for your sake, that you, by means of His poverty, might become *rich.* Let, therefore, this *pure love of Christ* prompt you to all that is good; let this be the motive of mortifying your flesh with all its desires: and let the remembrance of that death which He most willingly accepted for you, make you willing to lay down your life for Him. But of sincere gratitude for all His inestimable benefits, accept the cross at His hand, and resist sin and the world even unto blood.

8. Be not deceived; for not in tongue or in word, but in deed and in truth, is He to be loved by you. If you love Him, keep His commandments. He has told you, "If a man **IF YOU LOVE HIM KEEP HIS COMMANDMENTS** love me he will keep my words; and my Father will love him, and we will come unto him, and make our abode with him" (John 14:23). "For this," as the Holy Ghost witnesses, "is the love of God, that we keep his commandments; and his commandments are not grievous." For him who loves Christ with all his heart, it is pleasant, for His sake, to renounce the sweetness of worldly trifles. It is a light burden to bear what the Beloved is pleased to impose; to keep, from a principle within, the

commandments of love; to forsake and to be forsaken of the world, and by a total death thereto, to live in Christ.

But he who does not embrace the love of Christ from the heart does all things that concern Christian duty, heavily and awkwardly, and as it were with an ill will. And no wonder then, if everything in the exercise of a holy life, be found sharp and difficult to him.

Whereas, to a true lover of Christ, not even death itself is in any wise terrible; so far from it, that it produces in him joy and pleasure. **LOVE MAKES DUTY A PLEASURE** For it is the triumph of love to suffer for the Beloved. And therefore it is written, that "love is stronger than death." As a mark of true Christianity, it is delivered to us, that we be "in nothing terrified" by our adversaries, the world and the devil, but that we rather "rejoice and be exceeding glad," if we be persecuted for His name's sake. "For unto us it is given," says the apostle, "on the behalf of Christ, not only to believe on him, but also to suffer for his sake"; and that even to the laying down of our natural lives, if it should graciously please Him, for His name's sake, to call us to so great an honor.

9. Consider holy Paul, whose words are, "The world is crucified to me, and I to the world." Behold this blessed apostle, whose life was a life of continual crucifixion to the world, and all that is therein. By thus renouncing the world he became, with his beloved brother Peter, a true partaker of the divine nature. And thus trampling by faith upon the life of this world, received an eternal weight **IN THE WORLD BUT NOT OF THE WORLD** of glory. After whose example all good Christians are indeed in the world, but are not of the world. And although they live in it, yet no part of the love thereof cleaves to them; they accounting it a shadow which passes away. . . . All the desire of the eyes and flesh, all deceit and vanity—all are no better than shadows. . . . Vexation, disappointment, honors, riches, and pleasures are nothing esteemed by them. They account them all but as dung that they may gain Christ. For the world is dead and crucified to them, and they likewise are dead and crucified to the world.

10. Happy man, who is dead to the world and alive to God! Separated from the world and drawn into Christ! Blessed is the man **ALIVE TO GOD** into whose heart such divine graces are infused as withdraw it wholly from every tendency to inferior things, and exalt it to the supernal light and glory in the heavens. To obtain [this grace], it is needful to pray daily and instantly to God: seeing it is not possible for a Christian to live without it.

11. It is indeed a grievous cross to flesh and blood, to die thus to the world; yet the Spirit overcomes and triumphs in us over all difficulties and oppositions. So great is the force of the
THE SPIRIT TRIUMPHS IN US Spirit that Christians pass through all these things as a most easy burden for the sake of their Beloved. And although they are hated of the world, yet are they beloved of God. For the friendship of God is at enmity with the world; even as the friendship of the world is at enmity with God. For "whosoever will be a friend of the world, is the enemy of God," and whosoever consequently would be the friend of God must not count it hard to be treated as an enemy by the world or by the god of it.

The words of the disciple are, "Know ye not that the friendship of the world is enmity with God? Whosoever therefore will be a friend of the world, is the enemy of God" (James 4:4). And the words of the Master are, "If you were of the world, the world would love its own. But because you are not of the world, but I have chosen you out of the world, therefore the world hates you" (John 15:19). We ought therefore to remember that the world is an adversary to those who are dead to the world. But . . . as many as live in the pomp and splendor [of the world] it commends and favors. Let us consider then these things, my brothers, and remember the words of our Lord, "If the world hates you, you know that it hated me before it hated you."

12. . . . Now therefore if it be demanded, *what is it to die to the world?* The answer is plain. It is no other thing than not to love the world, or the things thereof, but for the sake of Christ to despise them utterly. Wherefore also the Holy Spirit says to these dying ones, "Love not the world, neither the things that are in the world." For we are sure, that he who loves the world is not of God, but of the world; neither can he be of God. For, "If any man loves the world, the love of the Father is not in him" (1 John 2:15). . . .

It is evident that this world was never designed to be the end of our creation. Another cause brought us into the world, and for that we were born. That cause is God himself, and the image of God
RENEWED BY THE SPIRIT which we bear in Christ Jesus and in which we are renewed by the Spirit. We are created for the kingdom of God and for life eternal, which our Savior Christ has recovered for us and into which we are regenerated by the Holy Spirit. How preposterous a thing then is it for anyone to fix his heart on the world; to spend his time on earthly things! How preposterous for

man, who is the most excellent of all the creatures; man, who was made to carry about with him the image of God in Christ, and who by Him is renewed after this image! *Man, who was not created for the world, but the world for man. . . .*

15. Man ought to love nothing but God alone. Whatever one loves, in that his heart is fixed; and where his heart is fixed, there he pays his devotion. He is a servant of it, whatsoever it be, and *devoted* to it. Consequently we have, in this broken and divided state, as many lords as we have objects which we love. But if your love, O

PERFECT LOVE TOWARD GOD

man, be simply directed towards God, then you are subject to no other lord; then you are at liberty. Wherefore you must be very circumspect, that you follow after nothing that may hinder the divine love in you; and that you suffer not your affections to run out into any creatures. If you desire to possess God alone, your *all* must be consecrated to Him. But if you

ALL MUST BE CONSECRATED TO HIM

please yourself, instead of loving and pleasing God, much sorrow and sadness will result. Whereas if you love God and rejoice in Him only, and dedicate yourself only to Him, then He will be your sure comfort. You shall never be overcome with sorrow, or fear, and never depressed with sadness and melancholy. . . .

17. Now the activities of this life, such as praise, honor, riches, pleasure, and even the world itself, which bestows them, are floating away, but the love of God endures forever. The delight which you take in the love of earthly things cannot be durable. Whereas the mind that is firmly set upon divine love can rejoice continually. Ah! How vain is all that which is not grounded upon God! . . . But you, O Christian, forsake all things, and you shall find all things by faith. For he who finds God finds all things; but the lover of the world finds not God.

"I am," says Christ, "the way, the truth, and the life." As if He was saying: Without the way, no man goes on; without the truth, nothing is known; and without life, no man lives. Therefore look upon *Me*, who is *the way*, which you ought to walk in; *the truth*, which you ought to believe in; and *the life*, which you ought to live and hope in. I am the *way* that endures for all ages; the infallible *truth;* and the *life* everlasting. The royal way to immortal life is through My merit. The truth itself is in My Word; and the life is through the power and efficacy of My death. Therefore, if you continue in this *way,* the *truth* will carry you on to eternal *life.*

PUT YOUR WHOLE TRUST IN ME If you will not err, come follow Me; and if you will possess *life eternal,* put your whole trust in Me, who for you endured the death of the cross.

And what is that royal *way,* that infallible *truth,* and that endless *life*—the best and most noble way, and truth, and life of all others? Truly other way there can be none, but the most holy and precious merit of Christ; nor other truth, but the Word of God; nor other life, but love on earth, and immortality of happiness in heaven.

Chapter 12
Of the Love of God and Our Neighbor

Now the end of the commandment is love, out of a pure heart, and of a good conscience, and faith unfeigned (1 Tim. 1:5).

In this assertion, the apostle sets before us the high and noble virtue of *love,* and certifies to us these four things concerning it.

1. First, that love is the end of all the commandments and the fulfilling of the law. Therein are comprehended and fulfilled all the precepts of God, both under the first and the second covenants. Without love, all gifts and virtues are fruitless and unprofitable.

2. The second is this, that true love comes "out of a pure heart" that is cleansed from the love of the world. Wherefore St. John warns us "not to love the world, neither the things that are in **OUT OF A** the world." Under these he specifies the "lust of the flesh, **PURE HEART** the lust of the eyes, and the pride of life." The mixture of any of these is absolutely inconsistent with the pure love of God. For, "If any man," says he, "love the world, the love of the Father is not in him."

3. The apostle, in the third place, teaches that love must be "out of a good conscience." Now this properly concerns the love of our neighbor. He instructs us that man ought to love his neighbor, not for the sake of interest or worldly advantage, which is a false love, and *out of a bad conscience.* One must love for the sake **LOVE OTHERS FOR** of God and of His commandments, and out of a **THE SAKE OF GOD** consciousness of our duty.

The last thing asserted here by the apostle is that love must be "out of faith unfeigned." [Under this head he lists a number of considerations.]

a. In the first place, "love is the end of the commandment"; it is a fulfilling of the whole law. It is a summary of all the precepts of Jesus Christ. It is both the beginning and motive, the end and perfection of all virtue. That love which is out of a right faith is the noblest,

LOVE IS THE HIGHEST FRUIT OF FAITH the best, and highest fruit of faith. God has changed the heavy yoke of the Old Testament service, and the "many commandments and ordinances" of that dispensation, into *faith* and *love: and this commandment is not grievous.* It is not so to an enlightened Christian because the Holy Ghost makes a free, willing, and ready heart. He is the inspirer of courage which does not fail, but surmounts all difficulties.

b. Neither does God require of us great skill or great ability; it is only love which He will have from us. And where this is present, God is more delighted therein than in all the knowledge and wisdom that any man upon earth can ever express in his best work. And where there is no love, all wisdom, all knowledge, all works, and all gifts are altogether unprofitable. Yes, he is dead—whoever lives without love. . . .

c. Without love every work is of no merit, and with it there is nothing but what is accepted of God. . . . It is the Christian's badge

LOVE IS THE SEAL OF THE HOLY GHOST and the seal of the Holy Ghost. It is love alone which unites us to God. For we know that "God is love, and he that dwells in love dwells in God, and God in him." Where love is not, God is not there; and he that abides not in love has no portion in God, in Christ, or in heaven, which is the kingdom of love. So then, where love is wanting there is no good; and where love is present no evil can abide, for God himself is there. Love is pleasant and acceptable with God because it is of His own nature; and so is every man that exercises it and brings forth the fruit thereof. There is no work *without* it but is a *dead* work: and there can be no work *with* it, but it is a *living* one. For in this love, there is an endless spring of life. It is the communication of the divine life itself and an essential ray of the infinite Goodness. . . .

d. This should be the spring of all our prayers; and without this, all is but lip-service. He that loves God prays well and praises well. But he who loves not God, neither prays nor praises as he ought because he neither prays to Him nor praises Him from the heart. The true prayer consists in spirit, in faith, in love. It consists not in bare words. Think upon Christ and how He prayed. Think out of what a tender merciful heart He cried, "Father, forgive them" (Luke 23:34). He that loves not God, that man prays not. But he who heartily loves God knows how to pray, and for him to pray is both easy and comfortable. In his heart is the prayer of peace. From his lips goes forth a *burning stream* of love as having been touched with a *coal* from the heavenly altar. . . .

e. Preserve the root of love always in you by faith, so that nothing but what is good may grow up. So shall you fulfill the commandments of God; seeing that they are all comprehended in love. Therefore a certain holy doctor spoke in this manner: "O love of God in the Holy Ghost, who is the ravishing sweetness of souls and the divine life of men, whosoever has not You is dead even while he lives; and whosoever has You, never dies before God. Where You are not, there the life of man is nought but a restless dying. Where You are, there man's life is made a foretaste of eternal life."

f. The love of man to God must be out of *a pure heart.* The heart of man that desires to love God should be cleansed from all worldly love.

CLEANSED FROM ALL WORLDLY LOVE

So shall God be to him the highest good, and he shall be able to say, "The Lord is the portion of my inheritance and of my cup: You maintain my lot."

g. God therefore should be the most beloved of our souls, and our hearts should rest in Him because He is our highest and best good, the good of all goods. He is all goodness, and all virtue. All that is, or can be called good, He is in the truest and most supereminent sense. God is the only good, and there is none besides Him. He is purely and only good, purely and only love. And if it be asked what God is, we may well answer: God is all that is grace, love, clemency, truth, consolation, peace, joy, life, and salvation. Now all these He has given us in Christ, and whosoever has Christ, has all of these. And if any man have the love of God, he has also the truth of God, with His mercy, His goodness, and the whole body of the virtues. Because he loves God he thereby loves . . . all the virtues, even as they are in God.

h. The right lover of God then has a love for all that God loves; and an aversion to all that God has an aversion for. He likes and dislikes all things, even as God likes and dislikes them. Hence if any man love God he must love righteousness. And therefore also should he have a love for truth, seeing God is truth. Moreover man ought to love mercy, seeing that God is mercy. For the same reason ought he to love meekness and humility in conformity to the meek and humble will of Christ.

And on the contrary, God's true lover cannot but hate all ungodliness and all the works of unrighteousness. For that which is unrighteous is against God and is the work of the devil. Therefore also the lover of God hates a lie because the devil is the father of lies. Moreover he must needs hate unmercifulness, pride, and all other sins because they are part of the devil.

i. But you must remember that when you pray to God for this love, which is *out of a pure heart,* through the grace of Christ, God will most freely kindle the flames of love in

GOD WILL KINDLE LOVE IN YOUR HEART your heart. He will give this love to you if you pray to Him for it, and cease not to importune Him by offering up to Him your heart every day, yes every hour. Every moment must be a constant habitual resignation of your will to Him. And if it happens that your love grows cold and weak at any time, rouse up your heart, faint not, but stir up the gift of divine grace within you, and never be discouraged.

Yes, should you, through weakness of your love sometimes fall; get up in the name of God, rise again, and go to work, and renew the acts of your love. For inasmuch as you are aware of this coldness and weakness, be sure that the eternal light of divine love is not extinguished, though it be eclipsed. And therefore never doubt but that God, your most gracious and tender Savior, will enlighten you again, and fire your heart with His love as in the days of your first commitment to Him. Again you may sit down under His shadow and rejoice in the light of His countenance.

Yet however it may be with you, be sure to abide humbly in Him. And whenever He visits you again with His gracious consolation, and shall enflame your heart with His love, you ought to pray. Pray that He may never at any time hereafter allow the bright fire of divine love in

PURIFIED FROM THE LOVE OF THE WORLD you to be quenched. In this way love is preserved— the love *out of a pure heart* which is *purified* from the love of the world and of the creatures.

j. The love of man to his neighbor must be *out of a good conscience.* The love of God and of our neighbor cannot be separated. But he who loves God will also love his brother who was made after the image of God. For the love of God cannot abide in a heart that is leavened with hatred or any unloving attitudes. And if you have no pity on your brother whom you know to stand in need of your help, how can you love God who needs not anything that is yours? And how can you profess to love God who has commanded you to show your love towards Him by the love you show to your brother?

k. Faith unites us to God, love unites us to our neighbor. It is the nature of love to feel compassion for the infirmities of others.

GIVEN LOVE FOR OTHERS This is so because they represent to us, as in a mirror, our own condition. Therefore when you see another overtaken in a fault, consider that you yourself are only *human.*

Then endeavor, if possible, to restore him *in the spirit of meekness.* Inasmuch as you bear his burden, you *fulfill the law of Christ,* which is the perfect law of love. Thus we are obliged to "receive one another," and to bear one with another, *as Christ also received us,* and bore with us, to the glory of God. This we are to do in all patience, humility, and gentleness, with brotherly kindness, considering ourselves, lest we also should be tempted.

l. Love must be *out of faith unfeigned.* Being so, it puts no difference for the sake of God, between what is bitter and sweet, painful and joyous. One loves them and embraces both alike. Love rejoices in adversity, even as in prosperity, and faints not when it is tried. The man who heartily loves God is well pleased with everything with which God is pleased. He who has a love for God cannot but have a love for His cross which God has given him to bear.

If this seems hard, let us look to our Lord and behold how willing He was to take His cross upon himself because it was God's will. "I have a baptism (says He) to be baptized with. And oh! how I am straitened (and in pain) till it be accomplished." In like manner have all the holy martyrs after Him carried their cross with joy. For to those who unfeignedly love God, out of a sincere faith, it is not hard to bear their cross. The magnet draws to itself heavy iron; and shall not the Heavenly Magnet, the love of God, draw that which is heavy to it? Shall not God lift up the burden of our cross as if it were most light and easy? Shall not the sweetness of divine love make the cross sweet, even when in its own nature it is ever so bitter to the flesh?

m. This love is a beautiful image and lovely foretaste of eternal life. There the saints mutually love each other sincerely and receive singular delight one from another. There they converse together in a wonderful fellowship with inexpressible sweetness and affection. Whoever therefore desires to have a foretaste of eternal blessedness, let him study *love.* He will be delighted with singular pleasure in the depths of his soul.

LOVE IS A FORETASTE OF HEAVEN

n. The purer and more frequent your expression of love is, the nearer it approaches the divine nature because in God, in Christ, and in the Holy Ghost, love is most pure and most fervent.

Now love is *pure* when we love not for private profit, but only for the cause of God alone. We know that He loved us for no good of His own, but for our need. The Christian loves his neighbor, God, and Christ without any ignoble or selfish ends. Thus is his love preserved pure and sincere, which is the true love.

And this love, as it is *pure,* so it is also *fruitful;* yes, nothing is more fruitful than love. Hence love is fitly called the fruitful mother of all the births both in heaven and on earth. It brings forth by the Holy Ghost all the fruits of righteousness from the heart, which is divinely impregnated with this *creative* principle.

Lastly, love is *fervent,* when it vehemently drives on the lover to act *vigorously* for the good of the beloved, when it is accompanied with abundant mercy and compassion, and when the affairs of our neighbor go as near to our heart as our own, so that we are ready even to *lay down our life* for him.

o. Yes, we ought to love even our enemies. According to our Lord's commandment, we are to: "Love your enemies; do good to those that hate you, and pray for them that persecute you, and revile you, that you may be the children of your Father who is in heaven. For if you love (only) them which love you, what reward have you? Do not the Publicans the same?"

In this love, then, the excellency and dignity of a true Christian consists. He subjects his nature to this divine principle. Love tames his flesh and blood and, by *goodness,* overcomes the world with the evil that is in it. Therefore, "If your enemy hunger, give him meat." Though he be your enemy, treat him as your friend and endeavor to make him so by all possible means, heaping as it were *coals* of love *upon his head.*

Lest we might think it sufficient not to hurt him, we are commanded to do good to him, to support him, to relieve him, and to provide him with food or other help that he may need. If any man refuses to do this, he cannot be the child of God, or a member of Christ because he does not love his neighbor, be he friend or enemy.

And who would not be moved to love his enemies by the patience and meekness of the Son of God himself? To this end our blessed Redeemer has set His example before our eyes, that He might be an ever-living guide to us in our whole life. That by His example whatever is proud or lofty in us might be abased; whatever is weak, should be strengthened; whatever is crooked, should be made straight; whatever was defective, should be made right. Let us constantly behold this blessed example so that we may
SHAPED BY THE
EXAMPLE OF CHRIST be conformed to it. For what pride of man may not be healed with the extreme humility of the Son of God? What wrath this meekness cannot subdue? What desire of revenge His patience cannot dissolve? What inhumanity so great

that Christ with His love and benefits shall not expel? Lastly, what heart so hard that it is not softened with tears of Jesus Christ?

p. Now who would not wish to be made like Him, and to represent Him in humility, patience, and love? Oh! Who would not bear the image of Him who loved His enemies to so high a degree? Or who would not wish from the bottom of his heart to be like God the Father, and His Son, and the Holy Ghost? . . . For it is the highest of all the divine attributes to have mercy, to spare, to pardon, and to be gracious. And doubtless, love is the highest of all virtues by which we become most like the Most High God.

MORE LOVE TO THEE, O CHRIST

q. On this consideration God was made man, that He might set before our eyes a living and breathing image of His own love. He came that He might manifest by His image His love . . . so that men should be transformed through love into this image of God. . . .

Book 2

Part 1, Chapter 1
An Introduction into the Holy Life of Christ

Jesus Christ is given us by our heavenly Father for an antidote against the deadly poison of sin, and a fountain, good, against all the calamities and evils both of body and soul.

As our sickness is exceeding great . . . it is needful that we should also have a remedy proportioned to the disease—a great, a high, a divine, an everlasting remedy flowing out of the pure mercy and love of God. Hence He has made the blood of Christ the grand restorative of our nature and the cleanser of it from all the contagion of sin. And He has given us His quickening flesh with its immortalizing power for our bread of life. He has given His precious death for an abolition of our death—both temporal and eternal. For He will swallow up death in victory and lead us to the living fountain of waters, clear as crystal, proceeding out of the throne of God, and of the Lamb. . . .

CLEANSED BY THE BLOOD OF CHRIST

Man is incapable of purchasing this most costly salvation. By his own skill or power it is impossible for him ever to reach it. What then is to be done? . . . By nature we strive against this heavenly cure and resist the remedy that should help us. . . . See, then, O God, that I take what You have ordered and trust me not to myself. I am lost because You know it is

O LAMB OF GOD, I COME

in the very nature of my malady to long for that which will hurt me and to shun whatever is likely to do me any good. I am abundantly more afraid of the cure than of the disease. O how You, therefore, urge me, that You may prevail upon me to accept life! . . . But unless You prevail, what would become of me? Or what would become of all that You have done for me? You know all my infirmity, and Your heart has pitied me and gently borne with me all this while.

O bear with me yet a little longer. Leave me not, lest I perish . . . out of the city of my God, and my name be written in the dust with them that go down to the pit. O tarry with me yet a little longer. Let not my folly and my reluctance drive You away, lest I descend into darkness, and the purchase of Your blood be lost. O let it not be! You have caused me to hope, blessed be Your name! Therefore, this sickness of my soul shall not lead to death, but to Your glory. Again and again You have asked me secretly in the deep of my heart, "What do you want?" Lord, what else should I want but that I may receive my health?

To receive health I am indeed willing, but not to receive the medicine which alone can give it. I shrink back when I hear it mentioned. And hence I did not seek You. But You have **YOU HAVE SOUGHT ME** sought me, and Your will is that I should be restored . . .

I find, alas, no disposition in me to take what You so kindly offer. But change my desire and I will be inclined to accept what You so freely offer. So manage my will that I may submit fully to Yours. Thus I may obtain that perfect cure which You are both willing and able to effect in me. O sweet constraint of love that breaks the will! Your love and your patience constrain me to yield. It is impossible longer to resist so great a love, so wonderful a patience.

I must follow when You thus draw me. I must obey when You so sweetly command me. For while You draw me with cords of Your love I run to You in whom alone is my health. Your commandments are sweeter to me than honey and more precious than diamonds. But without Your attraction, Your commandments would have been as bitter as gall . . . I would have dreaded Your presence above all things. I would have chosen death rather than life.

O draw me therefore, that I may run after You. O lead me to the springs of salvation. Give me the water to drink which is able to heal **LEAD ME TO THE SPRINGS OF SALVATION** all my infirmities and miseries. For You know that without You I can do nothing; there is no strength in me. I can destroy myself, but it is only You, Lord, who can restore me. Wherefore it is right that I should cast all upon You, so that You can in all things draw, lead, and move me as You will. If You permit me to run after the devices of my own will, I inevitably run to my own ruin. If You let me lie in my sickness . . . there is no remedy, even though help is near—I shall be forever lost. Let me not be left to my own care in this manner, but remain with me. Do all that You see fit with me, only trust me not in my own hands.

In You is all my hope. Were my heart converted to You, all would go well with me, and my life would henceforth be filled with You. O Eternal Fountain of eternal life, turn me, and I shall be turned, for You are the Lord my God. Heal me, O **HEAL ME AND I SHALL BE HEALED** Lord, so shall I be healed, for You are the health of my life and my glory. So long as You keep back Your mercy, I remain in the shadow of death. And so long as You delay to quicken me with Your salvation . . . just so long I am held in the chains of death. So long I am a captive to the powers of darkness. "Make haste to help me; You are my helper and my Redeemer. O my God, make no long tarrying."

AUGUST HERMANN FRANCKE (1663—1727)

Biographical Note

August Hermann Francke

In 1686 Elector Johann Georg III of Saxony invited Philipp Jakob Spener to Dresden as court chaplain. Spener was not Saxon—he was Alsatian— and by now he was well known, if not famous, for fearlessly exposing the sins of even the high and mighty. So we might expect exactly what happened. Jealousy arose among the Saxon clergy over the noted alien, and Spener, true to form, proved to be no respecter of persons. He admonished Duke Johann Georg to temper his drinking and to attend services more frequently. So the "father of pietism" remained as court chaplain only five years.

But in that time he met and won over a young lecturer in the University of Leipzig, August Hermann Francke. In 1685 Francke, as a student, had been one of the cofounders of the Collegium Philobiblicum, a type of Bible institute attached to the university. Its aim was Bible study with an emphasis on practical exegesis, and by 1687 it was making its mark in the university itself.

Even more significantly for our story, in 1687 that student, August Hermann Francke, was converted. Not that he had not been religious early on. He had been brought up in a pious Lutheran family and had read Johann Arndt's *True Christianity* and others of Arndt's works even before going to the university. But now he came to know Christ in a vivid and personal experience.

In 1688 Francke went to Dresden to visit Spener, largely because of their mutual interest in biblical exegesis aimed at practical ends. Francke found Spener most supportive of the Collegium Philobiblicum, and both found in each other a profound piety rooted in conversion experiences that were not to be doubted.

In 1692 the University of Halle called Francke to come as professor of oriental languages, and arrangements were also made that he serve as pastor in the township of Glaucha. He now settled in to give what would become 35 years of leadership in the university, the town, and the church.

This is not the place to review Francke's amazing record in the establishment and maintenance of social service organizations—everything from an orphanage to a bookstore to a pharmacy, from a divinity school to elementary schools for the children of both rich and poor. But it is the place to say what is not usually said: that Francke never failed to state that the impulse behind every one of his organizations was the love of Christ that he had first come to know in his conversion in 1687.

Francke also served very effectively as a preacher and a writer. In the century since Arndt, the Lutheran vocabulary had expanded, so Francke did not operate within the semantic restraints that Arndt had known. In fact, Arndt's work itself had opened that vocabulary somewhat. Some Lutheran theologians had developed ways to talk of sanctification and of broader possibilities of grace that Luther and even Melanchthon had simply not known.

Not that all was well. Controversy still swirled about the relationship between justification and sanctification, about the role of works in salvation, and about the freedom of the human will. The tendency among theologians to try to cover every conceivable angle and to ride every logical train to the end of the line had only begun to manifest itself in Arndt's day; in Francke's it was full-blown. And pastors reflected it in the pulpit by making the ordinary sermon a lecture in theology or philosophy. So Francke's concern was much the same as Arndt's had been: that the drive for orthodoxy not overshadow or replace holiness of heart and life as the fundamental concern of the Church.

Francke's strategy placed considerable emphasis on repentance and conversion, and in both cases he talked of them in ways that set orthodox Lutheran teeth on edge. The idea of repentance was no stranger at all to Lutheran theology, of course. One of the fundamental purposes of the liturgy, Sunday by Sunday, was to afford opportunity for confession and for hearing the gospel's promise to those who truly repented. Francke, concerned that too many were confessing only formally, talked about repentance in terms of struggle—a *busskampf,* he called it, a penitential combat that recognizes the heinousness of sin. Francke insisted that Christians understand and confess the depth and pervasiveness of sin, their own sin. But he also insisted that Christ's atonement provided a remedy that both forgives and transforms—a conversion, that includes regeneration.

Orthodox Lutherans were especially concerned that Francke was undermining baptism, for they believed that baptism regenerated. And in being an act of the church done in the name of God, baptism guarded the individual from thinking that he or she had done some good work that had merited salvation. They also feared that Francke's way of talking about repentance tempted people to think of it, too, as a good work meriting salvation. Francke's response was that baptism had indeed conferred regeneration but that most had lost that effect by living in a manner that deliberately contradicted the gospel. The gospel, he insisted, calls us to holiness of heart and life. Christ's atonement, the gospel, provides for such an experience, even for the possibility of its perfection in this life.

Francke, like Arndt, spoke biblical language with a Lutheran dialect. His pessimism concerning human nature in its sinfulness seems to intrude even his most optimistic convictions about what grace can do. So from a Wesleyan point of view, he sometimes appears to contradict himself. He would probably respond to any Wesleyan criticism at this point by suggesting that he is simply being true to the Bible itself. And such is indeed the case. But then this question surfaces: Which principle governs one's reading of Scripture—"sin abound[s]" or "grace . . . much more abound[s]" (Rom. 5:20, KJV)?

On Christian Perfection (1690)

1. We are justified solely by faith in the Lord Jesus. This is accomplished without merit and without added works inasmuch as the Heavenly Father accounts us to be free from all our sins because of the perfect satisfaction and treasured merit of His Son.

2. By means of this justification, which comes about through faith, the justified one becomes completely, totally perfect. It is like the righteousness of God himself, as St. Paul writes: "God made him who knew no sin to be sin for us, in order that we, in him, might become the righteousness of God." Just as God looked upon Christ as sin, because our sins were accounted to Him, so He looks upon the sinner as just and absolutely perfect because He grants the innocence and righteousness of Christ to the sinner as the sinner's own.

3. One who does not have this perfection cannot become holy. Perfection is nothing other than faith in the Lord Jesus. It is not ours, nor is it within us. It is in Christ and of Christ, for whose sake we are accounted perfect before God. Thus His perfection is ascribed to us.

4. However, if one be justified, one may be perfectly certain of blessedness. Nonetheless, one discovers straightaway the weakness of ORIGINAL SIN the flesh and inherited sinful tendencies. In the depths of one's heart, one wants nothing other than God and eternal life. One looks on all that is in the world as the lust of the eye, the lust of the flesh, and the pride of life—as filth with unexpected harmful effects. Still, one finds that original sin wakens in one's flesh and creates all sorts of doubts, evil thoughts, and, at times, evil tendencies in the will. He also discovers that because of the full-blown and long habit of sinning, one often rushes in word and deed into this or that evil practice.

5. Nonetheless, such disorderly patterns and practices as remain are not accounted to the justified person. There is now no condemnation for those who are in Christ Jesus, who walk not according to the flesh but according to the Spirit, though the flesh attracts them. So it is that as soon as the spiritually newborn recognizes an error that does not arise intentionally, he turns in true faith to the grace of Jesus Christ, because Christ in one's heart is an enemy of sin.

6. If the newborn Christian recognizes such sins of the flesh, he struggles wholeheartedly against the wickedness that arises in his flesh. And he does this not by his own power and **NEVER BY OUR OWN POWER** might. Rather, by means of the Spirit he destroys the works of the flesh. He depends upon the power of Jesus Christ, which is made God's sanctification for him and conquers the evil in him.

7. However, the justified man retains sinful habits and perseveres in offenses, never constant. But by the grace of God, he increasingly distances himself from evil and matures in **GROWTH IN GRACE** faith and love, day by day, just as one matures in one's physical life from child to youth to adult.

8. However, in his spiritual growth, one never can get as far as he might wish. He is never fully perfected. But he may grow and develop in good works as long as he lives. One who takes pride in his understanding of perfection deceives himself and others.

9. Nonetheless, it cannot be denied that, according to the Holy Scripture, some sort of perfection is attributed to the human being. In the same way I can call someone a master in an art, **THE BIBLE SPEAKS OF PERFECTION** though he has not completely learned that art and is surpassed in it by others. So Scripture would not teach that one can be fully perfect in this life—that he can be without sin or the attraction to sin. Rather, it would teach that one can come to such a human strength in Christianity that he may slay the old habits within himself and conquer his flesh and blood. It would also teach that the degree of perfection is not equal in all. So it is that the Epistle to the Hebrews says that for the perfect there is strong food. It describes the perfect as those who, because of practice, have mature discernment of good and evil, though they continue to be inclined to evil through sinful lust.

10. So it is that in a certain sense, both of the following statements are true: We are perfect; we are not perfect. That is to say, through Christ and in Christ, by way of our justification **PERFECT IN CHRIST** and according to the righteousness of Jesus Christ ascribed to us, we are perfect. However, in the sense that we will nevermore be able to grow, to put away evil and to put on that which is suitable for sanctification, we are not and will not be fully perfect.

11. One who does not wish to be mistaken in this matter needs to distinguish carefully between the doctrine of justification and the doctrine of regeneration or sanctification. If he does not, he will increasingly get tangled up in controversy.

12. It follows from this that after justification, one has no sin;

AFTER REGENERATION, ONE STILL HAS SIN but even after regeneration, because sin still clings to him (though, for Christ's sake, it is not laid to his account), one has sin.

13. When the justified person prays or goes to confession, he prays that God will, for Christ's sake, forgive the sins that are still within and not lay them to his account. On the other hand, as one who is in Christ Jesus, he knows and is assured that he is not under any condemnation.

14. Consequently, the justified person eats the sacramental meal in order to strengthen his faith and to improve his life.

15. However, in all of this, one must be careful that his repentance is not hypocritical; rather, that he is working out his salvation with fear and trembling. Otherwise, one can easily divert to personal gain the consolation received from the grace of Christ, and one who really loves the world will talk as if the love of God is in him. Such behavior is a charade and causes hell to rejoice.

13

EARLY MODERN ROMAN CATHOLIC PIETY

FRANÇOIS DE SALIGNAC DE LA MOTHE FÉNELON
(1651—1715)

Biographical Note

*Instructions and Counsel on Diverse Points
Concerning Morality and Christian Perfection*

Chapter 10: On the Imitation of Jesus Christ

Chapter 29: The Obligation to Abandon Oneself
to God Without Reserve

Chapter 30: Given Entirely to God

13

Early Modern Roman Catholic Piety

FRANÇOIS DE SALIGNAC DE LA MOTHE FÉNELON (1651—1715)

Biographical Note

Fénelon belonged to an aristocratic family in Périgord, a rather
sparsely settled area in west-cen-
tral France, northeast of Bordeaux.
In time he became one of the
most distinguished clerics in what
some historians call France's Glorious Epoch, the period dominated by the reign of Louis XIV
(1643—1715). Fénelon came to
the attention of the family of King
Louis XIV and was made the tutor
of two of the royal grandsons, one
of whom was Louis of France.
Had he lived, he would have suc-
ceeded his grandfather as king.

François Fénelon,
marble bust by
Jean Baptiste Lemoyne.

The royal tutor was to edu-
cate the children in all things—customs and manners, and religion
and ethics, as well as the usual academic subjects. But from the
point of view of the very worldly royal court, Fénelon did his work
too well. Detractors pointed specifically to his book *The Adventures
of Telemachus* (1699), which Fénelon wrote for his most important
pupil. It subtly but sharply criticized the moral and ethical careless-

ness of the government of the Sun King, as Louis XIV was known. And it brought about the tutor's exile from the court at Versailles.

Fénelon's trouble had actually begun two years earlier, in 1697. That year he had published a book titled *Explications of the Maxims of the Saints.* It was a response to a very strong assault on the theological position of one of his friends by another friend. One friend was Jacques Bénigne Bossuet, bishop of Meaux, who had been the royal tutor to the previous generation. He was probably the most popular preacher in France. Bossuet had attacked the quietistic teachings of Fénelon's other friend, Madame Jeanne Marie Bouvier de La Motte Guyon (1648—1717).

Quietism was a theology developed more than a century earlier in Spain by Miguel de Molinos. The papacy had condemned a number of propositions from the teachings of Molinos, and he had ended his days in one of the prisons of the Inquisition in Spain.

Molinos and those who either followed him or held similar views were mystics, so they insisted that the aim of the fully Christian life must be union with God. In turn, they said, the way to mystical union with God lay in a sort of internal, grace-given emptying of the self. It was a state in which one no longer thought of the world or of the self and no longer felt influences from them. The Christian prepared to receive the divine presence by allowing grace to make him or her completely passive and by awaiting the fullness of the Spirit "as wax awaits a seal." This spirit of complete passivity earned the name "quietism."

At base, the condemnation of quietism rested on what it implied, not on what it said. Being a form of mysticism, it did not speak precisely. It left a lot of room to read between the lines. Consequently, those who wished could see it as opposed to good works. Those who wished could see it as denying the goodness of creation, particularly the creation of human flesh. And those who wished could see it as denying the need for any external authority. Most damaging of all to the quietists' cause was the fact that those who wished could see it as denying the need for the hierarchical-sacramental system, the church.

Bossuet, who took himself to be one of the principal guardians of French orthodoxy and of the French hierarchical-sacramental system, saw Madame Guyon as a threat to that which he guarded. So he collected some of her less precise assertions, tearing some from their context. He deduced a number of implications from her work, stating some as if they were positive assertions. Madame Guyon, said he, had committed grave errors. Church and state must bring her to account.

Louis XIV apparently cared little about the theology of quietism, but some advisers led him to believe of all French quietists what may have been true of a few, that they tended politically to support Austria. Persons jealous of Fénelon's influence within the royal family and put off by his pious criticisms of their looser ways—matters having nothing to do with quietism—saw this as an opportunity for his undoing.

Fénelon, however, had some very powerful friends in court, and he did not lose altogether. He was acquitted of heresy and cleared of any hint of treason. However, it was the policy of the Sun King, when there were passionate public arguments among his courtiers, never to allow anyone to win completely, especially not the Jesuits or enormously popular persons like Bossuet. So Fénelon did not face prison as had been the fate of Molinos. But then came *Telemachus*, with its criticism of the inner circle—quite probably criticism of those who had plotted Fénelon's downfall two years earlier—and this time Fénelon could not save himself. The government ordered him out of Versailles and confined to the archdiocese of Cambrai, where he was the archbishop.

Was quietism really a heresy, and was Fénelon really a quietist? The answer to both is no. Quietism is not a particularly healthy form of orthodoxy, and out on its fringes it becomes heretical in that it attempts to be Christianity without the church and without external expression. But those are the fringes. Fénelon always insisted on the absolutely necessary role of the church in our salvation, and he gave witness to his faith continually in the care of his people. In his writings when he spoke of the church, he meant the priestly sacramental system, the Roman Catholic Church, and he allowed no validity to a faith without works.

In some sense, one may protest the inclusion of Fénelon's work in a collection of Holiness classics. But there is reason for including it as well. John Wesley included some of that work in his *Christian Library*,[1] and he spoke of Fénelon with affection and favor. Also, most of those within the Holiness Movement who have written of the history of the doctrine of Christian perfection have cited Fénelon as a pre-Wesley adherent of Wesley's point of view,

---

1. John Wesley, comp. and ed., *A Christian Library: Consisting of Extracts from and Abridgments of the Choicest Pieces of Practical Divinity Which Have Been Published in the English Tongue*, 50 vols. (London, 1749-55).

or of something like it. They have done this for three reasons: (1) Wesley's favorable mention of him and the inclusion of his work in the *Christian Library;* (2) the fact that Fénelon wrote a book titled *Instructions and Advice on a Number of Moral Points and on Christian Perfection,* which was translated into English and quickly became popular among pious persons in the era of the Evangelical Revival in England and on into and throughout the 19th century; and (3) the simple fact that other Holiness authors have cited it.

On the other hand, Wesley took away nearly everything positive that he had to say about Fénelon with a very sharp, negative critique.[2] What Wesley seems to have seen very clearly was Fénelon's extreme Augustinianism—the tendency to so emphasize the sovereignty of grace and the bondage of the human will that one resolutely refuses to do anything that might be understood as an attempt to participate in the process of salvation. Its formal name is quietism. Its principal advocate at the end of the 17th century was a spiritual disciple of Fénelon, Madame Guion (Guyon). Fénelon was not a quietist in any heretical sense, but he certainly leaned that way theoretically.

It is important to understand why Fénelon had taken that position. On the one hand, he was deeply disturbed with the pervasive patterns of works righteousness and superstition that he saw as spiritually ruinous in his own beloved Roman Catholicism. On the other hand, he was deeply disturbed with the individualism, even the spiritual egotism, selfishness, and self-righteousness that the orthodox Protestant doctrines of *sola gratia* and election were creating. As a spiritual guide, he sought to lead others to trust the sovereign grace of God and at the same time to place themselves in submission to the church. He, of course, understood the church to be the divinely appointed dispenser of that grace through its sacraments and its hierarchy. So he would emphatically agree that we are saved by grace alone, through faith. But he would insist that God has appointed the church as the sole dispenser of saving grace and that faith is precisely trusting in the church (and thus submitting to it) as that divinely appointed dispenser.

In Fénelon's view, Christian perfection is the process and the end of the process in which one learns fully to trust the church (and therefore fully to trust God and sovereign grace). And once

---

2. Cf., e.g., John Wesley, letter to "a young disciple," September 8, 1773 (Letter 517), in *Works* (ed. Jackson), 12:449-50.

one has come to that point, he may be justified—declared righteous, because he really *is* righteous. So Fénelon, characteristically of Roman Catholics, insists that Protestants have turned the divinely appointed order of salvation upside down. Protestants have taught that one must be justified before he or she may be sanctified. Roman Catholics have taught that (from their perspective) one must be entirely sanctified before he or she may be justified.

It is this inversion of the order of salvation and Fénelon's extreme Augustinianism that brought Wesley to speak of the dross, and even the poison, in Fénelon's works. These are no minor points of difference, and they certainly are not obscure differences that only theologians would argue over. They lie squarely at the heart of Christian practice. And they are, negatively, the guidelines for interpreting Scripture that Wesley uses as he edits Fénelon's work.

Still, Wesley could see that, with editing, Fénelon could be made to speak to those going on to perfection.

We remember all of that as we read the following extract from Fénelon himself, without the benefit of Wesley's antidote—editing and abridging.

Instructions and Counsel on Diverse Points Concerning Morality and Christian Perfection

Chapter 10
On the Imitation of Jesus Christ

One must imitate Jesus—live as He lived, think as He thought; **CHRISTLIKENESS** and one must be conformed to His image, a conformity that is the seal of our sanctification.

What a difference this makes in conduct! The nothing believes itself to be something, and the All-powerful makes itself nothing. I make myself nothing with You, Lord. I totally sacrifice my pride to You and the vanity that has possessed me right up to the present moment. Please help my goodwill. Keep me from occasions on which I might fall. "Avert my eyes so that I shall no longer give attention to vanity." Rather, may I see You alone, and may I see myself before You; then I shall know what I am and what You are.

Jesus Christ, born in a stable, constrained to flee into Egypt, spending 30 years of His life in the workshop of an artisan; He suffers hunger, thirst, weariness; He is poor, mistreated, and wretched. He teaches heaven's own tenets, but no one listens to Him. All of the

great and the wise pursue Him; they catch Him, and they make Him
suffer fearful torments. They treat Him as a slave. They make Him
die between two thieves, having preferred a thief to Him. Such was
the life that Jesus Christ had chosen. And we have a horror of any
sort of humiliation. For us, the least mistreatment is unbearable.

Let us compare our life with that of Jesus Christ. Let us remember that He is the Master, and we are the slaves; that He is all-powerful, and we are only feebleness; that He has abased himself, and we
would raise ourselves. Let us accustom ourselves to think [on these
truths].

Chapter 29
The Obligation to Abandon Oneself to God Without Reserve

Salvation does not depend solely upon ceasing to do evil. One
must add to that the habit of doing good. The kingdom of heaven is
too great a prize to be given to one who slavishly fears, to one who re-
frains from sin only because he dares not commit it. God wants children who love His goodness, not slaves who serve Him only because
they fear His power. So one should love Him and out of that love do
everything that inspires true love.

A number of otherwise well-intentioned people are mistaken
about this matter. But it is easy to disabuse them when they want to
go into it in good faith. Their mistake comes from not knowing either God or themselves. They are jealous of their freedom, and they
are afraid that they lose it in giving themselves over very much to
piety. But they should consider the fact that they are not their own;
that they belong to God, who has uniquely made them for himself
and not for themselves; that with absolute authority, He should lead
them as He pleases. Without conditions, without reservations, they
ENTIRE CONSECRATION should be entirely His. Properly speaking, we
have no right even to give ourselves to God, for
we have no rights at all over ourselves. But if we did not give ourselves to God as something that is absolutely His by nature, we
should be committing sacrilegious larceny, which would reverse the
natural order and violate the essential law of the creature.

Now it is not for us to make sense of the law that God imposes
upon us. It is ours to receive it, to adore it, and to follow it blindly.
God knows better than we what suits us. If we were fashioning the
gospel, we might, perhaps, be tempted to dilute it in order to accom-
modate our own weakness. But God did not consult us when He

made it. He gave it to us ready-made. And He has left us without any hope of salvation other than the fulfillment of this sovereign law—a law that holds under all conditions: "Heaven and earth shall pass away; but this word (of life or of death) shall never pass away."

One is not able to deduct a single word, not even the least letter, from it. Woe to the priests who would dare to lessen its force in order to dilute it for us. It is not they who have made this law. They are only its repositories. It is not necessary, then, to get after them if the gospel is a severe law. This law is just as awesome for them as it is for everyone else. In fact, still more for them than for others because they shall answer both for themselves and for others with respect to the keeping of this law. As the Son of God says, "Woe to the blind person who leads another blind person. Both will fall over the precipice." Woe to the ignorant priest, or one who is weak and a flatterer, who wants to broaden the narrow way. "The broad way is the one that leads to perdition."

So then, let human pride be stilled. One thinks one is free and is not. It is for one to bear the yoke of the law and to hope that God will give strength proportioned to the weight of the yoke. In fact, the

GOD EMPOWERS THE WILL

One who has this sovereign authority for commanding the creature gives that creature, through inner grace, the will to do what He commands.

Chapter 30
Happy the Soul That Is Given Entirely to God
How the Love of God Sweetens All Sacrifice
The Foolishness of Those Who Prefer the Benefits
of Time to Those of Eternity

Christian perfection does not consist in the rigors, listless melancholy, or constraints that one imagines it to do. It demands that one belong to God from the depths of one's heart. And if one be this way in his or her relationship to God, all that it does for Him becomes easy. Those who belong to God are always content when they are not of a divided mind, for they want only what God wills, and they want to do all that He wants them to do. They divest themselves of everything and find in this divestment a return of 100 percent: peace of conscience, a free heart, the sweetness of abandoning oneself into the

FULL COMMITMENT BRINGS JOY

hands of God, the joy in seeing an ever increasing light in the heart, and, finally, release from the tyrannizing fears and yearnings of the day. These multiply a hundred times the happiness that the true children of God have in the midst of some crosses, so long as they be faithful.

They sacrifice themselves, but to that which they most love. They suffer, but they wish to do so, preferring suffering to all false delights. Their bodies suffer sharp pains, their imaginations are troubled, their spirits languish; but their wills are set and peaceful at base, in their inmost being. And that will says an unceasing "Amen" to all of the blows with which God strikes it in order to sacrifice it.

What God asks of us is a will that is no longer divided between himself and some other creature. He asks a will that will be malleable in His hands, a will that yearns for nothing and rejects nothing, a will that wants all that He desires without reserve and **A WILL SUBMITTED COMPLETELY TO GOD** that wants nothing, under any pretext, that He does not want. When one is in this frame of mind, all is salutary, and the most useless diversions are turned into good works.

Happy is the one who gives himself to God! He is delivered from his passions, from mere human judgments, from human ill will, from the tyranny of human maxims, from cold and wretched railleries, from the adversities that the world attributes to luck, from the unfaithfulness and inconstancy of friends, from the wiles and snares of enemies, from one's own feebleness, from the misery and brevity of life, from the horror of a graceless death, from the cruel remorse that comes with criminal pleasures, and finally from God's eternal condemnation. One is delivered from this countless host of evils because, having placed his will in the hand of God, one wants only what God wants. And one has thus found one's consolation in the faith, and, consequently, hope in the midst of all of one's pains. What a mistake it would then be to fear giving oneself to God and to fear engaging oneself too early in such a desirable state.

Happy are those who throw themselves, head bowed and eyes closed, into the arms of "the Father of mercies and the God of all comfort." Then one wants nothing so much as to know what he owes to God. And one fears nothing more than not seeing sufficiently just what it is that He is demanding. As soon as one discovers new light on the faith, he is carried away with joy, as a miser who has found a treasure. The true Christian, whatever be the adversities piled upon him by Providence, wants all that comes to him and wishes for nothing that he does not have. The more that one loves God, the more content he is. The highest perfection, rather than overburdening him, renders his yoke lighter.

What folly it is to fear being entirely God's! It is to fear being too happy; it is to fear loving God's will in everything; it is to fear having too much courage among inevitable crosses, too much consolation from the love of God, and too much detachment from the passions that render us miserable.

So then, let us scorn the things of earth in order to be altogether God's. I would not say that we absolutely forsake them, for when one is already living a disciplined life of integrity, one has only to change the depth with which the heart loves, and we may do very nearly the same things that we were doing. This is so because God never inverts the human condition nor the roles that He has himself attached to it. Rather, to serve God, we do that which we were formerly doing to please the world and to satisfy ourselves, but with a difference. Instead of being eaten up by our pride, by our tyrannical passions, and by the world's ill-intended criticism, we act, on the contrary, with freedom, with courage, with hope in God. Confidence moves us. The expectation of eternal benefits, which are coming near at the same time that those here below are escaping from us, will sustain us in the midst of suffering. The love of God, which makes us sense that which He has in store for us, will give us wings with which to fly in His way, wings that will lift us above all of our misery. If we have difficulty believing this, experience will convince us. "Come, see, and taste," says David, "how sweet the Lord is."

COMPLETE TRUST IN GOD ENRICHES LIFE

Jesus Christ says to all Christians without exception, "Let him who would be my disciple take up his cross, and let him follow me." The broad way leads to perdition; one must follow the narrow way, which only a small number enter. Only those who do themselves hurt are worthy of the kingdom of heaven. One must be reborn, renounce himself, despise himself, become a child, be poor in spirit, weep in order to be consoled, and be not at all of the world, which is cursed because of its scandals.

BE DIFFERENT FROM THE WORLD

These truths frighten many because they know only that which religion exacts without knowing what it offers. They are ignorant of the spirit of love, which renders everything light. They are not aware that [religion] leads to the highest perfection by a sense of peace and love that sweetens the entire struggle.

Those who belong to God without reserve are always blessed. They know by experience that the Lord's yoke is easy and light, that one finds in Him repose of the soul, and that He "comforts those who are burdened and weary," as He himself says. But woe to those

THE PAIN OF THE DOUBLE-MINDED fainthearted and timid souls who are divided between God and the world! They desire and they don't desire; they are rent simultaneously by their passions and their remorse. They fear the judgments of both God and humankind. They have a horror of evil and are ashamed of the good. They have the sufferings of virtue without tasting its consolations. How unhappy they are! Ah, but if they have a bit of courage, in order to despise empty chatter, cold railleries, and rash criticisms—such peace they would savor in the heart of God.

How dangerous it is to the health, and unworthy of God and of ourselves; how very hurtful to our peace of heart, always to want to stay where one is! All of life is given us only in order that we might advance a long step toward our celestial homeland. The world flees like a misleading shadow. Eternity already moves toward us in order to receive us. What holds us back from moving forward while the light of the Father of mercy shines on us? Let us hasten to reach the kingdom of God.

Author Index

Subject Index

Index of Scripture References

The reader familiar with extensive Scripture references in other volumes of this series may wonder at the shorter list included here. These earlier Christian writers frequently quoted words of Scripture, but the convenience of chapter and verse divisions was not introduced in the Bible until the Geneva Bible was printed in 1560—after most contributors to volume 1 had died.